PETER DAWKINS

BUILDING PARADISE

THE FREEMASONIC AND ROSICRUCIAN SIX DAYS' WORK

The Master Series

FRANCIS BACON RESEARCH TRUST

Published by The Francis Bacon Research Trust
Warwickshire, United Kingdom

ISBN 0-86293-010-3

Copyright © Peter Dawkins, 2001

The moral right of the author has been asserted.

This book is sold subject to the condition that it shall not by way of trade or otherwise be lent, resold, hired out or otherwise circulated without the publisher's prior consent in any form of binding or cover other than that in which it is published and without a similar condition including these words being imposed on a subsequent purchaser.

Designed & Typeset by Starnine Design
Cover illustration by Samuel Dawkins.

Printed in Great Britain by Biddles Limited,
Guildford and Kings Lynn.

Dedication

This book I dedicate to the memory of Francis St Alban, with gratitude.

Acknowledgements

I would like to thank all my friends who have helped make this book possible, and in particular my wife Sarah and the Marquess of Northampton, Thomas Bokenham, the Brameld family, Gay Browning, John Dalhoff, Jonathan Kay, Colin McCallien, Mark Rylance, Suzy Straw, Robert Wilson, Ann Zoller, the Francis Bacon Society for the loan and use of its books, and members of both the Francis Bacon Society and the Francis Bacon Research Trust for information, help, support and feed-back over the many years that this book and series of books has been researched and prepared.

Illustrations in the book are reproduced by permission of the British Library, the United Grand Lodge of England or Lord Verulam, all as individually noted, or are reproduced from the Author's private library, the Francis Bacon Society library or the Francis Bacon Research Trust archives.

CONTENTS

CHAPTERS		PAGE
	Foreword	xi
1	**The Rosicrucian Light** *The Rosicrucian Master and the secret work of Francis Bacon and the Rosicrucians.*	1
2	**Life of Francis Bacon** *A brief summary of Francis Bacon's extraordinary life.*	9
3	**Tributes** *Tributes to Francis Bacon by his contemporaries acknowledging him as the greatest poet-dramatist as well as philosopher and judge.*	41
4	**The Great Instauration** *The Cabalistic Six Days' Work and the building of Solomon's Temple, the Temple of Light.*	59
5	**Bacon's Plan of Work** *Bacon's plan for the Six Days' Work, as described by himself.*	89
6	**Commentary on the Plan of Work** *The six stages of the Great Instauration leading to the seventh stage of peace and joy.*	103
7	**Solomon's House** *The Baconian-Rosicrucian College of the Six Days' Work; Freemasonry and its links with Bacon and Shakespeare; the Rosicrucian Father; Initiation and the Great Pillars; the Freemasonic and Cabalistic title-pages of Bacon's works.*	131

APPENDICES

A	Titles and Offices of Francis Bacon	166
B	Dates of Francis Bacon's Works	168
C	Ciphers of Francis Bacon	182
D	Bacon's Comments on Poetry	189
	Notes on the Text	191
	Select Bibliography	203
	Index	207

ILLUSTRATIONS

Page

xvi   **The Great Light**
19th century French lithograph depicting Francis Bacon as the Supreme Master and President of the Brotherhood of the Golden Rose-Croix.

1   **Grail Headpiece**
Headpiece: Francis Bacon's *Advancement and Proficience of Learning* (1640), Preface to the Great Instauration.

7   **Dove of Peace**
Titlepage emblem: *Saggi Morali* (Venice 1619) – Italian edition of Francis Bacon's *Essays*.

8   **Sir Francis Bacon, Lord Keeper of the Great Seal of England**
Engraving by Simon Passe, done from life after Bacon had been appointed Lord Keeper of the Great Seal of England (3 March 1617) and before he was created Lord Chancellor (4 January 1618).

9   **Double A Headpiece – Type 1 – The Cornucopic Grail**
Headpiece: first used in Baptista Porta's *De Furtivis Literarum* (1563). The design is also to be found in *The Essayes of a Prentise in the Divine Art of Poesie* (1584, 1585), *Striaticos* (1590), De Loque's *Single Combat* (1591), Shakespeare's *Contention of York and Lancaster*, Part 1 (1594), Shakespeare's *Taming of a Shrew* (1594), Hartwell's *Warres* (1595), *Regimen Sanitatis Salerni* (1597), Heywood's *Works* (1598), Shakespeare's *Henry V* (1598, 1600), Shakespeare's *Romeo and Juliet* (1599), Shakespeare's *Sir John Falstaffe* (1602), Shakespeare's *Richard III* (1602), Haywood's *Of the Union* (1604), and Paschal's *Coronae* (1671). Variations of the design were used in Shakespeare's *Richard II* (1597), Shakespeare's *Richard III* (1597), Shakespeare's *Henry IV* (1600), Shakespeare's *Hamlet* (1603), Shakespeare's *Sonnets* (1609), Matheieu's *Henri IV* (1612), and Lodge's English translation of Seneca's *Works* (1614).

32   **Sir Francis Bacon, Lord Keeper of the Great Seal and Lord High Chancellor of England**
Oil painting by Paul Van Somer (1618); from the Gorhambury collection.
Reproduced by kind permission of Lord Verulam.

39 **The Two Brothers**
Titlepage emblem: Francis Bacon's *Of the Coulers of good and evil* (1597).

40 **The Master and his Pupils**
Frontispiece: *Sermones Fideles* (1641)—Latin edition of Francis Bacon's *Essays*.

41 **Double A Headpiece – Type 2 – The Gemini and Cornucopic Grail**
Headpiece: first used in Sir Philip Sydney's English translation of De Plessis Mornay's *De la Verité de la Religion Christienne* (1587). The design is also to be found in *Arte of English Poesie* (1589), Sir John Harrington's English translation of Ariosto's *Orlando Furioso* (1591), *The Genealogies Recorded in the Sacred Scriptures* (1612), Hardy's *Le Theatre* (1624), Mayer's *Praxis Theologica* (1629), and Ben Jonson's *Works*, Vol. 2 (1640).

50 **Shaking a Lance at the Serpent of Ignorance**
Page 34: *Minerva Britanna* (1612) – emblem dedicated to Sir Francis Bacon.

51 **Pallas Athena, the Spear-shaker, Guardian of the Mysteries**
Title-page: Francis Bacon's *La Sagesse Mysterieuse des Anciens* (1641).

57 **Truth Revealed**
Titlepage emblem: Francis Bacon's *Essays* (1619) French edition.

58 **As Above, So Below**
Frontispiece: *Staats-Vernunfft* (1654)—German edition of Francis Bacon's *Wisdom of the Ancients*.

59 **Double A Headpiece – Type 3 – The Tied 'AA'**
Headpiece: first used in Sir John Harrington's English translation of Ariosto's *Orlando Furioso* (1591). The design is also to be found in Shakespeare's *Venus and Adonis* (1593), *Unnatural conspiracie of Scottish Papists* (1593), Spenser's *Faerie Queen*, Part II, Books 4-6 (1596), Marlowe's *History of Tamberlaine* (1597), Barckley's *Felicitie of Man* (1598), and *Nosce te ipsum* (1602).

70 **Bacon's Pillars**
Title-page: Francis Bacon's *Of the Advancement and Proficience of Learning* (1640).

72 **Bacon's Library**
Frontispiece: Francis Bacon's *Of the Advancement and Proficience of Learning* (1640).

74   Pyramid of Philosophy

80   Tree of Philosophy

84   The Two Pyramids (Divinity & Philosophy)

86   **The Cabala of the AV Bible**
Title-page: King James' Authorised Version of the Holy Bible (1611).
Reproduced by permission of the British Library.

88   **The Bacchanalia**
1st page emblem: Francis Bacon's essay *Of Honour and Reputation* (1597).

89   **Double A Headpiece – Type 4 – The Gemini and Wheatsheaf**
Headpiece: first used in *Daemonology* (1603). The design is also to be found in Spenser's *Faerie Queene* (1609). An expanded form of the design was used in the Shakespeare First Folio of *Comedies, Histories and Tragedies* (1623).

102   **'Every Surety of an even greater Art'**
Title-page emblem: Francis Bacon's *De Dignitate et Augmentis Scientiarum* (1624).

103   **Double A Headpiece – Type 5 – The Winged Eros**
Headpiece: first used in Spenser's *Shepheard's Calender* (1617).). The design is also to be found in *Discourse upon the meanes of well Governing* (1602), *The Rogue* (1622), Barclay's *Argenis* (1636), Bacon's *Remaines* (1648), and Bacon's *Mirrour of State* (1656).

107   Temple of Philosophia

111   Bacon's Method

122   **Hidden Truth brought forth by Time**
Title-page: Francis Bacon's *New Atlantis*—included as an appendix to the first edition of *Sylva Sylvarum* (1626).

124   **The Sabbath Book**
Detail: Frontispiece: Francis Bacon's *Of the Advancement and Proficience of Learning* (1640).

129   **Bacon, the Philosopher-Poet**
Title-page: Francis Bacon's *De Dignitate et Augmentis Scientiarum* (1645).

130 **The Twin Riders**
   1st page emblem: Francis Bacon's Essay *Of Expense* (1597).

131 **Double A Headpiece – Type 6 – The Arcadian Fleur-de-lis Shield**
   Headpiece: first used in Sydney's *L'Arcadie* (1625). The design is also to be found in Hardy's *Le Theatre*, Vol. 4 (1626), Barclay's *Argenis* (1625-6), and Aleman's *Le Gueux* (1632).

143 **'TT' Signature**
   Detail: The Shakespeare Memorial, Westminster Abbey.

144 **'TT' Signature**
   Dedication page: *Shakespeare's Sonnets* (1609).

145 **The Three Principals and Symbols of Freemasonry**
   Headpiece: The Benson Medley Edition of *Shakespeare's Sonnets* (1723).

146 **Shakespeare, the Rosicrucian Master**
   The Shakespeare Memorial, Westminster Abbey.

147 **Symbols of Freemasonry**
   Tailpiece: Dr. Peter Shaw's Collected Edition of Francis Bacon's Prose Works (1733).

148 **Beneath the Shadow of Thy Wings, O Lord**
   Emblem 6: *The Mirror of Modestie* (1618).

150 **The Cabalistic Tree of Life**
   Diagram: Tree of Life.

152 **The Johannine Eagle**
   Title-page: Anderson's *The Book of Constitutions of the Free-masons* (1723).
   Copyright, and reproduced by permission, of the United Grand Lodge of England.

158 **The Pillars of Initiation**
   Frontispiece: Anderson's *The Book of Constitutions of the Free-masons* (1723).
   Copyright, and reproduced by permission, of the United Grand Lodge of England.

160 **Entering the Temple**
   Title-page: Francis Bacon's *Novum Organum* (1620).

161 Passing beyond the Pillars
Title-page: Francis Bacon's *Of the Advancement and Proficience of Learning* (1640).

162 Raised into Light
Title-page: Francis Bacon's *Sylva Sylvarum or A Natural History* (1626).

165 The Master's Column
Title-page emblem: German edition, *Getreue Reden* (1654) of Francis Bacon's *Essays*.

INTRODUCTION

This book is about the work of one of the world's greatest geniuses to appear in a very long time—for many ages, as the poet laureate Ben Jonson said. He was not just a great genius but also one of the great Masters of Wisdom—and, moreover, the Master who was the 'Elijah' or herald of the Aquarian Age that we are now entering, the 'Apollo' of the Rosicrucians and the founder and first Grand Master of modern Freemasonry. His name was Francis Bacon. He was an Englishman who lived during the turbulent reigns of Queen Elizabeth I and King James I of England—years in which a brilliant light of culture shone and society made the transformational leap from medieval-renaissance to modern ways of thought.

This extraordinary man, Francis Bacon, is not well known today. Quite often, on the rare occasions when his name is mentioned, it is to abuse him—nearly always unjustly, although others see something of his greatness. A few centuries ago he was acknowledged as one of the greatest of philosophers who had an immense influence on the course of scientific thought and human development, helping us into the modern age. During his lifetime there were more than a few who saw and knew even more than this, but kept their knowledge guarded as a well-kept secret—for Francis Bacon was a Secret Master. Most of his work was deliberately concealed from the public eye. His own greatness was likewise veiled. Pointers were left, however—signposts for seekers after truth. It was never intended that he and his work should be left virtually unknown for evermore.

For nearly thirty years I have been researching the life of this man and his work, following the treasure trail that he and his friends established. Like most people, at the beginning I knew virtually nothing about him. Then one day I was, as one might say, hurled onto the path. Through the agency of someone who became a dear friend and mentor, I 'met' the Master. Then, having met him, as it were, I had to set out on the treasure trail, finding and following sign after sign, testing everything, seeking everywhere. It has not been easy, but it has been immensely joyful and fulfilling, and revelatory in so many unexpected ways. I have not been the first person by any means to do this. Without the help of others who have done valuable research or pointed the way, I would not have gone as far as I have—yet I suspect that my progress to date is along only a fraction of the route that is there to be followed. Others may well have gone further.

Different people come to find this Master and his work in different ways. Sometimes the finding is dramatic: it is always momentous. Mine was, I must admit, both—and it changed my life in ways that I never could have conceived possible. For one thing, it meant much more work, but joyful, meaningful work. As another great Master[1] once said, the only effective yoga for our age is karma yoga, which means hard work done as loving, devoted, effective service to each other, the world and the Divine Being. Bacon called this charity, as indeed did St Paul when he interpreted the teachings of Christ for us.

As you will read in this book, Bacon's mission was to bring us an Art of Discovery and to train us in this art. The idea is to be able to discover all things, all truth, in a proficient, beautiful and life-enhancing way—the way of a true artist. The purpose of this Art of Discovery is so as to know truth and to practice that truth in our lives for the benefit and beautifying of all life. In other words, to be able to build a paradise on earth for all people, all creatures, all nature, and in doing so to celebrate life itself—which life is, essentially and divinely, perfect love.

Bacon gave us a particular method by which this may be accomplished. It is a method based on ancient wisdom and traditional, proven usage, but updated in a major way. It was not a method for his time alone, but a method for this age we are now in and future ages. It is not a dogma, but a science. Moreover, it is a method that can grow and evolve with time. Unknown to the majority of people, it is in operation now, and its fulfilment needs only the goodwill and cooperation of you, me and whoever else wants to know and practise this art, this yoga of joy.

As Bacon said:-

> Truth, which only doth judge itself, teacheth that the enquiry of truth, which is the love-making or wooing of it, the knowledge of truth, which is the presence of it, and the belief of truth, which is the enjoying of it, is the sovereign good of human nature.[2]

> The essential form of knowledge… is nothing but a representation of truth: for the truth of being and the truth of knowing are one, differing no more than the direct beam and the beam reflected.[3]

In this book you will read how Bacon's project is known as the Six Days' Work and that this work is that of the Rosicrucians. Moreover, you will discover that Bacon was a great Master of Cabala as well as the President of the Rosicrucians and the founder and first Grand Master of modern Freemasonry. That one of his pseudonyms was Shakespeare is dealt with more fully in another book, part of this series.[4] A further book, also in this series, reveals in more depth the Cabalistic, Freemasonic and Rosicrucian symbolism and meaning of the various Baconian illustrations and works of art, illuminating Bacon's life, work and teachings in more detail.[5] This present book, **Building Paradise,** *tells you how the Six Days' Work works and how it can build paradise on earth.*

P.D.
Tysoe
December 27th 2000

---

[1] Babaji, the Mahaguru or Master of the Masters.

[2] *Essay*, 'Of Truth'.

[3] *The Advancement and Proficience of Learning.*

[4] *The Shakespeare Enigma.*

[5] *Beyond the Veil.*

THE GREAT LIGHT
19th century French lithograph depicting Francis Bacon as the Supreme Master
and President of the Brotherhood of the Golden Rose-Croix.

THE ROSICRUCIAN LIGHT

THE MASTER

SIR FRANCIS BACON, Baron Verulam, Viscount St Alban (1561-1626), was acknowledged by the poet laureate Ben Jonson and others as one of the greatest of Masters to appear in our world for many ages—a Socrates, Plato and Orpheus all rolled into one—an Apollo, leader of the Choir of Muses, and a Solomon, wisest of the wise. Like other great Masters, his birth and work was foretold by a prophet, Paracelsus,[1] who described him as 'a Great Light—Elias the Artist', who would renovate the arts and sciences and reveal many things.[2]

Paracelsus related this 'marvellous being' and his revelatory work to the appearance of a new star (a supernova) that would be 'the sign and harbinger of the approaching revolution'. The first supernova to occur after Paracelsus' death was in 1572-4, in the constellation of Cassiopeia, the Heavenly Virgin Queen. This was generally seen to be the harbinger of the birth of a great light upon the earth. To some, like Theodore Beza, the Calvinist biblical scholar, the 'new star' announced the Second Coming. For Tycho Brahe, the Danish astronomer, it marked the entrance of the world into the seventh revolution that would inaugurate the golden age. He wrote that 'Some great Light is now at hand which shall enlighten and by degrees expel the former darkness', and pointed out that the new star would be followed by a major conjunction of planets when the prophecies of the 1572 star would be fulfilled.[3] The appearance of this supernova, which for nearly two full years shone brighter than Venus, overlighted the period of Francis Bacon's great vision of his life's work.

Building Paradise

The next major 'new star' appearance was connected with the great planetary conjunction foretold by Brahe. Paracelsus had conceived of Elias the Artist as being an adept of chemical science and prophesied that he would come fifty-eight years after his own (Paracelsus') death. According to most reports Paracelsus died in 1541, although others state that his death occurred in 1544. These dates render 1599 and 1603 respectively, when Bacon was at a critical juncture in his life. The latter date is particularly significant, for in 1603 there was a rare conjunction of Saturn, Jupiter, Mars, Venus and the Sun in the sign of Sagittarius in the ninth house, preceded by a nova in Cygnus (1602) and followed by a supernova in Serpentarius (1604).

These starbursts and conjunctions were generally believed to correspond to the positions pertaining on the Fourth Day of Creation, when the sun, moon and stars were created in the heavens as signs and to give light upon the earth.[4] Many people thought that it meant a completely new beginning—a new Creation. Robert Fludd interpreted the celestial phenomena, in a treatise defending the Rosicrucians (*Tractatis Apoligetica*), as a sign to the Rosicrucian brotherhood to emerge from their period of secrecy that had begun in 1572, during which they had prepared their work, and to both expand their membership and begin the restoration of the world. The 'Instauration' or restoration of the world, through the renovation of the arts and sciences, was Bacon's great work. 1604 was the date when the tomb of 'Fra. C.R.C.', the 'Father' of the Rosicrucians, was opened, according to the Rosicrucian manifestos.[5] In the following year (1605), thirty-three years after 1572, the first of Bacon's books on the Great Instauration—*The Advancement of Learning*—was published. (33 is a symbol for illumination: for initiatic 'rebirth' or resurrection into glory. It is also the Cabalistic cipher number for BACON.)[6]

Rosicrucian records show that Bacon was the President of the 'invisible' fraternity of Rosicrucians in Europe in the late 16th/early 17th century, whilst many cryptic pointers indicate that he was almost certainly the founder and Grand Master of speculative English Freemasonry, the 'mother' of all subsequent branches of Freemasonry—and all this for a purpose still to unfold. Other evidence, cryptic and otherwise, reveal him as having been the great English Bard, Shakespeare, masked

The Rosicrucian Light

deliberately by the actor of that name, and the leader of other poets, scholars and artists.

This period was the high point of the English Renaissance, when, in a matter of half a century (1575-1625), the English language was properly formed, classical and foreign works were translated into the newly enhanced language, dictionaries were begun, histories were compiled on all manner of things, and great poetry, literature and drama appeared. Through Bacon's work, both publicised and secret, a major revolution in thought took place, and the seeds of modern science and society were sown.

However, society worldwide has continued to grow in two disparate ways: ethically and corruptly, charitably and selfishly. This is nothing new. But what is new is the power that modern science gives to the human race, for good or evil. Bacon came to give power to the good.

Bacon's science is based on love and the practice of love, as charity or good works. It is an ethical science whose purpose is to produce things both useful and good, to raise mankind out of its misery, and in particular to encourage and develop a philanthropic goodness of nature in people, assisted by a thoroughly tested, practical knowledge of how love operates and how it is best served. As for nature, our environment, Bacon urges us to love nature, to care for her, as a lover loves his beloved.

Bacon forewarned us (like a prophet) that science is only valid insofar as it is dedicated to love and goodness, or charity, and that if carried out purely for profit or commodity it would be to the infinite loss of mankind. He warned us against a purely mechanistic and materialistic approach to life, and the forcing of nature against her will by mechanical arts. He fervently prayed that such evils might not happen, although he feared they would. One of the reasons for his method, his gift to humanity, is so as to counter the growth of such evils. He sensed the approach of an age of materialism, but saw beyond that, to an age of peace and enlightenment that could, with help, ensue. In an almost super-human way Bacon set about to provide us with that help.

Bacon's art is his method for the discovery of all truth—an 'Art of Discovery' by means of which all things might be known. He teaches this art by means of a treasure trail or game of hide and seek. By discovering what he has hidden we train ourselves in the

Building Paradise

art of discovery, which we can then use to discover whatever we wish to know.

Part of Bacon's life and work is 'in the light' and able to be easily seen, and part of it is 'in the shadow', veiled from immediate sight. This dual openness and secrecy forms the basis of his treasure trail, which is Cabalistic in nature and follows the practice of the schools of the Ancient Wisdom. The open aspect is represented by his work known under his personal name of 'Francis Bacon'. His veiled aspect is signified primarily by his work under the mask of 'William Shakespeare', although he had other pseudonyms too. These constitute the twin pillars that stand at the entrance to the Baconian temple of light, built as a landmark or starting point for a worldwide temple of enlightened humanity that he envisioned as possible of construction. His special gift to us is a sure method by means of which the temple—which is a temple of the mind or soul—might be constructed.

> I am not raising a capitol or pyramid to the pride of man, but laying a foundation in the human understanding for a holy temple after the model of the world. That model therefore I follow. For whatever deserves to exist deserves also to be known, for knowledge is the image of existence; and things mean and splendid exist alike.
>
> Francis Bacon, *Novum Organum*, Bk I, Aph.120.[7]

Like Elias or John the Baptist, Bacon referred to himself as the herald or harbinger of a new age—an age of universal enlightenment.[8] Like Orpheus he was a renovator or reviver of the ancient and original wisdom teachings taught via the Mysteries and based on love—a 'music' by means of which all things can be brought to a harmonious perfection.

Bacon is not a dead Master but a living Master. His work was designed for the benefit not just of our generation but of generations and ages to come. His spirit imbues it all, and his soul overlights and guides all those who draw close and take part.

The Rosicrucian Light

THE ART OF SCIENCE

The aim of Bacon's art is to discover truth itself, and in particular the ultimate truth, which he recognised as being divine love—the single, summary law or 'desire' of the universe.

With Bacon's method the discovery of truth goes hand in hand with the practice of truth. Science is knowledge, and knowledge is not true knowledge without the practical experience of it. As we can never discover the ultimate truth of love without practising love, Bacon's science is an ethical science, its philanthropic purpose being to relieve the poverty, misery and ignorance of all who suffer in such a state and thereby to glorify God, or Love, through the practice of charity or good works. By this means Love, or God, the Truth, is made manifest and known.

To do this well and efficiently is not necessarily easy, as the history of the human race proves. It is an art which, when practised well, produces a science of love which is an illumination. Moreover, it is an art and science that requires discovery and practice on many levels of existence, physical and metaphysical, from the outer world of effects to the innermost world of causes. The former is a key to the discovery of the latter, whilst the latter is the creative cause of the former. Since causes produce the effects, if we do not like the effects, and if we know the causes, by altering or modulating the causes we can change the effects. Likewise, if we discover the supreme cause, the law of love, and learn how to work with it, and if we put that law into operation in our lives and surroundings, we can bring about works of love and produce miracles.

This is the supreme art, which is alchemical in nature. It has the capacity to transmute all base matter into spiritual gold, to change all gross and ugly conditions into fine and beautiful ones, and to transform all ignorance into true science or illumination.

It is an ancient art, practised down the ages by the adepts or 'scientists' of the Hermetic wisdom. The Hermetic Master, Francis Bacon, improved the art still further, for the benefit of humanity and the whole world.

But it has to be practised. The art is known by means of itself. This is the great teaching.

Building Paradise

A YOGA OF LIFE

Francis Bacon is probably best known as one of the Western world's greatest philosophers, although he was also a profound mystic and a supreme poet who attributed most of his vast knowledge to divine inspiration and revelation.

The word *philosophy* is from the Greek, *philo-sophia,* which means 'the love of wisdom'. A philosopher is described, therefore, as a lover of *Sophia*—a seeker after Wisdom, wooing her with love. The first person to call himself a philosopher was Pythagoras, with whom Bacon has much in common; for Pythagoras felt himself unworthy to be called a wise man but only a seeker after wisdom.

True wisdom is love. Wisdom is the radiance of love. This is truth. When the philosopher has discovered the truth and brought it to light, he or she becomes illumined by the wisdom, thereby fulfilling the purpose of love by being love. Such a person is a true Gnostic—a seer or knower who sees and knows truth because he/she has discovered it, is in love with it and knows it by living or being it.

Francis Bacon referred to the revelations and guidance given to us by Wisdom as 'Divinity'. Divinity includes religion, prophecy and the sacred scriptures, but also the intuitive knowledge inspired into our heart that illuminates the mind. He consistently emphasised that philosophy should go hand in hand with divinity and should serve divinity as a handmaiden serves her mistress.

Just as science and art are the twin pillars of the temple of philosophy, so divinity and philosophy are the twin pillars of all knowledge. The balance and union of the two fulfils the purpose of human existence, just as the phoenix and turtledove of Shakespeare's poem become one flame in their mutual love and then vanish together into the bosom of God. Such union, deliberately and willingly undertaken, is yoga, enabling the conscious union of the human soul with God, the supreme yoga. This is also known as the mystical marriage.

The real Baconian foundations and purpose of science are to do with such yoga. The Baconian science and art has not yet been properly recognised let alone practised by society at large, and has nothing to do with any purely mechanistic, utilitarian and

The Rosicrucian Light

exploitative aspects of modern science and society, or with any materialistic philosophy. Bacon's philosophical and practical foundation of science and service has within it a graduated plan of action and development leading ultimately to the blessing and illumination of all mankind. This is a yoga of science and service for the benefit of all. When practised on a large scale it can help to bring the whole world into a golden age of wisdom, peace and prosperity, which is its intention.

As the original 17th century Rosicrucian manifestos state, such a science entails, and will entail, the reformation of the whole wide world—and this reformation is already, quietly and subtly, under way.

Building Paradise

SIR FRANCIS BACON, LORD KEEPER OF THE GREAT SEAL OF ENGLAND
Engraving by Simon Passe, done from life after Bacon had been
appointed Lord Keeper of the Great Seal of England (3 March 1617)

LIFE OF FRANCIS BACON

THE ELIZABETHAN PERIOD

Francis Bacon was born at York House, Charing Cross, London, on 22 January 1561. He was baptised at St Martin-in-the-Fields on 25 January 1561 as second son of Sir Nicholas and Lady Ann Bacon. His father was Lord Keeper of the Great Seal of England and his mother was one of the most highly educated and accomplished women of her time. As a child he showed more than unusual promise and attracted the attention of Queen Elizabeth, who called him her 'young Lord Keeper' and 'baby Solomon'. He was given a privileged private education by the best teachers of the time, which took place mainly at York House, the Lord Keeper's London residence—a thriving hub of State business that adjoined York Place, the Queen's Palace of Whitehall. In the vacations the family lived at Sir Nicholas' country home of Gorhambury, St Albans, where several scenes in the early Shakespeare play *Henry VI* are laid. There were also tours with the court, visiting the many country mansions and palaces of the Queen and her courtiers.

Because of his father's high office and his other family connections (his uncle, Sir William Cecil, later Lord Burghley, was the Queen's Secretary of State until 1573 when he was made the Queen's Lord Treasurer), Francis was almost certainly present at various court entertainments, such as the regular Christmas festivities and the two great entertainments of 1575. These latter entertainments, which were pivotal events in the Queen's reign, were the Arcadian Woodstock Tournament presented by Sir Henry Lee, the Queen's Champion, and the sumptuous Kenilworth Entertainment laid on for the Queen at Kenilworth

Building Paradise

Castle by her favourite, Robert Dudley, Earl of Leicester. The Woodstock Tournament was the forerunner of the annual Accession Day Tournaments, whilst the Kenilworth Entertainment was designed by Leicester to persuade the Queen to marry him, which offer she turned down. Twenty years later Francis Bacon was to incorporate some of what he witnessed at the Kenilworth Entertainment in *A Midsummer Night's Dream,* which he wrote specially for the wedding of his niece, Elizabeth Cecil, when she married William Stanley, 6th Earl of Derby, in January 1595.

In April 1573, at the age of twelve, with a highly dramatic 'new star' (supernova) blazing away in the heavens, brighter than Venus,[1] Francis Bacon entered Trinity College, Cambridge University, accompanied by his brother Anthony.[2] They were already learned in the Classics and could read, write and speak Latin, Greek, French, Italian and Spanish fluently. They also knew Hebrew. They were placed under the direct charge and tuition of the Master of Trinity, Dr John Whitgift, and lodged in rooms under his roof. (Whitgift afterwards became Archbishop of Canterbury, and was the authority who granted the licence to publish *Venus and Adonis* in 1593.) Their contemporaries and friends at Cambridge included John Lyly, William Clerke, Edmund Spenser, Philemon Holland and Gabriel Harvey—the latter being their tutor in rhetoric and poetry as well as being a member of Sir Philip Sydney's group of philosopher-poets, the English 'Areopagus'.

Whilst a student at Cambridge, Francis became thoroughly disillusioned with the Aristotelian system of thought and teaching. As a reaction to this, and inspired with prophetic vision as to what to do to improve matters, his Grand Idea was born—an illumination matching the brilliance of the supernova shining overhead. For him it was like a spiritual birth or awakening, revealing to him his mission in life. Less than three years later, at Christmas 1575, with nothing more left that the university could teach him, he and Anthony left Cambridge, carrying with them the embryo of a plan by means of which Francis' grand idea might be set in motion and gradually achieved. In this Anthony was a dedicated partner, even though for the next fifteen years their respective paths would separate them physically for most of the time.

Life of Francis Bacon

On 27 June 1576 Francis, aged fifteen, and Anthony, aged seventeen, were entered as law students at Gray's Inn, one of the four Inns of Court in London, to follow in their father's footsteps. Other members of that learned Society included the Earl of Southampton (to whom the Shakespeare poems *Venus and Adonis* and *Lucrece* were dedicated), Francis and Anthony's uncle, Lord Burghley (upon whom the Shakespeare character of Polonius in *Hamlet* is modelled), Lord Strange (in whose company of players the actor Shakspere played), William Herbert (later Earl of Pembroke to whom the First Folio of the Shakespeare plays was dedicated), Sir Francis Walsingham (founder of the Elizabethan secret service, and a patron and employer of poets and dramatists), Edward de Vere, Earl of Oxford (a patron of writers and actors as well as a poet in his own right), and Sir Philip Sydney (a renowned poet and leader of the Areopagus of English lawyer-poets until his premature death on the battlefield in 1586). Five months later Francis and Anthony were admitted, as sons of a judge, to the Grand Company of Ancients by Order of Pension dated 21 November 1576, which gave them certain privileges. However, by that time Francis was abroad on the continent.

Francis did not immediately take up residence at Gray's Inn but, instead, went 'from the Queen's hand' to France with Sir Amyas Paulet, the newly-designated English Ambassador,[3] landing in Calais on 25 September 1576 and remaining in France with the French court for nearly three years. This was just at the time when, on one hand, the functions of the French State were in disorder because of corrupt and feeble administration, and, on the other hand, the French Renaissance was still at its height, with its poets, writers and artists encouraged and patronised by the French monarchy. During this time Paulet entrusted Francis with an important commission to the Queen, and Francis returned briefly to England in June 1578 for this purpose. Sir Amyas Paulet was recalled in October 1579, but Francis continued on at the French court.

During Francis' three years in France he travelled with the French court to Fontainebleau, Blois, Tours, Poitiers and Chenonceaux, as well as living in Paris where the French court was normally based. He was privy to historical and current affairs, both private and State, and witnessed not only the politics of

Building Paradise

France but also the spectacular court entertainments and the Italian Commedia dell'arte. (Several Shakespeare plays are set in France and incorporate first-hand knowledge of the French court and other privileged information, whilst the Commedia dell'arte was a strong influence in many of the plays.) Francis made some kind of dangerous journey during August-September 1577, and in the following year he appears to have travelled with Catherine de Medici and Marguerite de Navarre's entourage to the south of France, where he took part in the Court of Love festivities at Nérac. (Some of his experiences there, and subsequently, were incorporated into the early Shakespeare play, *Love's Labour's Lost*.)

It was in Paris, after his return from Nérac, that on 17 February 1579 Francis dreamt his father's country house was plastered all over with black mortar.[4] Since Gorhambury was actually plastered white and known as the 'White House' or 'White Temple', this was an ominous dream. In fact, three days later Sir Nicholas Bacon died of a chill caught at his official home in London, York House.[5] As soon as news of the death arrived in Paris, Francis immediately set about organising his return home, arriving in England on 20 March 1579, unfortunately just a few days after Sir Nicholas' funeral.[6] Carrying out the wishes of his deceased father and his uncle Lord Burghley, who now acted *in loco parentis* towards him and Anthony until they should each come of age, Francis entered Gray's Inn to study law. He took up residence in May 1580, with benefit of 'special admittance' on account of his health, which meant that he was freed from the obligation of keeping Commons. According to Francis' mother, Lady Anne, the explanation of Francis' special admittance was that he suffered from indigestion caused by untimely going to bed, then musing about goodness knows what when he should sleep, and then in consequence of this rising late from bed. The 'special admittance' meant that Francis could choose his diet and take meals in the chambers that he shared with Mr. Fulwood in Fulwood House.

However, law was not Francis' great interest. It was not what he wanted to do, and about it he writes later that 'the Bar will be my bier'. In later years he informed Dr William Rawley, his chaplain, secretary and biographer, that law was to him but an accessory, not his principal study, even though in law, according to Rawley, 'he obtained to great excellency' and 'in the science of the grounds and mysteries of law he was exceeded by none'.[7] Francis' passion in life was literary and educational, and devoted to the realisation of his Grand Idea. He had been both shocked and inspired by what he saw and experienced in France. The French court was dissolute and its government was corrupt, but its culture otherwise was refined and glorious, whereas English culture at that time was uncouth and the English language still a sorry patchwork of almost incomprehensible dialects. Francis' mission, therefore, was to create, with the help of others suited to the task, a magnificent English language and culture just as the French poets and philosophers had created theirs, but one that would promote virtue, not corruptness, and would be a vehicle for the new avenues of thought and discovery that he wished to encourage. He desired to do this as a service to both his country and his Queen, to make Elizabeth's reign even more glorious and memorable than it might otherwise have been, and to leave a heritage for future ages to build upon. His design was, literally, a renovation of all arts and sciences based upon the proper foundations, and one which, by means of a special method that he was to test out and then teach, could spread to other countries for the benefit of the whole world It was a truly grand concept.

To help him in his educational and cultural endeavours he applied to his uncle Lord Burghley to exert influence with the Queen on his behalf, in recognition of his special abilities and circumstances, so that he might have not only royal approval but also a position whereby he could have sufficient influence and income, without having to practice law, to give him 'commandment of more wits' than his own to assist him in his proposed task, since his own inherited resources were far too limited.[8] The Queen, who was interested in the French Academies, did voice her approval and support, and gave Francis to believe that such a place would be found for him; but, other than moral and verbal encouragement, in this 'rare and unaccustomed suit' he was to meet with little success.

For fifteen years Francis was to be kept on a string concerning his suit. Nevertheless, devoting himself whole-heartedly to his great project and continually being buoyed up by promises of

Building Paradise

support from both Burghley and the Queen, Francis immersed himself in his writings and his study of human nature and the nature of all things, as well as studying law. From this time on he began to ring the bell that 'called the wits together'—and there were many. Philip Sydney's scholarly circle of philosopher-poets (the English *Areopagitae* or 'Areopagus') was already in existence (from *c*.1574) and in the throes of developing English poetry. The Renaissance magus, Dr John Dee, was at the height of his influence and making available his magnificent library at Mortlake—the largest in England—to the philosopher-poets and mathematicians. The Earl of Leicester, still dear to the Queen, provided an enthusiastic patronage of the poets and artists, making his London house available to them as well as patronising his own company of actors. Then, from 1579 and onwards through the 1580's, the 'University Wits' began to appear, who raised the level of English drama and helped lay the foundations for the Shakespeare plays. The University Wits were, in order of appearance, John Lyly, Thomas Lodge, George Peele, Robert Greene, Thomas Nashe and Christopher Marlowe. The Areopagitae included Sir Philip Sydney, Gabriel Harvey, Edward Dyer, Daniel Rogers, Thomas Drant and 'Immerito' (Edmund Spenser)[9].

Francis Bacon was called to the Bar as Utter Barrister on 27 June 1582, but seems to have remained a briefless barrister for a further twelve years, until forced by circumstances in 1594 to take up some court briefs and plead at the King's Bench in the Courts of Westminster. However, during this time, and in fact right up to her death in 1603, the Queen many times asked for Francis' advice and used his talents to draw up various reports and papers for her on difficult matters—religious, political and legal. Francis also assisted in the gathering of political intelligence, helped by his brother Anthony who first started going abroad in 1578 on missions as a spy, culminating with travelling Europe from 1579 to 1592 as the Queen's Intelligencer at Burghley's request. The head of Intelligence was the Queen's Secretary of State, Sir Francis Walsingham, who had set up one of the most efficient intelligence networks in Europe, with a training school in London. (Walsingham had succeeded Lord Burghley as Secretary of State in 1573 when Burghley became the Queen's Lord Treasurer.)

Life of Francis Bacon

In 1580 the Queen commissioned Francis, via Sir Thomas Bodley,[10] to make report and compile notes of observations respecting the 'laws, religion, military strength and whatsoever concerneth pleasure or profit' in the countries of Europe. This was a specially prepared 12-month tour of Italy, Spain, Germany and Denmark, to observe life and gather information, both for the Queen and for his own purposes.[11] For the planning of the journey Francis was aided by his brother Anthony, who was able to advise, arrange contacts and prepare a route. Anthony returned briefly from France to England in November-December 1580 for this purpose, and then was sent back again to the continent, remaining abroad for the next eleven years (except for one visit to England in 1588) gathering political intelligence.

Francis left England sometime in the spring 1581 and was back home at Gray's Inn by the beginning of April 1582. On his return to England he wrote up a report of his travels and findings for Lord Burghley and the Queen. This report, including additional information from his brother Anthony and Nicholas Faunt,[12] was presented to the Queen as a State Paper entitled *Notes on the Present State of Christendom*.[13] The countries covered included not just France, Italy and Spain, but also Austria, Germany, Portugal, Poland, Denmark and Sweden. Florence, Venice, Mantua, Genoa and Savoy are dealt with in most detail. Some of this information was used in the Shakespeare plays. (N.B. These *Notes* were not made available to the public until 1734.)[14]

Cryptography was one of Francis' interests, and he assisted Burghley and Walsingham with decoding various correspondence. He also invented some new ciphers, one of his earliest creations being the Biliteral cipher which he invented in his youth whilst at Paris, which later became the basis of the Morse code and the binary code of all computer technology today.

In 1581 Francis began his thirty-six years of Parliamentary service as a Member of Parliament.[15] Other than this he seems to have led the life partly of a courtier and partly of a recluse, and we hear little of him until 1587, except that in March 1584 he visited Scotland,[16] and on 10 February 1586 he became a Bencher of Gray's Inn.[17]

Nearly two years later, on 23 November 1587 Francis was appointed a Reader of Gray's Inn. As a Reader he was allowed his

Building Paradise

own private chambers. In fact, just two days previous to this, confirming a grant made nine years earlier, several buildings were leased to Anthony and Francis Bacon for a term of fifty years, with leave to add additional rooms (which Francis eventually did). These buildings contained the original chambers of Sir Nicholas Bacon, which had been kept for Edward and Anthony Bacon's use. By then Edward, Francis and Anthony's half-brother, had ceased studying law and had acquired the lease of Twickenham Park from the Queen, as well as having estates elsewhere. Since Anthony was still abroad, this meant that Francis had the unimpeded use of all the chambers, both to live in and to pursue his great project. Conveniently, the Great Library of Gray's Inn was adjacent to and on the same level as Francis' chambers.

From that time onwards we learn that Francis was regularly associated with other gentlemen of Gray's Inn in devising and presenting masques and entertainments at Gray's Inn and the royal court at Greenwich, and writing speeches and devices to be used in the Queen's Accession Day Tilts.

Francis' movements tended to oscillate between Gray's Inn, the royal court when he was in attendance on the Queen, and Twickenham Lodge. The latter was situated in Twickenham Park, the Crown property leased by Edward Bacon, with land leading down to the River Thames immediately opposite the Queen's palace of Richmond. The lodge with its park was a tranquil and beautiful place where Francis could write in peace, together with his friends and 'good pens'. It was almost certainly here as well as at Gray's Inn that Bacon began writing, in 1588, the extraordinary series of plays that were later (from 1598 onwards) published under the pseudonymous mask of 'William Shakespeare'. Edward seems to have allowed Francis the use of Twickenham Lodge whenever he wanted, and in November 1595 Francis took over the lease himself. Gorhambury, the fine country house and estate at St Albans, although owned by Anthony Bacon, was, under the terms of Sir Nicholas Bacon's will, Lady Anne Bacon's home and residence until she should die. It was, in any case, rather far from London, whereas Twickenham Park was close to the city and linked to it by river. All the main royal palaces and noblemen's houses in or just outside London, from Greenwich to Hampton Court Palace, fronted onto this one great Thames thoroughfare.

Life of Francis Bacon

Twickenham Lodge was thus an ideal place. Francis had the use of it and part of its park until 1607, when the lease was surrendered to Lucy, Countess of Bedford, the new owner.

1588 saw the Spanish Armada approach the coast of England in July and suffer defeat, and the Earl of Leicester's fever and death in September. Robert Devereux, the Earl of Essex, took on the mantle of his stepfather, becoming Elizabeth's principal favourite, and Leicester House became Essex House.

In 1591 Francis appears to have almost given up his fruitless suit with Burghley and the Queen, threatening that if his lordship would not carry him on he would sell the small inheritance he had in order to purchase some means of quick revenue, and thereby give up all care of service (*i.e.* to Burghley and the Queen) in order to become some 'sorry bookmaker or a true pioneer in that mine of truth which (Anaxagoras) said lay so deep'.[18] Suspecting Burghley's motives, Francis tried to make it absolutely clear to his uncle that just as he had vast contemplative ends so he had moderate civil ends, and that he did not 'seek or affect any place whereunto any that is nearer unto your Lordship shall be concurrent'. In this Francis was particularly referring to his hunchback cousin, Robert Cecil, Burghley's son by his second wife, Mildred, the sister of Lady Ann Bacon. Besides being Lord Treasurer and Master of the Court of Wards, the most lucrative office in the land, Burghley was doing his best to advance Robert as high and as quickly as possible to a similar status, although unlike Francis (and Burghley himself) Robert had no official legal training. Not without cause, it was the astute but wily Robert Cecil who, seen from the point of view of Francis Bacon, provided the character study for the hunchback King Richard in the Shakespeare play of *Richard III*.

Richard III was written in 1591 and first performed in 1592. One of Francis' main endeavours in his work was not only to study human nature and raise the level of people's consciousness, but to improve people's moral behaviour and purge corruption from wherever it might lurk—including corruption in high places. His ideal was to discover truth and practice philanthropy; and, like the Ancients, to teach wisdom through entertainment. One of the main points about the Shakespeare plays is that they hold a mirror up to human nature, so that both good and bad might be

Building Paradise

seen for what they are and what they do. Each character in the plays embodies qualities and characteristics drawn from real life, and sometimes the analogies go close to the bone. Increasingly, from 1591 onwards, the Shakespeare plays subtly attacked or satirised the abuses and weaknesses of the Cecil combo and others, even the Queen, as well as of society in general.

However, Francis did carry on serving the Queen with his legal and political advice, and with the use of his pen, and about this time (perhaps in response to his letter to Burghley threatening to retire) she made him Queen's Counsel Extraordinary—an honorary, unpaid position with duties that were not clearly defined, except that examining prisoners suspected of treason or other grave offences, protecting the Queen's interests and drawing up official reports were some of the services Francis was called upon to perform. Moreover, it was about this time that the Queen asked Francis to assist Robert Devereux, the Earl of Essex, as an advisor.

Francis had in fact already struck up a good friendship with Essex. The Earl at that time was the foremost favourite of the Queen and, with his sparkling charisma and gallantry, popular with the people. Francis set out to assist Essex in every way possible, believing him to be 'the fittest instrument to do good to the state'. Essex in turn promised to help Francis, such as with his suit to the Queen and in obtaining other patronage. Ultimately this turned out to be a perilous mistake for Francis. Essex's temperament was so hotheaded and imperious that, rather than helping Francis, he repeatedly made matters worse, with the Queen and he clashing like gladiators. Burghley and Robert Cecil came to loathe him, resulting in their declared policy of doing their utmost to block the advancement of any of Essex's friends, including the Bacon brothers. It was Essex's character that was used as the model for the fiery, gallant Hotspur in Shakespeare's *Henry IV*, about which Essex complained to the Queen, saying that Francis and Anthony Bacon 'print me and make me speak to the world, and shortly they will play me in what form they list upon the stage'.[19] However, most importantly, it was with the group of writers that were associated with or were to become associated with Essex and his friends that Francis had already launched his literary endeavours.

Life of Francis Bacon

The Essex group, which had been linked with Robert Dudley, Earl of Leicester, Sir Francis Walsingham and Sir Philip Sydney until their deaths in the 1580's, and with the Areopagitae of English poets that used to meet at Leicester House (later Essex House), included the Earl of Oxford, the Earl of Southampton, Lord Mountjoy, Lady Frances Essex, Penelope Rich, Elizabeth Vernon and Mary Sydney, the Countess of Pembroke, all of whom periodically resided at Essex House. Associated with them were the circle of poets, writers and dramatists patronised by Essex, Southampton and the Pembrokes, who included Samuel Daniel, Ben Jonson, John Florio, George Wither, Edmund Spenser, Thomas Nashe and John Lyly. The other 'University Wits'—Thomas Lodge, George Peele, Robert Greene and Christopher Marlowe were also connected with this group—the wits who acknowledged Shakespeare (but *not* the actor Shakspere) as their head.

Southampton—a scholar, poet, gentleman and soldier, and a patron of poets, scholars and playwrights, and of libraries and places of learning—considered himself to be, like Essex, the successor to Philip Sydney. To Southampton was dedicated, in 1593, the 'first heir' of Shakespeare's 'invention'—the erotic narrative poem *Venus and Adonis*. His wife, Elizabeth Vernon, was Essex's cousin. Essex's wife, Frances, was the daughter of Sir Francis Walsingham and widow of Sir Philip Sydney. Penelope Rich was Essex's golden haired, black-eyed, beautiful sister, who had previously been considered as a bride for Sir Philip Sydney; but sadly her father died before the match could be arranged and her guardian (Huntingdon) married her in 1581 to 'the rich Lord Rich'. Sydney remained passionately in love with Penelope all his life and addressed her as 'Stella' in his sonnets.[20] After Sidney's death in 1586 Penelope became the mistress of Sir Charles Blount, Lord Mountjoy.

Mary Sydney, Countess of Pembroke, was Sir Philip Sydney's sister and the mother of 'the Two Noble Brethren' to whom the Shakespeare First Folio was dedicated. Her husband, Henry Herbert, the 2nd Earl of Pembroke, whose country estate at Wilton bordered on the Wiltshire River Avon, was the patron of his own professional acting company, the Lord Pembroke's Men, who owned and performed the early Shakespeare plays. Mary was a

Building Paradise

devoted patroness of the arts and learning, and of poets, who saw to it that her brother's epic poem *Arcadia* was completed and published after his death. The poet Samuel Daniel was a tutor to Mary's eldest son, William Herbert.

John Florio, a poet and scholar, was a friend of Giordano Bruno[21] who came to England in 1585. Florio, who was previously in the service of the Earl of Leicester, entered Southampton's household in the early 1590's. He tutored Essex in Italian whilst working on his own Italian-English dictionary and the English translation of the essays of Anthony Bacon's friend, Michel de Montaigne.[22] Influences from these essays are to be found in *The Tempest, Hamlet* and *King Lear*, whilst Florio himself is thought to be caricatured as Holofernes in *Love's Labour's Lost*. Florio's wife was a sister of the poet Samuel Daniel.

Oxford, the hereditary Lord Great Chamberlain who was brought up as a ward of Burghley, was noted as a poet and writer of comedies as well as being a patron of poets and dramatists. He also had his own acting companies, Oxford's Boys and Oxford's Men. His harsh treatment of his wife, Anne Cecil, Burghley's daughter, became a matter of great concern to the group of family and friends, as well as to the Queen, who between them contrived an eventual reunion of the couple. Much of *All's Well That Ends Well,* written in 1598, ten years after Anne's death in 1588 and seven years after Oxford's second marriage to Elizabeth Trentham in 1591, is largely based upon Oxford's marriage to Anne. The play's title was first recorded in Francis Bacon's private notebook in 1594.[23]

The novelist and dramatist John Lyly, who had been at Cambridge University at the same time as the Bacon brothers, entered the service of the Earl of Oxford as Oxford's secretary from 1580 onwards, writing plays for Oxford's Boys from 1583 to 1590. The style of *Love's Labour's Lost* was derived from Lyly's romance, *Eupheus, the Anatomy of Wit,* published in 1578. Lyly eventually became one of Anthony Bacon's 'good pens' at Essex House. Later, however, he was suspected of being a spy at Essex House, acting for Burghley.

In February 1592 Anthony Bacon returned home from the continent. Anthony, whom Francis called his 'dearest brother' and 'comfort', shared Francis' aspirations. His main love was literary and, like his brother, he was a secret poet, known only as such to his friends, as revealed in their letters to him. But his wit and his talents as a multi-linguist were much in demand, and he put them at the service of the Queen and Burghley, who sent him on his twelve-year mission. All the time he was abroad he kept in constant correspondence with his brother Francis as well as with his uncle and Sir Francis Walsingham.

Anthony Bacon's foreign contacts were widespread and he enjoyed friendship in many high places, 'being a gentleman whose ability the world taketh knowledge of for matters of state, specially foreign'.[24] His contacts and friendship with Henri of Navarre, later Henri IV of France, were later incorporated into the Shakespeare play, *Love's Labour's Lost*, as also was the result of his association with the King of Spain's Secretary of State, Antonio Perez, who defected to England and upon whom the character of Don Adriana de Armado is based.

When Anthony returned to England he joined his brother at Gray's Inn, and started to pour all his energy and financial resources into his brother's project whilst at the same time continuing his intelligence work. Together the brothers formed a scrivenery of secretaries and writers ('good pens') to assist them, dealing with political intelligence, cryptography, translations of correspondence and books in foreign languages and the classics, invention of new words, and literature generally. Moreover, it was about this time that Francis Bacon started that part of his *Promus of Formularies and Elegancies* which has survived—a 'storehouse' or notebook containing nearly two thousand observations and expressions in several languages, most of which were incorporated into the Shakespeare plays.[25] Anthony Bacon's extensive correspondence with princes, statesmen, ambassadors, poets and writers across Europe was also used as a resource for the plays, as well as his twelve years of experience abroad as the Queen's intelligencer.

With Anthony back in England with his brother, it soon became clear to them that their uncle Burghley, far from helping them as much as he had repeatedly promised, in return for their services, had in fact been holding back on his help, blocking Francis' advancement and taking most of the credit for Anthony's intelligence work to himself. He was full of promises and pleasant

Building Paradise

words to the brothers, but time proved that he did not exert himself much on their behalf or give much in return, and in fact was suspicious and at times antagonistic towards them. He and the Queen took all but gave little. He was the Queen's chief counsellor and friend, and in charge of the Queen's treasury and the lucrative Court of Wards. She held Francis in special regard and affection, and used him 'in her greatest causes'. Francis' official and financial situation could and should have been different, as also Anthony's: they had both served the Queen and Burghley faithfully and unceasingly. As it was, it was hard, with Lady Fortune (the 'Dark Lady' of the Shakespeare Sonnets) acting many times cruelly.

There was already a 'Shake-scene' in England when Anthony arrived home, with several Shakespeare plays being owned by acting companies—first by Lord Strange's Men (with whom the players from Leicester's Men, led by Burbage, had amalgamated in 1588), and then by Lord Pembroke's Men.[26] Sussex's Men were also credited with having performed *Titus Andronicus*, in addition to the other two companies. However, except for Robert Greene's brief mention (in August 1592) of the 'Shake-scene' and his associated complaint that there was an actor taking the credit for plays that were not his,[27] it was an anonymous dramatic output. This was soon to be changed.

In April 1593 the 'William Shakespeare' pseudonym was made public with the printing of the highly erotic and scholarly poem, *Venus and Adonis*, dedicated to the Bacon brothers' close friend, 'cousin', co-student and patron, the Earl of Southampton,[28] as a sign to both contemporary and future students of the wisdom traditions as to what was afoot.[29] This was quickly followed in 1594 with another poem, *The Rape of Lucrece*, carrying the same signature. Whether this was done because Anthony had now rejoined Francis, or because two further 'new stars' or novae appeared in the constellation of Cassiopeia in November-December 1592, is an open question, but the 'new stars' were certainly like heavenly signs of the two brothers' partnership and the herald of something important, as had been the supernova in Cassiopeia in 1572-4. Except for these two poems, however, it was not until 1598 that any plays were printed with the Shakespeare signature. When they were, some of them deliberately made the pseudonym more visible by printing the name as 'Shake-speare'.

Just as the 'Shakespeare' name was launched onto the public scene for the first time, a major crisis arose for Francis. When Parliament was called in February 1593 Francis, as a Member of Parliament representing Middlesex, dared to stand up in the House of Commons against an attempt by the Queen and Lord Burghley not only to demand some exorbitant grants to pay for debts incurred in helping the King of France and sending troops to the Netherlands, but also to take away the Common's vitally important prerogative of raising taxes, which was their only real power. When the Queen heard of this stand she was furious and Francis was made to feel her displeasure, being denied access to her presence, which hitherto he had enjoyed with an unusual freedom. She told him 'that he must nevermore look to her for favour or promotion'.

Such a royal excommunication precipitated a major crisis for Francis, who supported himself and his literary work mainly by loans and credit; and, although helped by his mother and Anthony, who sold two estates to assist Francis (and eventually beggared himself on his brother's behalf), Francis was driven by necessity to practice law seriously. So it was that on 25 January 1594 Francis pleaded his first case in the King's Bench, with others to follow. His first pleading was so successful that Burghley, content with Francis as a lawyer and pressured by his own family who had taken pity on Francis' predicament, undertook to make a report 'where it might do him the most good'.

The Queen played a game of punishment or reward with Francis, trying to make him her creature in all ways, including the Parliamentary one. In 1594 the position of Attorney General fell vacant and was kept vacant for a whole year, and several times it was intimated to Francis that the Queen might appoint him to this position and that it was only his conduct in Parliament that stood in the way. Essex, eager to help Francis, urged the Queen to appoint him to this position. But Francis would not recant, and there were other factors afoot. Robert Cecil suggested to Essex that if Sir Edward Coke, the Solicitor-General, were to be appointed as Attorney-General, which he felt the Queen would prefer, then perhaps Francis might be content with the lesser position of

Building Paradise

Solicitor-General instead. But Essex would not have it. Only the higher office would do for the friend of Essex! As Essex saw it, his own reputation was at stake. The result was that the Attorney-Generalship went instead to Coke, and Francis was also by-passed for the office of Solicitor-General.

Essex was mortified by this result, feeling it as a matter of pride, and bestowed on Francis a gift of land in Twickenham in token recompense for what he felt was his failure to help his friend. Francis was able to raise money on the land to ease his situation; later he sold it.[30]

But, despite the fact that (or perhaps because) Francis thought of retiring to Cambridge with a couple of men to spend his life in studies and contemplation, matters between him and the Queen did improve that year. In the summer the Queen appointed him one of her Counsel learned in the Law and conferred on him some woodland in Somerset at a nominal rent.[31] Then for her Accession Day celebration on 17 November 1594 Francis wrote *The Device of the Indian Prince,* filled with flattering and adulatory references to the Queen, which helped to reconcile her to Essex, who had, thanks to a book published abroad, been under a shadow of suspicion concerning his influence with the Queen upon the matter of succession. The Device was sponsored by Essex and took place at York House. It was so successful that Her Majesty was extremely pleased. She was reconciled to Francis and on that very day made over to him the reversion of the lease of certain lands in Twickenham Park—a concession on the basis of which he could raise some more money to satisfy his creditors for a while.[32]

Creditors were a continual problem, as Francis's project was costly and he never ever had enough money. His brother Anthony was the main source of his help on this matter. The friendship between the two brothers, and the difficulties they endured through being forced year after year to raise loans from usurers, and the eventual bankruptcy of Anthony on his brother's behalf, was strongly reflected in the Shakespeare play, *The Merchant of Venice.* In the play Antonio is a good caricature of Anthony, who did trade abroad (but in intelligence rather than merchandise) and who hazarded all for his brother's sake. Likewise Bassanio is a self-portrait of Francis, whose 'Portia' he sought after was, in a philosophical sense, Wisdom on her Mount of Beauty ('Belmont'), and, in a personal sense, his rich cousin Lady Hatton (see below), whose London garden was renowned for its beauty. Many times either one or the other brother had to attend court and pay the forfeits demanded for late repayment of the loans. Being a lawyer and 'learned in the law', Francis often pleaded his own case. He was even arrested for debt at one time (September 1598), unjustly as it happened, because of the maliciousness of a particular debtor, and had to be rescued from the awful possibility of incarceration in the Fleet.

At the end of 1594, during the Gray's Inn Christmas Revels, a dramatic work by Francis Bacon hinted publicly at the existence of a Rosicrucian society associated with the pseudonym of 'William Shake-speare'. The twelve days of revels included certain 'Grand Nights', the first of which became known as the 'Night of Errors', named after the Shakespeare comedy, *The Comedy of Errors*, that had been performed there that evening (Holy Innocents' Day, 28th December) and the general commotion that had taken place. This supposedly brought the good name of Gray's Inn into disrepute and so a second Grand Night was arranged five days later to put matters right. The entertainment for this was called 'The Honourable Order of the Knights of the Helmet', written by Francis Bacon, in which he presented some of his philosophical ideals and an Order of knighthood dedicated to carrying them out. The purpose of the Order was to correct the errors and bring order out of chaos. The name of this philosophical Order relates to the divine spear-shaker, Pallas Athena, the tenth Muse and Patroness of the Arts and Sciences, who presents helmets of illumination to her knight-heroes. These helmets are said to bestow 'invisibility' on the wearer as well as being 'will helms' (*i.e.* William)—helmets of divine will and light.

In 1595, at the Queen's behest, Francis 'knit' Anthony's service to the Earl of Essex.[33] As a result, in August 1595 Anthony moved into Essex House to act as the Earl's 'Secretary of State', partly in the hope of counter-balancing the increased power base of the Cecil faction. 1595 was the year in which the Lord Treasurer Burghley completed his personal *coup d'état* by seeing his son Robert, who was knighted in 1591 and made a member of the Privy Council, and who had been unofficially filling the vacant office of Secretary of State for several years, achieve the politically

Building Paradise

powerful position of Chancellor of the Duchy of Lancaster. This climb to power culminated the following year when Robert was officially made the Principal Secretary of State, cementing the father-son combo which together held the reins of power in the Queen's Government. (When Burghley died in 1598, Robert continued as Secretary of State, maintaining his position of power.)

Only two years later, in 1597, a hazardous situation arose, in which the Shakespeare play of *Richard II* was involved. Again, this had to do with the royal succession, but this time it was a question of the deposing and 'voluntary' abdication of a king. When first performed, the historical deposition scene was included; but the Queen was both horrified and incensed by it, seeing herself regarded by certain of her courtiers as 'Richard' and Essex as 'Bolingbroke'. Subsequently the play was performed with the offending deposition scene omitted. Simultaneously both it and other plays that followed were published with the name of 'William Shakespeare' appearing on their title-pages for the first time. The actor Will Shakspere suddenly acquired a lot of money, reportedly from the Earl of Southampton, and set himself up in Stratford-upon-Avon with a fine house and trading business, and Essex continued in the Queen's high favour. It was also in that year that Francis had a book published under his own name of 'Francis Bacon' for the first time, this being the first version of his *Essays*, which he dedicated with affection to his 'Loving and beloved Brother', Anthony, referring to Anthony as 'you that are next myself'.

Anthony was not the only person Francis loved deeply, howbeit as a brother, friend and partner in his grand scheme. Francis was also enamoured of his cousin, Elizabeth Cecil, one of Burghley's granddaughters, with whom he had flirted when younger. He continued his friendship with Elizabeth after she was married to Sir William Hatton in 1594, which friendship deepened over the following years. When Elizabeth was widowed in 1597 Francis courted her seriously, requesting her hand in marriage. But another disappointment was in store for Francis, and once again Sir Edward Coke, now Attorney General and wealthy, won the day.

In 1599 trouble between the Queen and Essex flared up dangerously, Essex consistently acting against the advice of both

Life of Francis Bacon

Francis and Anthony, who urged Essex not to seek a military position and not to go to Ireland at the head of the English army—both of which he did. Just before Essex set out for Ireland in March 1599, a potentially volatile situation arose for both Francis and Essex in which the Shakespeare play of *Richard II* was again involved. This time a book based on the play had been published by a young doctor of civil law, John Hayward, a friend of both Essex and Bacon, which in its preface likened Essex to Bolingbroke and seemed to exhort Essex to rise up against the Queen and usurp the throne.[34] Hayward was arrested and Francis was immediately called before the Queen to explain and sort matters out, the Queen seemingly knowing of Francis' authorship of the Shakespeare play. Fifteen months later Francis was again involved on the same subject, when Essex was arraigned before the Queen's Council on a charge of disobeying Her Majesty's orders in Ireland. Francis, as one of the Queen's Counsel, was given the specific role of charging Essex concerning the use of Hayward's book, a role to which he objected, remarking that 'it would be said that I gave in evidence mine own tales'.[35]

When all this culminated in February 1601 with Essex's abortive attempt to raise an armed insurrection against the Queen and her government, which led to his trial for treason and subsequent execution (25 February 1601), the Bacon brothers were devastated. Essex, who had been secretly plotting and preparing his insurrection for several years, had misled both of them, and they only learnt the full truth during and after the trial. Both brothers had worked hard to try to prove the supposed innocence of Essex, and Francis did all he could to mediate with the Queen on Essex's behalf, right up to the end, at the expense of his own relationship with her. Francis was ordered by the angry Queen to take part in the trial as her Counsel Learned, assisting the State Prosecutor. As if these tragic events were not enough, a few months after Essex's execution Anthony, who had not been well, was reported to have died (27 May 1601). It is perhaps not surprising that in this and the following five years the deeply introspective great Shakespeare tragedies were produced—*Hamlet* (1601), *Othello* (1604), *King Lear* (1604-5) and *Macbeth* (1605-6).

Building Paradise

THE JACOBEAN PERIOD

Queen Elizabeth went to her grave just two years later (24 March 1603), and in July 1603 King James VI of Scotland was crowned King James I of England. Anthony Bacon had, over the years, done some good service for the Scottish king, and Francis, who pleaded his case as a 'concealed poet' who was for the most part one with his brother in 'endeavour and duties', was helped by King James as a result. In Queen Elizabeth's reign Francis had been continually by-passed in terms of being given a position where he could command both a sufficient income and influence for the needs of his great project, and his service under the Tudor queen had gone largely unpaid, except for the promise of the reversion of the position of Clerk to the Star Chamber when it became vacant, the granting under favourable terms of the lease of Twickenham Park, which became Francis' favourite retreat and home for his scrivenery, the lease of the Rectory of Cheltenham, and the payment of a fee of £1200 for his services at Essex's trial. With James, after a cautious start, it was to be different.

The Stuart king soon came to rely on Francis' exceptional talents and to recognise them officially; but, as with Elizabeth, it was primarily in the highways and byways of law that he drew Francis' services to him, although Francis eventually became the principal adviser to the King on all matters. (Not that James always took notice of the advice: if he had done so more often, many unfortunate situations might have been avoided, including the mismanagement and rape of Ireland.[36])

Francis' philanthropic literary work in the reign of Elizabeth, and the largely unpaid legal work for his sovereign, had left him in dire straights financially. Anthony had died with debts that had to be paid, whilst Francis had his own debts, to cover which his Twickenham Park lease was mortgaged. The literary work was still continuing and had to be supported, and meaningful and sufficient patronage was still not forthcoming. Therefore, even though he inherited the manors and estates of Gorhambury from his brother, which brought a modicum of financial security, Francis still needed to earn a reasonable income, even if it meant practising law more fully and trying to obtain an official position in the King's service.

Life of Francis Bacon

First Francis was knighted on 23 July 1603, along with three hundred others at Whitehall, two days before the coronation of King James and his Queen, Anne of Denmark, in Westminster Abbey. Then, a year later, in August 1604, he was confirmed by letters patent as a member of the King's Counsel Learned with a pension of £40 per annum. It was at this time that he started writing the tracts that were the forerunners of his *Great Instauration*, including his first version of *The Advancement of Learning*, to be published in October 1605.

Francis also met in 1603 Alice Barnham, a wealthy alderman's daughter, 'an handsome maiden,' to whom he took a liking with a view to marriage when she was old enough (she was only eleven years old when they first met). A little over two years later, on 10 May 1606, when she was fourteen and he forty-five, they married. She brought with her a dowry of £6000 plus an annual income of £220,[37] which Francis allowed her to keep for herself, whilst he settled on her a further income for life of £500 per annum. Francis treated his wife with much conjugal love and respect, and for all the years of their marriage (*i.e.* until his death) they appear to have lived together happily, in peace and contentment, and with style. It is noteworthy that it was after his marriage (a condition that Francis had longed for) that the four great Shakespeare romances were written—*Pericles* (1607), *Cymbeline* (1609-10), *The Tempest* (1610) and *The Winter's Tale* (1611).

On 25 June 1607, the year after his marriage to Alice, Francis was appointed Solicitor-General with a pension of £1000 per annum. This was not a particularly onerous position but one that Francis hoped would allow him to enlarge his private practice.[38] In 1609 the reversion of Clerk of the Star Chamber fell to him at last, which happily boosted his financial resources even further. One of the legal works that he became engaged in during this time was the preparation of a royal charter for the Virginia Company. He had long been involved with the dream of establishing a new and enlightened society—a commonwealth—in the 'virgin land' of North America, and was a council member of the Virginia Company along with his young friends, William, Earl of Montgomery, and Philip, Earl of Pembroke, the 'Incomparable Paire' to whom the 1623 Shakespeare Folio was later to be dedicated. Another member was the Earl of Southampton, to whom

Building Paradise

the poems *Venus and Adonis* and *Lucrece* had been dedicated, but with whom Francis was now out of favour because of his enforced role in the Essex affair, for which Southampton, misunderstanding the situation, never forgave Bacon.

The London Virginia Company was the first to succeed in establishing a permanent English settlement in North America, founding Jamestown on 14 May 1607. The new 1609 charter that Sir Francis Bacon, as the King's Solicitor-General, prepared for James' signature established a new governing council for the colony.[39] (This charter of 1609, and the later one of 1612 that Francis was also involved in, were the beginnings of constitutionalism in North America and the germ of the later Constitution of the United States.) The fleet carrying the new governor and much-needed supplies and men set sail for Virginia in May 1609, but before it reached the shores of America a storm blew up that separated the flagship, the *Sea-Adventure*, from the other ships and forced it towards the rocky coast of the Bermudas (on the 25 July 1609). The other ships of the fleet, with one exception, managed to reach Jamestown safely, but in the belief that the *Sea-Adventure* and all aboard her had perished. A confidential report to the Virginia Company's council was sent back to England before the end of 1609, giving news of the storm and the supposed foundering of the *Sea-Adventure*. However, the *Sea-Adventure* and all aboard her survived unharmed and, after living on the island for a further nine months, they managed to refloat the ship and sail on to Virginia, reaching the Jamestown colony in May 1610. An official but confidential report on this 'miracle' as well as on the state of Virginia generally was sent by William Strachey, Sir Thomas Gates' secretary, to the council members of the Virginia Company.[40] This report was a primary inspiration and source of detail for *The Tempest*, which Francis began to compose soon afterwards.[41]

In 1611 Sir Francis Bacon was appointed President of the Court of the Verge and Chief Advisor to the Crown. On 26 October 1613 he became the Attorney General, and on 9 June 1616 a Privy Councillor. With the Attorney Generalship Francis became far more fully immersed in the King's business, with little time left for writing. What precious moments he had for literary matters he mainly devoted to perfecting the writing and presentation of his

Life of Francis Bacon

New Method, the first two books of which he wrote in Latin and published in 1620 as the *Novum Organum*. *Henry VIII* thus became the last Shakespeare play to be completed (c.1612-13), but as this was done with the collaboration of John Fletcher, it is *The Tempest* that is traditionally said to be Shakespeare's last play.[42]

Finally, to cap his political and legal service to the Crown, on 7 March 1617 the King appointed Sir Francis Bacon as his Lord Keeper of the Great Seal (the 'keeper of the King's conscience'), and immediately left him to act as his virtual regent in England whilst he departed for Scotland for a six-month visit—the first of his reign as King of Great Britain. Even with the King absent Lord Bacon took his place in Chancery with magnificent ceremony. In his procession to Westminster Hall he was escorted by 200 knights and gentlemen mounted on horse, together with lords of His Majesty's Council, the nobility, courtiers and followers of the Queen and Prince of Wales, plus the judges and fellows of the Inns of Court. He himself was dressed in purple satin, as he was on his wedding day—a privilege normally reserved for royalty.

Having taken up his new position Francis worked exhaustively to make up for the delays in Chancery caused by the illness of his predecessor, his old friend Lord Ellesmere, and by the workings of Chancery generally. He doubled the amount of time that he personally, together with his staff, were traditionally expected to spend on Chancery matters, in order to expedite and clear the causes of the court, although he made sure to reserve the depth of the vacations 'for studies, arts, and sciences', to which, he said in his inaugural speech, he was in his nature most inclined.

Ten months of hard work later, on 4 January 1618, King James bestowed the honour of Lord Chancellorship upon Francis. By this time Francis had moved into York House, the home of his father as Lord Keeper and of all subsequent Lord Keepers, and where his father had died and he had been born and bred. This was a home which meant a great deal to him and he set about making it into a beautiful mansion, repairing and furnishing it lovingly and lavishly, connecting it by pipe to the City's main water supply, building an aviary in its gardens, and installing in it a huge household of servants and retainers, all dressed in his livery. When he had money Francis was a big spender and

Building Paradise

SIR FRANCIS BACON, LORD KEEPER OF THE GREAT SEAL AND LORD HIGH CHANCELLOR OF ENGLAND
Oil painting by Paul Van Somer (1618);
from the Gorhambury collection.

exceptionally generous. As a lover of theatre he thoroughly enjoyed pageantry and ceremony, and believed it was an important part of statecraft.

Francis also at this time had the lease of Canonbury Manor, a fine mansion on Islington's hill, with panoramic views over London and fine oak-panelled rooms decorated with Masonic and Rosicrucian symbolism. He took on a forty-year lease of this house and its park in 1616, the year when the Rosicrucian 'Invisible College' was reputedly founded. (The Invisible College eventually gave rise to the Royal Society and other societies, academies and orders, based on Francis' proposals and inspiration). Francis referred to this Invisible College in his *New Atlantis* as 'the College of the Six Days' Work'—Bacon's whole project or 'Great Instauration' being based on his understanding of the biblical Six Days of Creation. The following year (1617) this College made a brief public appearance when Bacon's friend, Edmund Bolton, presented James I with a proposal to found an official Society or College for the advancement of learning along Baconian lines, to be called 'King James' Academy or College of Honour', the members of whom were to 'love, honour and serve each other according to the spirit of St John'. Regrettably this never obtained Parliament's approval.

Fittingly, on 12 July 1618 His Majesty raised Francis to the peerage, creating him Baron Verulam. Two and a half years later, on 3rd February 1621, in celebration of Francis' 60th birthday and of over three years of faithful unstinting service as Lord Keeper and Chancellor, the King created Francis Viscount St Alban.

Almost immediately upon receiving the last title, at the height of his public glory, a plot that had been hatched against Francis by those who envied him and his position came to fruition. It fell upon him like a bombshell, even though friends such as Tobie Matthew had tried to warn him that something dangerous was afoot. The result of the plot led to Francis' impeachment in Parliament (during March-April 1621) on concocted charges of corruption. The King, in order to move attention away from the extravagant behaviour of his favourite Buckingham and his own weakness, ordered his Lord Chancellor to offer no defence and to plead guilty. Sentence was given on 3 May 1621. Francis was stripped of his office and banned from holding any further office, place or employment in the State or Commonwealth, or from sitting in Parliament. He was banished from the verge of court, fined the enormous sum of £40,000 (the equivalent of about £20 million today) and imprisoned in the Tower of London.

Francis' imprisonment at the end of May was, however, brief. After a few days he was released, although banished from London and commanded to retire to Gorhambury until the King's pleasure should be further known. Gorhambury was a beautiful and relaxing place for vacations, but to live there month after month meant that he and his wife were cut off from society and their friends, and he from his books and papers and helpers, and the stimulating company of other good minds. Francis longed to return to the metropolis so as to work on his writings, and he grieved greatly that his wife had to suffer on his behalf. He pleaded with the King to be allowed to return to London. He begged also for financial help in order just to live, having sold his plate and jewels and other commodities in order to pay his creditors and servants what he owed them, so that they should suffer as little as possible.

On 16 September 1621 King James issued a licence permitting Francis to return to London (but to lodge at Sir John Vaughan's house, not York House, and only for six weeks), and on 20 September 1621 he assigned the fine of £40,000 to four trustees of Francis' own choosing, which meant in effect that Francis was freed of its burden. Moreover, on 12 October 1621 King James signed a warrant for Francis' pardon. From the historical evidence and the tone of Francis' letters to Buckingham and the King, this pardoning of Francis would seem to have been because of an understanding Francis had with the King, as part of the agreement whereby he would plead guilty to the charges made against him: but nevertheless the damage was done and Francis' good name was and remains to this day tarnished in the eyes of the world as a result.

Francis' bitter experience was not yet over. Although the King had granted his pardon, the new Lord Keeper, Bishop Williams, delayed putting his seal on it. Until this was done Francis was still not legally a completely free man and, more to the point, was shut out of London (his six weeks at Sir John Vaughan's house having elapsed) and could not return to his beloved York House.

Life of Francis Bacon

Eventually it was made known to Francis that the delay was caused by Buckingham, who desired York House for his own purposes. Until Francis surrendered the house he would not be given either his full pardon or his freedom. Francis tried every way he could not to lose his beautiful and convenient London home, with its strong sentimental value and into which he had poured so much of himself and his finances, but eventually he had to give way. In mid-March 1622 he surrendered York House to Buckingham, the Marquis contracting to buy the lease for £1,300. Immediately Francis' pardon and freedom arrived, signed, sealed and delivered, and by November his pension and a grant from the petty writs, both of which had been illegally stopped, had been restored to him—but not without him having to borrow money from friends and write to the King as a supplicant in great extremity.

To begin with, sometime at the end of March 1622, Francis moved with his wife and household to a house in Chiswick, but this was only temporary; for by June that year they had taken up residence in Bedford House on the Strand. This now became their London home, Gorhambury still being their country abode and family estate in Francis' ownership (unlike Bedford House, which was leased).

During his time of banishment from court and forced retirement at Gorhambury (June 1621–March 1622) Francis would have been able to spend time on the final planning and organisation of the presentation of his Great Instauration to the world at large, gathering further material for his Natural History, the third part of his Great Instauration, and writing his revised and greatly enlarged final version of the *Advancement of Learning*. This latter work was to represent the first part of the Great Instauration, the second part (the *Novum Organum*) having already been published in 1620. Moreover, it was probably during the six weeks in London (September-October 1621) that he issued instructions for the collecting together of the Shakespeare plays and the purchasing of the publishing rights for them, so that they could be published collectively as his example of the fourth part of the Great Instauration—his working model or 'machine' as he called it, by means of which the data collected concerning natural, human and divine nature might be 'set as it were before the eyes'.[43] For this he

Building Paradise

had Ben Jonson to help him, one of his 'good pens who forsake me not'. His other remaining 'good pens' included George Herbert, Thomas Hobbes, Peter Böener, Dr. William Rawley and Sir Thomas Meautys.

Once back in London the composition and translation into Latin of the *Advancement of Learning* went full steam ahead, although it was not until the autumn of 1623 that it was finally published (as the *De Dignitate et Augmentis Scientiarum*). The timing of this went hand in hand with the publication of the Shakespeare plays, the printing of which was set in motion early in 1622, probably under the supervision of Ben Jonson. The famous folio of plays was published during the last two months of 1623, entitled *William Shakespeare's Comedies, Histories and Tragedies*. The parallel publication of these two works—the *De Augmentis* and the Shakespeare plays—was important and obviously carefully planned, as they are twinned in the Cabalistic design of the Great Instauration. (See Chapter 4.)

Francis also busied himself at this time with researching and writing a history of the reign of King Henry VII, as part of his intended collection of histories of the later sovereigns of England, and with making a start on a collection of studies that would comprise his example of a Natural History. Both *The History of the Reign of King Henry VII* and the first of six essays on natural history (*Historia Ventorum*, 'The History of Winds') were published in 1622.

Always Francis did his best to maintain his wife in a state befitting a viscountess, and had settled on her a suitable income, in addition to her own private one, which she enjoyed throughout their marriage. This meant that by February 1623 Francis was again in financial difficulties. He tried to sell Gorhambury to Buckingham, but the Marquis was at that time about to embark for Spain with Charles, the Prince of Wales, to pursue the proposal for the marriage of the King of Spain's daughter to the Prince. Failing to sell Gorhambury, Bedford House had to be given up, as being too expensive to run. This left Gorhambury as their only stately home, so that when in London Lady Bacon had to rely on staying with family or friends, whilst Francis retired to his 'cell'—his chambers at Gray's Inn—where he could carry on with his writings.

Life of Francis Bacon

When the provostship of Eton fell vacant in April 1623, Francis applied to the King for the position, as it would have fulfilled his original desire to have a suitable position with a small but sufficient income to sustain him wherein he could 'command wits and pens' and oversee the education of bright young minds. But even in this he failed. the position having already been promised to another, and King James being unable to believe that his ex-Lord Keeper and Lord Chancellor, who in title was a viscount, would want to take up such a humble position. The truth of the matter was, though, that beyond granting the pardon (which was never given in full, as Francis was denied being able to sit in parliament for the rest of his life), neither the King nor Buckingham did anything whatsoever to help Francis, other than to say friendly and encouraging things in answer to his letters and pleas.

So Francis remained at Gray's Inn, writing copiously and urgently, and living at Gorhambury with his wife from time to time. Each year, usually in the summer months, he was subject to bouts of sickness, but always seemed to recover. He never lost his profound hope, his extraordinary mental faculties or his zest for completing his great work. Yet within three years he was to die, outliving by one year the King whom he had served so well, who died on 27 March 1625 and who was succeeded by his son Charles I.

Even though Francis never completed his work to his own satisfaction, yet by the time he died he had produced remarkable examples of the first four parts or stages of the Great Instauration (and possibly of the fifth and sixth if we could but find or identify them), constructed a treasure hunt to teach and train others, and set in motion a work that others could take up—a work that Francis knew would grow and evolve, and take many ages to complete.

In the early years of King James' reign Francis had been able to continue writing the Shakespeare plays and other works. In addition, as his experiments began to bear fruit, he started to develop and publish his philosophical works under his own name of Bacon; but this he did carefully, a little at a time, not revealing the critical role of drama until his final 1623 version of the *Advancement of Learning*—the *De Augmentis Scientiarum*. Like the *Novum Organum* that he had published in 1620, the *De Augmentis*

Building Paradise

was written in Latin with the help of George Herbert, Ben Jonson and others as translators—the reason being, he said, so that other nations might have the benefit of reading the work as well as his own countrymen, Latin being at that time the universal language of the learned.

During the early Jacobean period Francis had become directly involved with the Virginia Company and its schemes to colonise North America, sitting on its council together with the Earls of Pembroke and Montgomery, and the Earl of Southampton. Moreover, Francis was largely responsible for drawing up, in 1609 and 1612, the two charters of government for the Virginia Colony. These charters were the beginnings of constitutionalism in North America and the germ of the later Constitution of the United States of America. The confidential report[44] sent to the Virginia Company council members by William Strachey in 1609, concerning the shipwreck of the Company's flagship, the Sea Adventurer, on the Bermudas, gave Francis some good material on which to base his account of the island and shipwreck in *The Tempest,* the so-called 'last' Shakespeare play.

The very last Shakespeare play, however, appears to have been *All is True,* thought to have been written sometime between the end of 1612 and June 1613, when the Globe Theatre accidentally burnt down during a performance of the play. This play, or a later version of it, was first published in the 1623 Shakespeare Folio as *The Life of King Henry the Eight*, with certain additions that Francis wrote after his impeachment. These additions include the prologue and Cardinal Wolsey's farewell speech, and details of Wolsey's fall as Lord Chancellor and Keeper of the Great Seal, that are purposely mixed with details of Bacon's own personal experience when he had the Great Seal taken from him, thus making a kind of signature.

Francis' impeachment in 1621, although a severe blow to his good name, was to him a release from the burden of legal and State service, enabling him to devote himself entirely to his greatest love and real mission in life. During the last five years of his life he worked like a superman, collecting together, revising, polishing and finishing works already commenced, completing or at least making a start on other projects already planned, and seeing his greatest works through publication, including the Shakespeare Folio of comedies, histories and tragedies. For all this he was helped by those 'good pens' of his who, after his fall, forsook him not—men whose names should be remembered with gratitude.

Ever a master of drama and symbolism, it was on Easter Day, 9th April 1626, that Sir Francis Bacon, Baron Verulam, Viscount St Alban, died. He left copious manuscripts and letters, a library of books and a generous will—although he died so much in debt due to his misfortune that the benefits of his will could not be fully realised. Some of his letters and manuscripts were given into the care of his principal secretary and friend, Sir Thomas Meautys, others to his chaplain Dr William Rawley, and some to be looked after by his brother-in-law Sir John Constable and his literary friend Sir William Boswell, the English Ambassador at The Hague. Francis left them instructions to publish some of the material and to reserve others to a 'private succession' of literary 'sons'. His extensive library he bequeathed to Constable, but it seems that the books had to be sold because of the insolvency of his estate when he died. Upon his death tributes poured forth from many men of letters, praising him not only as the greatest philosopher who had lived in many ages but also as the Star of Poets, the Apollo who led not only the other writers and poets but the Muses themselves. From then on, as Ben Jonson remarked, 'wits daily grow downward'. The unique half-century of brilliant English Renaissance culture was over. The 'light' had vanished, but not the inheritance that it has left behind for us to enjoy.

Building Paradise

THE MASTER AND HIS PUPILS
Frontispiece: *Sermones Fideles* (1641)
Latin edition of Francis Bacon's Essays.

TRIBUTES TO SIR FRANCIS BACON

During Francis Bacon's lifetime, and especially on his death, various tributes were given to him which identify him as a supreme poet and author as well as a philosopher and lawyer, who renovated philosophy by means of the stage and who was the acknowledged leader of the other wits and poets of his time. Highly talented people, including the poet Ben Jonson, both reverenced and adulated Bacon, referring to him as a secret poet, the best of them all, and one of the greatest of men who ever lived—a genius or Master soul who was entirely dedicated to philanthropy, and who devised a sure method and global plan for the gradual but certain upliftment and enlightenment of humanity. Indeed, the tributes identify Francis Bacon as the author Shakespeare, the great English Bard, and neither Bacon nor his vast philanthropic work can be understood correctly without realising this.

The first example given here of these tributes is by the poet, physician and Gray's Inn man, Thomas Campion, who wrote an epigram referring to Bacon's combination of 'prudence' and 'silent gravity' with 'celestial nectar' and 'merry wit' (*i.e.* his 'thorny' law and 'sweet' poetry) as well as to his Neoplatonic philosophy ('the Academy'):-

> To the Most High Chancellor of all England.
>   FR. BA. [Francis Bacon]
> How great thou stand'st before us, whether the thorny volumes of the Law
> Or the Academy, or the sweet Muses call thee, O Bacon!
> How thy prudence rules over great affairs!
> And thy whole tongue is moist with celestial nectar!

Building Paradise

How well combinest thou merry wit with silent gravity!
How firmly thy love stands by those once admitted to it.

Thomas Campion, *Epigrammatum. Lib II.*(1619).[1]

Another poet, John Davies of Hereford (?1565-1618), who published various poems from 1603 to 1617 and who was writing-master to Henry, Prince of Wales, likewise wrote a revealing epigram that refers to Bacon as both a lawyer and a poet, whose law was enriched by his poetic Muse and whose poetry was infused with his law:-

To the Royall Ingenious and All-learned Knight, Sir Francis Bacon.
Thy bounty and the beauty of thy witt
Compris'd in lists of Law and learned Arts,
Each making thee for great Imployment fitt,
Which now thou hast (though short of thy deserts,)
Compells my pen to let fall shining Inke
And to bedew the Baies that deck thy Front,
And to thy Health in Helicon to drinke,
As to her Bellamour the Muse is wont,
For thou dost her embosom; and dost use
Her company for sport twixt grave affaires:
So utter'st Law the livelyer through thy Muse.
And for that all thy Notes are sweetest Aires;
  My Muse thus notes thy worth in ev'ry line,
  With ynke which thus she sugars; so, to shine.

John Davies of Hereford, *Scourge of Folly* (c.1610).

This is in fact a fitting description of Bacon as Shakespeare, his nom-de-plume, for the Shakespeare plays are indeed infused with law and learning, and were Bacon's 'sport' or pleasure, which he far preferred above his law or 'grave affairs'. Elsewhere in his *Scourge of Folly* Davies refers to Shakespeare (the actor) as 'Our English Terence', truly giving the game away to those who know that Terence was a Roman slave famed for allowing his name to be used as a mask for the writings of great men, such as Scipio and Laelius. A few years earlier (1597) the Elizabethan writer, Joseph Hall, had also drawn back the veil of secrecy surrounding Shakespeare by attacking the author of

Tributes to Sir Francis Bacon

Venus and Adonis for concealing his identity under another name (William Shakespeare). Hall declared the real author 'Shakespeare' to be another Labeo,[2] referring to Antistius Labeo who was a celebrated lawyer in the time of the Roman Emperor Augustus and who lost favour with the Emperor for opposing his views, just as Bacon did when he opposed Elizabeth's views in Parliament in 1593, the same year in which *Venus and Adonis* was published.

Sir Tobie Matthew, linguist, translator, diplomat and son of the Archbishop of York, in one of his letters written to Bacon from France, refers to Bacon as not only being the 'most prodigious wit' in both England and on the continent, but also being masked by another person:-

> The most prodigious wit, that ever I knew of my nation, and of this side of the sea, is of your Lordship's name though he be known by another.
>
> Sir Tobie Matthew, Letter to Lord Bacon (1619)

Tobie Matthew had good reason to know Bacon well. He was another Gray's Inn man and a friend with whom Bacon frequently communicated by letter when Matthew was in exile because of his Roman Catholicism. Bacon used to send Tobie the manuscripts of his writings for Tobie to peruse and comment upon; and when Matthew was in England, Bacon, when Lord Chancellor, took Tobie under his wing, rescuing him from prison and protecting him from further persecution. Tobie Matthew translated Bacon's *Essays* and *Wisdom of the Ancients* into Latin whilst living in Bacon's home (1617-1619), and Bacon once referred to him as his 'alter ego'. The following quotation, from the dedicatory letter with which Matthew prefaced his Italian translation of Bacon's *Essays,* reveals the truly great and loving nature of Bacon:-

> And truly I have known a great number whom I much value, many whom I admire, but none who hath so astonished me and, as it were, ravished my senses, to see so many and so great parts which in other men were wont to be incompatible, united, and in that eminent degree in one sole person. I know

not whether this truth will find easy belief... The matter I report is so well understood in England, that every man knows and acknowledges as much, nay hath been an eye and ear witness whereof; nor if I should expatiate upon this subject, should I be held a flatterer, but rather a suffragan to truth...

Praise is not confined to the qualities of his intellect, but applies as well to those which are matters of the heart, the will and moral virtue; being a man both sweet in his ways and conversation, grave in his judgments, invariable in his fortunes, splendid in his expenses, a friend unalterable to his friends, an enemy to no man, a most indefatigable servant to the King, and a most earnest lover of the Public, having all the thoughts of that large heart of his set upon adorning the age in which he lives, and benefiting, as far as possible, the whole human race. And I can truly say (having had the honour to know him for many years as well when he was in his lesser fortunes as now he stands at the top and in the full flower of his greatness) that I never yet saw any trace in him of a vindictive mind, whatever injury was done to him, nor ever heard him utter a word to any man's disadvantage which seemed to proceed from personal feeling against the man, but only (and that too very seldom) from judgment made of him in cold blood. It is not his greatness that I admire, but his virtue; it is not the favours I have received from him (infinite though they be) that have thus enthralled and enchained my heart, but his whole life and character; which are such that, if he were of an inferior condition I could not honour him the less, and if he were my enemy, I should not the less love and endeavour to serve him.

Sir Tobie Matthew, Dedicatory Letter prefacing an Italian translation of Bacon's *Essays* and *Wisdom of Ancients* (1617).

Later on, when Bacon had been dead some years, Tobie Matthew continued his tribute to Bacon by describing him as not only one of the greatest men of the age, but perhaps the most knowledgeable and eloquent of men since the world began:-

It will go near to pose any other nation of Europe, to muster out in any age, four men, who in so many respects should excel four such as we are able to show them: Cardinal Wolsey, Sir Thomas More, Sir Philip Sydney and Sir Francis Bacon. The fourth was a creature of incomparable abilities of mind, of a sharp and catching apprehension, large and faithful memory, plentiful and sprouting invention, deep and solid judgement, for as such as might concern the understanding part. A man so rare in knowledge, of so many several kinds endued with the facility and felicity of expressing it in all so elegant, significant, so abundant, and yet so choice and ravishing a way of words, of metaphors and allusions as, perhaps, the world hath not seen, since it was a world.

> Tobie Matthew, Preface to his Collection of Letters (published 1660).

The famous poet Ben Jonson thought the same. He described Bacon as being the 'mark and acme' (*i.e.* the summit or culminating point of excellence) of the English language:-

Yet there happened in my time one noble speaker who was full of gravity in his speaking; his language, where he could spare or pass by a jest, was nobly censorious. No man ever spake more neatly, more pressly, more weightily, or suffered less emptiness, less idleness, in what he uttered. No member of his speech but consisted of his own graces. His hearers could not cough or look aside from him without loss. He commanded where he spoke, and had his judges angry or pleased at his devotion. No man had their affections more in his power. The fear of every man that heard him was lest he should make an end…

But the learned and able (though unfortunate) successor [Bacon] is he who hath filled up all numbers, and performed that in our tongue which may be compared or preferred either to insolent Greece, or haughty Rome. In short, within his view, and about his times, were all the wits born that could honour a language, or help study. Now things daily fall: wits grow downward, and Eloquence grows backward. So that he may be named and stand as the mark and acme of our language…

Building Paradise

> My conceit of his Person was never increased toward him by his place or honours. But I have and do reverence him for the greatness that was only proper to himself, in that he seemed to me ever, by his work, one of the greatest men and most worthy of admiration that had been in many ages. In his adversity I ever prayed that God would give him strength: for greatness he could not want. Neither could I condole in a word or syllable for him, as knowing no accident could do harm to virtue, but rather help to make it manifest.
>
> Ben Jonson, Discoveries (1641), p 102.

In this tribute Jonson uses the same descriptive accolade, borrowed from Seneca, as he used when adulating 'the Author' Shakespeare in his tributary poem in the Shakespeare Folio: namely, that Bacon had produced works that were greater than anything produced by 'insolent Greece or haughty Rome'.[3] The phrase, 'he who hath filled up all numbers,' is also noteworthy, for Jonson uses the word 'numbers' in the same well-known sense in which Cicero, Virgil, Horace and Ovid all used its Latin original, and which was likewise used in the Shakespeare works—*i.e.* referring to musical measure, verse or poetry.

> If I could write the beauty of your eyes,
> And in fresh numbers number all your graces,
> The age to come would say, 'This poet lies'.
>
> Shakespeare Sonnet 17.

> *Longaville.* I fear these stubborn lines lack power to move;
>   O sweet Maria, empress of my love,
>   These numbers I will tear, and write in prose.
>
> Shakespeare, Love's Labour's Lost, IV, iii, 52-54.

In other words, Ben Jonson proclaims that Bacon is supreme as a poet. Pope and Milton, in the 17th and 18th centuries, continued the use of the word in the same sense.

In Jonson's tribute to Bacon, he hints that in some way Bacon influenced all the wits of his time who could 'honour a language', and that with Bacon's death (in 1626) 'things daily fall: wits grow downward, and Eloquence grows backward'. That Bacon was

Tributes to Sir Francis Bacon

indeed the leader and inspirer of the wits is made abundantly clear in the tributes published upon his death. These tributes, known as the *Manes Verulamiani*,[4] are in the form of thirty-two Latin poems or elegies, plus a preface written by Bacon's private chaplain, William Rawley. The elegies, selected by Rawley from a much larger number of tributes to Francis Bacon, were largely written by scholars and Fellows of the Universities, and members of the Inns of Court, including a bishop, two royal chaplains and a Regius Professor of Divinity. They give ample proof that a large number of contemporaneous scholars, lawyers, poets, writers, and at least one printer, knew Bacon to be a supreme poet as well as an extraordinary philosopher. A full twenty-seven of them deal with the outstanding poetic genius of their deceased master.

The writers of these tributes include John Williams, Fellow of St John's College, Cambridge, chaplain to James I and Bishop of Lincoln, who became Lord Keeper of the Great Seal after Francis Bacon and later Archbishop of York; Henry Ferne, Fellow of Trinity College, Cambridge, who became Bishop of Chester in 1661; Samuel Collins, Regius Professor of Divinity at Cambridge; William Boswell, Fellow of Jesus College, Cambridge, diplomat, scholar, man-of-letters and, for a time, secretary to Sir Dudley Carleton, the Ambassador at the Hague; George Herbert, poet and musician, Fellow of Trinity College, Cambridge; Robert Ashley, Middle Temple barrister and writer; Thomas Randolf, poet and dramatist, one of Ben Jonson's adopted 'sons'; and John Haviland, the finest printer of the time. William Rawley, Fellow of Corpus Christi College, Cambridge, and Bacon's private chaplain (1619-1626), who wrote the preface to the *Manes*, became chaplain to Charles I and Charles II in turn after Bacon's death.

Rawley states that the elegies he chose to publish were by no means the best ones, which is rather extraordinary. Usually the case is that the best tributes are selected with which to publicly commemorate a person. But perhaps the best ones would have revealed too much too soon? However, even the thirty-two second-best elegies selected by Rawley manage to identify Bacon as the author Shakespeare and the leader of the poets and artists. The descriptions and symbolic analogies that are used for Shakespeare, which are carved on the Shakespeare Monument at Stratford-upon-Avon and set down in print, are repeated in these

Building Paradise

thirty-two remarkable Latin tributes to Francis Bacon—which, with Rawley's preface, make thirty-three contributions. These unique references are such that they cannot apply to two different people: there can only be one person, one supreme poet, one Shakespeare, and that Shakespeare is clearly Bacon.

First of all, 'E.F.' makes it clear that Bacon was a concealed poet:-

> Let expediency consider the better part of counsel, but add, a concealed poet from Ithaca, and you hold all.
>
> E.F., *Manes Verulamiani* (1626), Elegy 17.

'R.P.' explains that Bacon renewed philosophy by means of poetry in the form of comedy and tragedy—that is to say, stage drama:-

> So did Philosophy, entangled in the subtleties of Schoolmen seek Bacon as a deliverer... He renewed her, walking humbly in the socks of Comedy. After that, more elaborately he rises on the loftier buskin of Tragedy...
>
> R.P., *Manes Verulamiani* (1626), Elegy 4.

This passage not only clearly declares that Bacon was a playwright, writing for the stage and not just masques for Gray's Inn, but, more than this, that his plays were not just written as a pasttime or as entertainment only, but were an integral part of his Great Instauration.

Thomas Randolf goes further and associates Bacon with Pallas Athena (Minerva), whose name literally means 'Spear Shaker' or 'Shake-speare' (which is how the name of Shakespeare is often spelt on quartos of Shakespeare plays). Apollo, Athena's female counterpart, was also known as a Spear-Shaker, and Bacon is described as another Apollo who restores the honour of Athena and dispels the clouds that hid her light:-

> The ardour of his noble heart could bear no longer that you, divine Minerva, should be despised. His god-like pen restored your wonted honour and as another Apollo dispelled the clouds that hid you. But he dispelled also the darkness which

murky antiquity and blear-eyed old age of former times had brought about; and his super-human sagacity instituted new methods and tore away the labyrinthine windings, but gave us his own. Certainly it is clear that the crown of ancient sages had not such penetrating eyes. They were like Phoebus rising in the East, he like the same resplendent at noon… They begot the infant muses, he the adult. They were parents of mortal muses, he produced goddesses… Pallas too, now arrayed in a new robe, paces forth, as a snake shines when it has put off its old skin.

Thomas Randolf, Manes Verulamiani (1626), Elegy 32.

In the same tribute Randolf not only states that Bacon taught the Pegasean arts to grow with proper roots, but likens this to the spear of Quirinus which grew into a laurel tree.

When he [Bacon] perceived that the arts were held by no roots, and like seed scattered on the surface of the soil were withering away, he taught the Pegasean arts to grow, as grew the spear of Quirinus swiftly into a laurel tree.

Thomas Randolf, Manes Verulamiani (1626), Elegy 32.

The Pegasean arts are the poetic arts in particular, Pegasus being the winged white horse whose hoof struck the side of Mount Helicon and brought forth the Hippocrene, the Muses' stream of poetic inspiration. Quirinus, meaning 'Spearman', was the title of Romulus, the founder of Rome, whose laurel wood spear grew into the fragrant laurel or bay tree from which was obtained the wreaths given to the most highly acclaimed heroes, philosophers and poets of ancient Rome. In reference to the idea of the 'shaking spear', it was the custom for the Roman consul, before embarking upon any expedition, to visit the Temple of Quirinus upon the Quirinal Hill, where he would offer prayers and, in a solemn ritual imitating Romulus, shake a replica of the laurel spear.

Apollo, the Phoebus ('Brilliant') and Daystar, was known as the Leader of the Choir of Muses, whilst Pallas Athena was entitled the tenth Muse, chief of the other nine. Bacon's contemporaries, who mourned him and missed him greatly when he died, likened him to both Apollo and Athena. As an Apollo, he was their

Building Paradise

Ex malis moribus bonæ leges. 34
To the moſt iudicious, and learned, Sir FRANCIS BACON, Knight.

THE Viper here, that ſtung the ſheepheard ſwaine,
(While careles of himſelfe aſleepe he lay,)
With Hyſope caught, is cut by him in twaine,
Her fat might take, the poiſon quite away,
 And heale his wound, that wonder tis to ſee,
 Such ſoveraigne helpe, ſhould in a Serpent be.

By this ſame Leach, is meant the virtuous King,
Who can with cunning, out of manners ill,
Make wholeſome lawes,* and take away the ſting,
Wherewith foule vice, doth greeue the virtuous ſtill:
 Or can prevent, by quicke and wiſe foreſight,
 Infection ere, it gathers further might.

* vitiorum emendatricem legem eſſe oportet Cic 1 r. de legibus.

Salus Civitatis in legibus. Ariſt :

Afra venenato pupugit quem vipera morſu,
 Dux Gregis antidotum læſus ab hoſte petit :
Vipereis itidem leges ex moribus aptas
 Doctus Apollinea conficit arte SOLON.

vitiis quæ plurima menti
Fœminex natura dedit humana malignas

Cura dedit leges, et quod natura remittit
Invida iura negant &c.

Ovid Metamor: lib 10.

GI.   TO

SHAKING A LANCE AT THE SERPENT OF IGNORANCE
Page 34: *Minerva Britanna* (1612)
emblem dedicated to Sir Francis Bacon.

Tributes to Sir Francis Bacon

PALLAS ATHENA, THE SPEAR-SHAKER, GUARDIAN OF THE MYSTERIES
Title-page: Francis Bacon's *La Sagesse Mysterieuse des Anciens* (1641)

Building Paradise

leader—but not just their leader: he was the leader also of the choir of Muses, of whom the other poets, writers and artists were the disciples.

> Muses pour forth your perennial waters in lamentations, and let Apollo shed tears... The very nerve of genius, the marrow of persuasion, the golden stream of eloquence, the precious gem of concealed literature, the noble Bacon (ah! the relentless warp of the three sisters) has fallen by the fates. O how am I in verse like mine to commemorate you, sublime Bacon! and those glorious memorials of all the ages composed by your genius and by Minerva.
>
> R. C., T. C., Manes Verulamiani (1626), Elegy 9.

And you, who were able to immortalise the Muses, could you die yourself, O Bacon?

R.L., Manes Verulamiani (1626), Elegy 29.

> Finally he [Bacon] dies full of an unusually rich vein of arts, and dying demonstrates how extensive is art, how contracted is life, how everlasting fame; he who was in our sphere the brilliant Light-Bearer, and trod great paths of glory, passes, and fixed in his own orb shines refulgent.
>
> Anon., Manes Verulamiani (1626), Elegy 25.

The daystar of the Muses has set before his hour!

Anon., Manes Verulamiani (1626), Elegy 18.

Is it thus falls the rarest glory of the Aonian band? And do we decree to entrust seed to the Aonian fields? Break pens, tear up writings, if the dire goddesses may justly act so. Alas! what a tongue is mute! what eloquence ceases! Whither have departed the nectar and ambrosia of your genius? How is it happened to us, the disciples of the Muses, that Apollo, the leader of our choir, should die?

John Williams, Manes Verulamiani (1626), Elegy 12

If none but the worthy should mourn your death, O Bacon! none, trust me, none will there be. Lament now sincerely, O

Tributes to Sir Francis Bacon

> Clio! and sisters of Clio! Ah, the tenth Muse and glory of the choir has perished. Ah, never before has Apollo himself been truly unhappy!
>
> <div align="right">Anon., <i>Manes Verulamiani</i> (1626), Elegy 20.</div>

> Bacon... a muse more rare than the nine Muses.
>
> <div align="right">Samuel Collins, <i>Manes Verulamiani</i> (1626), Elegy 2.</div>

Besides the references and allusions to Bacon as a secret poet, and to him being both Apollo and Athena, included in these elegies of the *Manes Verulamiani* is a set of clever and more direct hints that Bacon was the author Shakespeare. These hints, comprised of allusions to Shakespeare's tomb and the inscription on his monument, seem to be intended to form part of the treasure trail—the game of hide and seek that Bacon, like Solomon, wished us to play:-

> Think you, foolish traveller, that the leader of the choir of the Muses and of Phoebus is interred in cold marble? Away, you are deceived. The Verulamium star now glitters in ruddy Olympus...
>
> <div align="right">Anon., <i>Manes Verulamiani</i> (1626), Elegy 23.</div>

> Some there are though dead live in marble, and trust all their duration to long lasting columns; others shine in bronze, or are beheld in yellow gold, and deceiving themselves think they deceive the fates. Another division of men surviving in a numerous offspring, like Niobe irreverent, despise the mighty gods; but your fame adheres not to sculptured columns, nor is read on the tomb, 'Stay, traveller, your steps'...
>
> <div align="right">Thomas Vincent, <i>Manes Verulamiani</i> (1626), Elegy 7.</div>

The Shakespeare Monument refers to Shakespeare as being held in Olympus (*'Terra tegit, populus maeret, Olympus habet'* – 'The Earth encloses, the people mourn, Olympus holds him'). A few lines further on the inscription poses a remarkably strange and unique question: 'Stay Passenger, why goest thou by so fast?' A 'passenger' is a traveller. The whole inscription is as follows:-

Building Paradise

IVDICO PYLIVM, GENIO SOCRATEM, ARTE MARONEM:
TERRA TEGIT, POPVLVS MAERET, OLYMPVS HABET.

STAY PASSENGER, WHY GOEST THOV BY SO FAST?
READ IF THOV CANST, WHOM ENVIOVS DEATH HATH PLAST,
WITH IN THIS MONVMENT SHAKSPEARE; WITH WHOME,
QVICK NATVRE DIDE; WHOSE NAME DOTH DECK YS TOMBE,
FAR MORE THEN COST: SIEH ALL, YT HE HATH WRITT,
LEAVES LIVING ART, BVT PAGE, TO SERVE HIS WITT.

OBIIT AÑO DOI 1616
ÆTATIS o 53 DIE 23 APR.

There is no other tomb with such an extraordinary question on it: only the Shakespeare 'tomb' or monument.

As can be seen, the first two lines of the Shakespeare tomb inscription are in Latin. The first of these lines describes Shakespeare as 'A Pylus in judgement, a Socrates in genius, a Maro in art'. This refers to Nestor, Socrates and Virgil, and is a description that certainly cannot be suited to the actor Will Shakspere of Stratford-upon-Avon.

Pylus was the appellation of Nestor, King of Pylus, who was a statesman, prince, ruler and judge. He was renowned for his eloquence, address, wisdom, justice, good judgement and prudence of mind. In addition he was one of the Argonauts and the most perfect of Homer's heroes in the Trojan War.

Socrates was the most celebrated philosopher of all antiquity, who was proclaimed by the Delphic Oracle as the wisest of mankind. He was a renowned orator as well as the principal instigator of the great philosophies which have constituted the major traditions of Western civilisation ever since. He was the advocate of clarity and the inductive procedure, for which he was particularly famed. He was said to have drawn down philosophy from heaven to earth by deriding the more abstruse enquiries and ungrounded metaphysical researches of his predecessors, and encouraging his countrymen to learn from experience. By introducing moral philosophy he induced mankind to consider themselves, their passions, their opinions, their duties, faculties and actions.

Socrates' aim was the happiness and good of his countrymen, and the reformation of their corrupted morals. The tragedies of his pupil Euripides are said to have been at least partly composed by him, although he remained hidden as a playwright behind the mask of his pupil. He was attended by a number of illustrious pupils, whom he instructed by his exemplary life as well as by his doctrines. However, his irreproachable character, independence of spirit and visible superiority of mind and genius over the rest of his countrymen created many enemies, who set out to ridicule and defame the great philosopher, and finally to incriminate him, relying upon the perjury of false witnesses and the envy of the judges whose ignorance and gullibility would readily yield to misrepresentation. Socrates was unjustly condemned and forced to drink poison.

Maro was the surname of Virgil, the greatest of the Roman poets, known as the prince of poets and Homer's successor. He was not only a scholar and writer but also a high initiate of the Orphic Mysteries as practised at Cumæ near Naples, where he lived for the last part of his life. His *Æneid* was based upon the Mysteries and Homer's epic tales, the *Iliad* and *Odyssey*. In his early years he was forced to live in an impoverished state, but later he managed to reach Rome where he formed an acquaintance with the celebrated Roman knight, Mecænas, the favourite of Augustus, who recommended Virgil to the Emperor. From then on the Emperor patronised the poet, restoring his lands, and Virgil in return dedicated many of his poems to Augustus. Mecænas was himself a liberal patron of men of learning, but his life became effeminate and debauched, he being censured by Seneca for his dissipation, indolence and effeminate luxury. Virgil dedicated his *Georgics* to him. Virgil also wrote pseudonymously under the name of Tityrus.

These three analogies—to Nestor, Socrates and Virgil—are applicable to one person only, and that person is Francis Bacon. The three-fold description fits him like a glove. The Maro and Nestor analogies are made in the *Manes Verulamiani*. The Socrates analogy was publicly well known.

> You have written, O Bacon! the history of the life and death of us all... Nay, give place, O Greeks! give place, Maro, first in Latin story. Supreme both in eloquence and writing, under every head renowned...
>
> Anon., *Manes Verulamiani* (1626), Elegy 16.

Building Paradise

> For if venerable Virtue and the wreaths of Wisdom make an Ancient, you [Bacon] were older than Nestor.
>
> Gawen Nash, Manes Verulamiani (1626), Elegy 27.

The trinity of Nestor, Socrates and Virgil—of statesman, philosopher and poet—relate to the attributes of Hermes Trismegistus, expressed by Bacon as 'that triplicity, which in great veneration was ascribed to the ancient Hermes; the power and fortune of a king, the knowledge and illumination of a priest, and the learning and universality of a philosopher'.[5] The relationship is clearly intended, since the second line of the Latin inscription ('The Earth encloses, the people mourn, Olympus holds him') refers to the three Worlds of Hermetic philosophy—Nature, Mankind and God.

Apparently, it would seem, many people knew of Bacon's secret, but they kept it faithfully veiled under a cloak of allegory, allusion and cryptic writing. They appear to have constituted a school or society bound by vows of silence, of which the rose was a symbol and whose chief was Bacon. Yet they also gave out deliberate hints, so that the secret might not be lost but discovered by those who earnestly seek. This sort of game of hide and seek is an ancient Cabalistic and Classical method of education, which forms an essential part of Bacon's method of training people in his Art of Discovery.

Fittingly, both Ben Jonson and Thomas Powell refer to Francis Bacon in terms of a veiled mystery, whilst Archbishop Tenison, the inheritor of some of Bacon's 'reserved' works, points out that those who have true skill in the works of Bacon can, like great masters in painting, tell by the design, the strength, the way of colouring, whether Bacon was the author of this or the other piece, even though his name of Bacon is not affixed to the work.

> Hail, happy *Genius* of this ancient pile!
> How comes it all things so about thee smile?
> The fire, the wine, the men! and in the midst,
> Thou stand'st as if some Mystery thou did'st!
>
> Ben Jonson, Ode for Lord Bacon's Birthday (1621).[6]

Tributes to Sir Francis Bacon

TO
TRUE NOBILITY,
AND TRYDE LEARNING,
BEHOLDEN
To no Mountaine for Eminence,
nor Supportment for Height, FRANCIS,
Lord *Verulam*, and Viscount St,
Albanes.
O Give me leave to pull the Curtaine by
That clouds thy Worth in such obscurity.
Good Seneca, stay but a while thy bleeding,
T' accept what I received at thy Reading:
Here I present it in a solemne strayne,
And thus I pluckt the Curtayne backe again.

Thomas Powell, Dedication, *Attourney's Academy* (1630)

And those who have true skill in the works of the Lord Verulam, like great Masters in Painting, can tell by the Design, the Strength, the way of Colouring, whether he was the Author of this or the other Piece, though his Name be not to it.

Archbishop Tenison, *Baconiana or Certaine Genuine Remains of Sir Francis Bacon* (1679).

Building Paradise

AS ABOVE, SO BELOW
Frontispiece: *Staats-Vernunfft* (1654)
German edition of Francis Bacon's *Wisdom of the Ancients*.

THE GREAT INSTAURATION

Solomon's Temple

Francis Bacon was, according to his own personal chaplain and confessor, Dr. William Rawley, not only a deep philosopher but also a religious person, and able to render a reason of the hope which was in him.[1] His writings are infused with quotations from, comments on and interpretations of scriptural teachings—more even than from the ancient philosophers, to whom Bacon makes abundant references. But more than this, Bacon was a master of Cabala, and the whole project of his Great Instauration is designed accordingly.

Cabala (Hebrew: *Kabbalah*, meaning the 'Received Wisdom') is a name for the inner doctrine concerning the Scriptures that was known to Moses and handed on by him to the 'select' of Israel and developed further by successive masters of Cabala, both Hebraic and Christian.[2] It includes what is known as initiation into the 'Mysteries of the Torah', which is direct revelation or illumination concerning the nature of divinity and design of the universe. King Solomon of Israel was reputedly one of the great masters of Cabala, and it is notable that King James and others referred to Francis Bacon as Solomon as well as Apollo, Solomon's Greek archetypal counterpart. Bacon himself declared, in a prayer filled with Freemasonic symbolism and written just before his impeachment, that the Scriptures had been his principal books of study and knowledge, and that it was in God's temples that he had found God:-

> (O Lord) Thy creatures have been my books, but thy Scriptures much more. I have sought thee in the courts, fields, and gardens, but I have found thee in thy temples.[3]

Building Paradise

King Solomon was renowned for building the great temple at Jerusalem, known as Solomon's Temple. According to Freemasonic legend he formed a Masonic fraternity to design and construct the building. Furthermore, Solomon wrote both a book of wisdom and a natural history.

All this should be taken into account when trying to understand Francis Bacon and his work; for Bacon was, by design and recognition, a second Solomon. Moreover, Cabala itself is known as *Sod*, 'the Mystery', denoting the secret magic and initiation into *Hokhmah*, 'Wisdom'. This is fundamentally the spiritual knowledge and application of the first chapter of Genesis, concerning the creation of light and the universe, with the addition of an inner knowledge concerning Ezekiel's vision of the Divine Chariot, and the revelation of Christ in the life and teachings of Jesus.

Bacon uses his Cabalistic knowledge and biblical imagery in the design of his Great Instauration—his *magnum opus*. He referred to it as the Work of Six Days, in imitation of the Six Days' Work of Creation that leads to the Seventh Day of Rest and Illumination. He was fond of the Wisdom of Solomon, likening himself to the king who searches out truth after God has hidden it—a proverb which can be applied to all seekers after truth, but which was particularly used by Solomon in reference to himself. Bacon always hoped that King James would become, or at least act, like Solomon, but in fact James always referred to his Lord Chancellor, Bacon, as his Solomon.

> For he [Solomon] sayeth expressly, the glory of God is to conceal a thing, but the glory of a King is to find it out;[4] as if according to that innocent and affectionate play of children, the Divine Majesty took delight to hide his works, to the end to have them found out; and as if Kings could not obtain greater honour, than to be God's play-fellows in that game; specially considering the great command they have of wits and means, whereby the investigation of all things may be perfected.
>
> Francis Bacon, *Advancement of Learning* (1605), Bk I.

Bacon sought, like Solomon, to construct a natural history, a temple of light and a fraternity in learning and illumination. He

The Great Instauration

began to build these three related things from the age of eighteen onwards, on his return from France:-

> I am not raising a capitol or pyramid to the pride of men, but laying a foundation in the human understanding for a holy temple after the model of the world.
>
> Francis Bacon, *Novum Organum* (1620), Aph. 120.

> And surely, as nature createth brotherhood in families, and arts mechanical contract brotherhoods in commonalities, and the anointment of God superinduceth a brotherhood in kings and bishops; so in like manner there cannot but be a fraternity in learning and illumination, relating to that paternity which is attributed to God, who is called the Father of illuminations or lights.
>
> Francis Bacon, *Advancement of Learning* (1605), Bk II.

The reference to God as 'Father of lights' is from the first chapter of St James' Epistle, verse 17. This verse and the following verses hold a key to Bacon's own life and the Great Instauration:-

> Every good gift and every perfect gift is from above, and cometh down from the Father of lights, with Whom is no variableness, neither shadow of turning.
> Of his own will begat He us with the word of truth, that we should be a kind of firstfruits of His creatures...
> But be ye doers of the word, and not hearers only, deceiving your own selves. For if any be a hearer of the word, and not a doer, he is like unto a man beholding his natural face in a glass: for he beholdeth himself, and goeth his way, and straightway forgetteth what manner of man he was.
> But whosoever looketh into the perfect law of liberty, and continueth therein, he being not a forgetful hearer, but doer of the work, this man shall be blessed in his deed.
>
> James i, 17-25.

The law of liberty is the law of love: for freedom, derived from the Sanskrit word *pri*, meaning 'love', is a state of love—

Building Paradise

hence the Masters of humanity have always been known as the liberated ones. Bacon's intention with his Great Instauration is that mankind should not only hear about the law of love and understand it, but also practise it. He pointed out that in fact this is the only way that the law, which is truth, can be truly known, and that such knowledge is illumination.

Bacon's allegory, *The New Atlantis*, describes his utopian vision based on how he hoped his Great Instauration would work. He describes the society of Bensalem (the New Atlantis) as being founded by a Second Solomon (*i.e.* himself), who established at its heart the College of the Six Days' Work, the brethren of which wear a red cross as their special mark. The work of the College is the labour of love, in order to discover and know love, the truth, which is light. Hence all of Bacon's work and that of his fraternity is, as he states, dedicated to charity.

In terms of Freemasonic allegory, the Great Instauration constitutes the rebuilding of the Temple of Solomon by a fraternity in learning dedicated to charity and led by a Second Solomon.[5]

THE SIX DAYS' WORK

Francis Bacon's Great Instauration is a project he conceived for the step-by-step restoration of a state of paradise upon earth, but coupled with the illumination of mankind. In other words, whereas mankind was innocently ignorant in the original paradise, in the new paradise all human souls will have reached a state of knowledge of truth. Such illumined knowledge will be one based on experience or practice of the truth, which truth (as all great Masters teach) is love: for it is one thing to speak of love and believe in it, but quite another to really know the truth of it from living experience and practice.

A worldwide state of illumination or golden age is an ancient dream and prophecy of all the great sages who ever lived on earth, for which they laboured. Bacon's great gift to the world was his ability to see this anew, and to both devise and inaugurate a particular scientific method by which it might be more certainly

The Great Instauration

achieved, suitable for the approaching era. This new method he referred to as an art—the Art of Discovery—whilst the Great Instauration itself he conceived of as being comprised of six stages of work leading to a final stage of rest and enjoyment of the results of the labour—the state of paradise.

Bacon planned his Great Instauration in imitation of the Divine Work—the Work of the Six Days of Creation, as defined in the Bible, leading to the Seventh Day of Rest or Sabbath. He saw his own work, which is itself built upon that of Jesus Christ, his exemplar, as being like the light of the First Day, which would inaugurate and illumine the unfolding of the rest. He also understood that the Seven Days of Creation constitute an eternal archetype for a cyclic occurrence, associated for instance with the seven-day cycle in which the solar wind or 'breath' from the Sun bathes the Earth with its light-energy and then switches polarity for the next seven days, and so on. The Six Days' Work of the Great Instauration plus its Seventh Day is therefore also cyclic, just like life itself, with each cycle building upon the previous one so that knowledge and ability steadily increases in cycle after cycle, and with there being smaller cycles within greater cycles.

All good teachers practice what they teach, and so Bacon left not just an idea for posterity but also a practical example, a working model for the rest of us to study, learn from and, if necessary, develop further. Although it is not generally realised, he provided us with examples of each of the individual parts or stages of the Great Instauration, which he symbolised as individual volumes, seven in all. These volumes may be seen illustrated in the frontispiece engraving to the 1640 edition of Bacon's *Advancement of Learning,* as well as on the title-page illustration to the same publication.

In some instances there was in fact one particular volume of writing published for the part of the Great Instauration it illustrates, such as the 1623 *De Augmentis Scientiarum* to illustrate Part 1, the 1620 *Novum Organum* to illustrate Part 2, and the 1623 Folio of *Shakespeare's Comedies, Histories and Tragedies* to illustrate Part 4; but for Part 3 several publications comprise Bacon's example of a Natural History and not all of them were published in his lifetime. However, even the *De Augmentis* volume consists of nine books and the *Novum Organum* of two books (with a total of three intended), whilst the Shakespeare Folio comprises a collection of thirty-six individual plays.

It is important to realise that Bacon set out to teach his method by examples, and that not all Bacon's examples are to be found written down and published. They are either to be discovered elsewhere in other forms or are reserved for posterity and private study by his 'successors'. Moreover, even those examples which he published were written and printed purposely in such a way that they would 'not be to the capacity or taste of all' but rather single out and 'adopt' the reader. In doing this Bacon was following the example of all great Cabalists, such as Moses and Solomon and Jesus, who revealed some things and hid others according to the capacity and readiness of the student.

> These words shalt thou declare and these shalt thou hide...
>
> Esdras: Exodus II, 14: 5-6.

> That the discretion anciently observed, though by the precedent of many vain persons and deceivers disgraced, of publishing part, and reserving part to a private succession, and of publishing in a manner whereby it shall not be to the capacity nor taste of all, but shall as it were single and adopt his reader, is not to be laid aside, both for the avoiding of abuse in the excluded, and the strengthening of affection in the admitted.
>
> Francis Bacon, *Valerius Terminus*.[6]

> It was said by Borgia of the expedition of the French into Italy, that they came with chalk in their hands to mark out their lodgings, not with arms to force their way in. I in like manner would have my doctrine enter quietly into the minds that are fit and capable of receiving it; for confutations cannot be employed, when the difference is upon first principles and very notions and even upon forms of demonstration.
>
> Francis Bacon, *Novum Organum*, Bk I, Aph 35.[7]

Bacon's successors are those he refers to as his 'sons of science'. They comprise those to whom the secret knowledge is handed down by teachers and those who discover the truths for themselves by 'piercing the veil'.

The Great Instauration

[The Method of Discourse] is either *Magisterial* or *Initiative*. Observe however that in using the word 'initiative', I do not mean that the business of the latter is to transmit the beginnings only of sciences, of the former to transmit the entire doctrine. On the contrary I call that doctrine *initiative* (borrowing the term from the sacred ceremonies) which discloses and lays bare the very mysteries of the sciences. The magisterial method teaches; the initiative intimates. The magisterial requires that what is told should be believed; the initiative that it should be examined. The one transmits knowledge to the crowd of learners; the other to the sons, as it were, of science. The end of the one is the use of knowledges, as they now are; of the other the continuation and further progression of them... But knowledge that is delivered to others as a thread to be spun on ought to be insinuated (if it were possible) in the same method wherein it was originally invented. And this indeed is possible in knowledge gained by induction...

Another diversity of Method there is, which in intention has an affinity with the former, but in reality is almost contrary. For both methods agree in aiming to separate the vulgar among the auditors from the select; but then they are opposed in this, that the former makes use of a way of delivery more open than the common, the latter (of which I am now going to speak) of one more secret. Let the one then be distinguished as the Exoteric method, the other as the Acroamatic; a distinction observed by the ancients principally in the publication of books, but which I transfer to the method of delivery. Indeed this acroamatic or enigmatical method was itself used among the ancients, and employed with judgment and discretion. But in later times it has been disgraced by many, who have made it as a false and deceitful light to put forward their counterfeit merchandise. The intention of it however seems to be by obscurity of delivery to exclude the vulgar (that is the profane vulgar) from the secrets of knowledges, and to admit those only who have either received the interpretation of the enigmas through the hands of teachers, or have wits of such sharpness and discernment as can pierce the veil.

Francis Bacon, *De Augmentis Scientiarum*, Bk VI, Ch 6.[8]

Building Paradise

The idea of passing or piercing the veil is taken from the ancient and classical Mystery Schools and refers to initiation. Each level or degree of initiation involved passing a veil, which until the moment of passing obscured the truth (or mystery) of the higher degree from those still in the lower degrees. This occulting of knowledge and method of approach is entirely in keeping with a Cabalistic and Freemasonic-Rosicrucian scheme, and is one that Bacon carefully adopted and developed. His 'Art of Transmission' or 'Method of Discourse' is, therefore, what he calls 'Initiative' whilst he himself is the originating Initiator and Hierophant.

Like a good teacher who wishes to exclude no one fit for the task, Bacon provides enough signposts for the discovery of all that is needed by the earnest seeker after truth. The search for such truths is itself a training in the 'Art of Discovery', which is what Bacon wishes to teach us.

Bacon set great store on the compilation of a Natural History; but it should be emphasised that by 'Natural History' Bacon means a history or factual record, suitably organised, that embraces natural, human and divine nature, not just nature in the sense of our natural, corporeal world. That is to say, the Great Instauration concerns the acquisition of *all* knowledge for entirely philanthropic or charitable purposes, and therefore includes knowledge of the human psyche and human ethics as well as knowledge of the nature and operations of divinity within all manifest life, physical and metaphysical. All too often Bacon is called materialistic and utilitarian (in a materialistic sense), which is a travesty of the truth and a point of view that misses the point of the Great Instauration.

Moreover, it should be noted that Bacon's examples were made as starting dissertations and experiments, providing inspiration and guidance as well as material to get things going. They were not intended to be dogmatic examples that have to be repeated *ad infinitum* without change. He foresaw his method, like the whole project, as evolving, and designed it accordingly. Part of the reason for his concealing some of his examples is so as to leave a seeming gap in his explanation of the method, so as to encourage others to try to fill that gap themselves by 'spinning on the thread', as he puts it. In this way, by following Bacon's intimations and using the process of induction, the 'sons of science' can

The Great Instauration

initiate themselves into the method and discover Bacon's 'lost' examples in the process; for Bacon is not a magisterial teacher but an initiator.

Bacon's six stages of work can be summarised as:-

(1) **Design.** A survey of the state of philosophy and science together with a design of the relationships of the various aspects of knowledge and a plan of action.

(2) **Method.** The discovery, acquirement or development of a method by means of which to accomplish the work.

(3) **Data Bank.** The collection of a history—a suitably organised data bank drawn from observation and experience of the nature of life—natural, human and divine.

(4) **Presentation & Inquiry.** The presentation of the data to the eyes and heart by means of drama, illustrated examples and suitable experiments, in order to discover the underlying laws, followed by an inquiry into and testing of what is discovered, and new experiments. Bacon refers to this as 'the Art of Discovery'.

(5) **Temporary Axioms.** The collection of unproven but useful axioms or speculations for temporary use pending being tested by the method.

(6) **Proven Axioms.** The collection of final axioms or more certain conclusions as a result of testing the ideas in action according to the method—the test being that 'truth prints goodness'.

Bacon's own names for the six stages of work are:-

(1) Partitions of the Sciences.

(2) New Method.

(3) Natural History.

(4) Ladder of the Intellect.

(5) Anticipations of the Second Philosophy.

(6) The Second Philosophy or Active Science.

Building Paradise

These stages of the Great Instauration are mentioned specifically in the first Rosicrucian manifesto, the *Fama Fraternitas*. For instance, the manifesto begins by urging the learned of all nations to unite together for the purpose of collecting a *Librum Naturae* ('Book of Nature') or 'a perfect method of all arts'. Later on the *Fama* names three prize volumes in the library or *Bibliotheca* of the Fraternity of the Rose Cross—the *Protheus*, which is referred to as being 'the most profitable', the *Rota Mundi*, called 'the most artificial', and the *Axiomata*, which 'was held for the chiefest'. These specifically relate to the second, third, fourth and sixth stages of the Great Instauration, although the 'Book of Nature' and 'perfect method of all arts' can also refer to the whole scheme:-

(1) Survey of all Knowledge.

(2) New Method: 'a perfect method of all arts'.

(3) Proteus (**'Matter'**): 'the most profitable'. (See Bacon's essay, 'Proteus or Matter' in *The Wisdom of the Ancients*.) Bacon considered that the collection of such a history of life was the most profitable thing that could be done, without which the Great Instauration could not be achieved. This 'matter' can also be described as the *Librum Naturae* ('Book of Nature') in the sense of the Natural History that Bacon describes.

(4) Rota Mundi (**'Wheel of the World'**): 'the most artificial'. In particular this refers to the grand art of drama that mimics life in such a way that it can be seen, heard, felt and experienced in an emotional but 'scientific' fashion, in the 'laboratory' of a theatre. (*i.e.* Such theatre mimics the stage of the world upon which we are all actors). It has an inference to the Globe theatre, but it also alludes to 'all the arts and secrets' of Father C.R.C. which the *Fama* says 'he knew would direct them [the learned], like a globe or circle, to the only middle point and *Centrum*'. The middle point is the supreme or summary law of the universe, pointed out by Francis Bacon as being love, the divine emotion.

(5) Temporary Axioms.

(6) Axiomata (**'Collection of Axioms'**): 'the chiefest', also referred to in the *Fama* as 'the true and infallible *Axiomata*'.

The Great Instauration

As shown in the title-page illustration to the 1640 edition of Bacon's *Advancement of Learning,* these six parts or 'volumes' of the Six Days' Work are organised into two sets of three, which cross-relate to each other as well as being related to the symbolism and meaning of the Six Days' Work of Creation:-

1.	Partitions of the Sciences *(De Augmentis Scientiarum)*	4.	Ladder of the Intellect *(Scala Intellectus)*
2.	New Method *(Novum Organum)*	5.	Anticipations of the 2nd Philosophy *(Anticipationes Philosophiæ Secunda)*
3.	Natural History *(Historia Naturalis)*	6.	The Second Philosophy or Active Science *(Philosophia Secunda aut Scientia Activæ)*

The corresponding biblical Six Days' Work of Creation are as follows:-

1.	Creation of Light *Division of Light from Darkness*	4.	Creation of the Lights *Distinction of Day from Night, seasons, days, years*
2.	Creation of the Firmament *Division of the Waters by Air*	5.	Creation of Creatures of the Water and Air *To be fruitful and multiply*
3.	Creation of Earth *Earth brings forth vegetation, fruit, seed*	6.	Creation of Creatures of the Earth & Man *Man to be fruitful, multiply, have dominion, eat fruit, etc*

Light is wisdom or knowledge of truth: darkness is ignorance. The sciences identified by Bacon in the first stage of the Great Instauration constitute the light that he carefully separates out from dark ignorance, so that the light is identifiable, just as the

Building Paradise

BACON'S PILLARS
Title Page: Francis Bacon's
Of the Advancement and Proficience of Learning (1640)

The Great Instauration

First Day of Creation concerns the creation of light and the division of this light from darkness. The method by which the nature of the universe might be recognised and known corresponds to the division of the waters (*i.e.* the matter of the universe) by the firmament in the Second Day of Creation. The creation of Earth with all its vegetation and life processes in the Third Day is a straightforward archetype for Bacon's natural history. The 'ladder of the intellect' concerns the identifying of the various laws of life, in imitation of the distinguishing of the signs, seasons, days, years, sun, moon and stars in the Fourth Day of Creation, which takes place in the firmament or 'Air' of the divine Intellect. Bacon refers to this Day or stage as the particular operation of the new method, which method corresponds to the firmament or divine Intellect that was created on the Second Day. The axioms correspond to the creatures that are created during the Fifth and Sixth Days, of which 'man' is the highest and most perfect, being made in the image of God.

The division of the six into the two sets of three is illustrated and explained in the 1640 *Advancement of Learning* title-page. It is a Cabalistic knowledge, represented by the two pillars of Solomon's Temple—the Temple of Solomon or Tree of Life. The right-hand pillar is known as being 'in the light' and associated with the sun and day, whilst the left-hand pillar is 'in the shadow' and associated with the moon and night. The one gives light, the other reflects it. The right-hand side represents the truth, which Bacon refers to as a 'naked and open daylight', whilst the qualities and functions of the left-hand side are intellectual and represented by moonlight or 'candlelights'.[9] The point of this in Bacon's scheme is that the right-hand side (*i.e.* Parts 1-3) signifies the light, wisdom, truth or law, which is then going to be studied, speculated upon and eventually known by the left-hand side (*i.e.* Parts 4-6), by means of putting Bacon's method (*i.e.* a proven law or set of laws) into operation. Whilst the right-hand side signifies the light of truth, the left-hand side is equated with the form or *persona* that masks and veils that truth, yet which can in the process make the truth understandable and capable of being practised. In later chapters of this book this will be explained and illustrated in more detail.

Building Paradise

BACON'S LIBRARY
Frontispiece: Francis Bacon's
Of the Advancement and Proficience of Learning (1640)

The Great Instauration

Pyramid of Philosophy

In the frontispiece illustration to the 1640 edition of Bacon's *Advancement of Learning*, a different organisation of the six parts is shown, together with the addition of a seventh part that corresponds to the Seventh Day or Day of Rest. These seven parts or 'volumes' of the Six Days' Work are organised into three sets. The first set is comprised of volumes 1 and 2, stacked lying down, one on top of the other, on the end of the table to Bacon's left. The second set consists of volumes 3 to 6, stacked upright on the bookshelf. The third set is the single volume, the mystical seventh, in which Bacon is shown writing.

This whole arrangement relates to Bacon's 'Pyramid of Philosophy', wherein the second set of volumes forms the pyramid itself, whilst the first set provides the survey or plan together with the method by which the pyramid is built.

Bacon describes philosophy, which is human learning, as having three faculties—history, poesie (poetry) and philosophy. History forms the base of the pyramid, philosophy is the structure (*i.e.* the pyramid) raised upon it, and poesie is the ladder (*i.e.* 'ladder of the intellect') by which the mind is uplifted from earth to heaven so as to grasp the higher laws. Poesie is, therefore, not only part of the method but also part of the structure, like the winding staircase within Solomon's Temple. These three faculties of human learning relate to the three faculties of the human soul:-

> That is the truest partition of human learning, which hath reference to the three faculties of man's soul, which is the seat of learning. History is referred to Memory, Poesie to the Imagination, Philosophy to Reason.
>
> Francis Bacon, *Advancement of Learning* (1640), Bk III, i.

To Bacon, philosophy and science are two words for virtually the same thing, like mind and soul, but with this difference: just as the soul signifies the mind that becomes illumined with wisdom, so science signifies the knowledge that philosophy develops into when put into practice. Hence Bacon's 'Second Philosophy' is also called by him the 'Active Science', emphasising his intention that such a new philosophy, based upon his method, will be an

DIVINE PHILOSOPHY

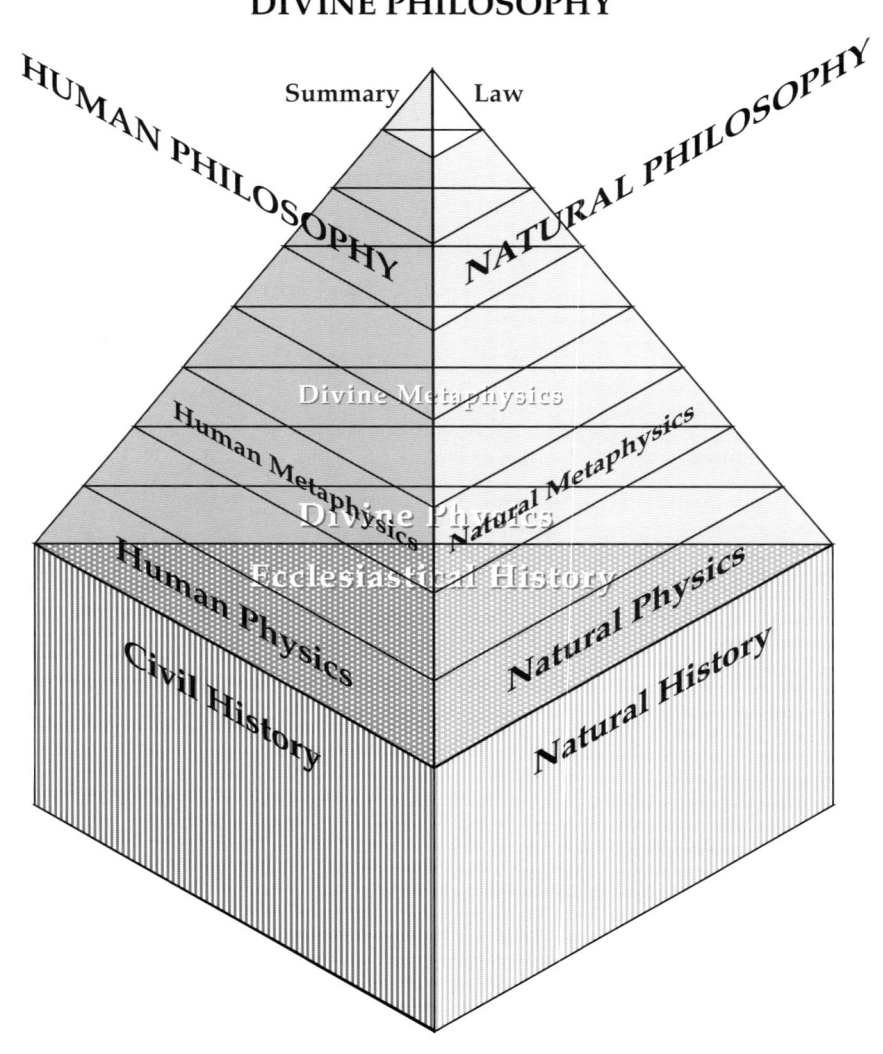

HUMAN PHILOSOPHY

NATURAL PHILOSOPHY

Summary   Law

Divine Metaphysics

Human Metaphysics   Natural Metaphysics

Divine Physics

Human Physics   Natural Physics

Ecclesiastical History

Civil History   Natural History

THE PYRAMID OF PHILOSOPHY

The Great Instauration

enlightened one. This 'Second Philosophy' or 'Active Science', therefore, is nothing less than philanthropy, or charity.

> I take Goodness in this sense, the affecting of the weal of men, which is that the Grecians call *Philanthropia*; and the word *humanity* (as it is used) is a little too light to express it. Goodness I call the habit, and Goodness of Nature the inclination. This of all virtues and dignities of the mind is the greatest; being the character of the Deity: and without it man is a busy, mischievous, wretched thing; no better than a kind of vermin. Goodness answers to the theological virtue Charity, and admits no excess, but error. The desire of power in excess caused the angels to fall; the desire of knowledge in excess caused man to fall; but in charity there is no excess; neither can angel or man come in danger by it…
>
> Francis Bacon, 'Of Goodness and Goodness of Nature,' *Essays* (1625).

> In sum, I would advise all in general, that they would take into serious consideration the true and genuine ends of knowledge; that they seek it not either for pleasure, or contention, or contempt of others, or for profit, or fame, or for honour and promotion, or such like adulterate or inferior ends; but for the merit and emolument of life; and that they regulate and perfect the same in charity. For the desire of power was the fall of angels, the desire of knowledge the fall of man; but in charity there is no excess, neither man nor angels ever incurred danger by it.
>
> Francis Bacon, *Advancement of Learning,* The Preface (1640).

Bacon's 'temple', which is to be constructed in the human mind according to his principles and method, and on which he has made a start, is his Pyramid of Philosophy. A pyramid is a pyre of flame—a temple of light.

Bacon's Pyramid of Philosophy has history for its base, upon which is built, layer upon layer, and with the help of poetry, first physics, then metaphysics, and finally the crowning knowledge of the supreme law of love. Physics is concerned with material and efficient causes, and metaphysics with formal and final causes. These causes are laws, which Bacon, like Plato, calls 'Forms'. Of these, the 'formal causes' are the living ideas (*i.e.* angels) of God that lie behind all Creation. The 'final causes' are the greatest of those living ideas (*i.e.* archangels), of which the supreme cause, the 'Summary Law of Nature', is Divine Love. Bacon urges us to discover and know these causes, and most of all the supreme cause, so that we may do good by practising them. Therefore, because love is an emotion—a passion or desire of the highest kind—he urges us to study emotions, for these essentially are the laws. Thought gives it shape, but emotion (desire) is the cause.

> For the principles, fountains, causes, and forms of motions, that is, the appetites and passions of every kind of matter, are the proper objects of philosophy.
>
> Francis Bacon, *Thoughts on the Nature of Things.*

> It is a correct position that 'true knowledge is knowledge by causes'. And causes again are not improperly distributed into four kinds: the material, the formal, the efficient and the final.
>
> Francis Bacon, *Novum Organum* (1620), Bk II, Aph.2.[11]

> For knowledges are as pyramids, whereof History is the basis. So of Natural Philosophy, the basis is Natural History; the stage next the basis is Physique [Physics]; the stage next the vertical point [apex] is Metaphysique. As for the vertical point, *opus quod operatur Deus à principio usque ad finem*,[12] the Summary Law of Nature, we know not whether man's enquiry can attain unto it.
>
> Francis Bacon, *Advancement of Learning* (1605), Bk II.

> On a given body to generate and superinduce a new nature or new natures is the work and aim of Human Power. Of a given nature to discover the Form, or true specific difference, or nature-engendering nature or the source of emanation (for these are the terms which come nearest to a description of the thing), is the work and aim of Human Knowledge.
>
> Francis Bacon, *Novum Organum* (1620), Bk II, Aph. 1.[13]

The last quotation given above describes a Form in three ways, which can be seen to relate to the Cabalistic Worlds of

The Great Instauration

Formation (the 'true specific difference'), Creation (the 'nature-engendering nature') and Emanation (the 'source of emanation'). The World of Emanation refers to the supreme or absolute sphere of divine principles, the summary laws of life and existence. In Cabalistic teaching these number ten, yet are One. The first direct expression of these principles is the World of Creation, the spiritual sphere of creative forces that create, or engender, the multitude of differentiated natures of the next World. The next World is the World of Formation, the celestial sphere of individual souls, including angels (*i.e.* the individual thought-forms or ideas created by the spiritual forces), each with their own nature and purpose to fulfil. The fourth and final sphere of existence is the World of Fact, the body of the universe in which the work may be done that enables each angel and soul to fulfil its purpose. This last World is what we would call the physical universe, containing the physical forms (bodies) of Nature, including that of human beings.

This same aphorism of Bacon's also reveals clearly that Bacon's philosophy and Great Instauration is an active, creative one, co-creating with God. It is not a philosophy of passively letting things be as they are, as if everything is preordained and therefore fixed, but a philosophy that recognises, firstly, that the universe is in constant movement and evolution, and secondly, that there was a 'Fall' in which corruption and sin entered into the original paradisiacal state of existence. The essence of Cabalistic teaching is that God taught (and continues to teach) the Divine Wisdom to mankind so that we might, with effort, find our way back to the paradisiacal state of being; and, since we are created to be the gardeners of nature, to bring all creatures, all nature, back to that pristine and utterly beautiful state as well. How to do this is mankind's great challenge. By doing it we gain knowledge of truth, which is mankind's destiny, joy and illumination, and the reason for the Fall being allowed in the first place. That is what the Great Instauration is all about, and Bacon is very clear in his belief (or knowledge) that by knowing and working with the higher laws it is possible to change the nature and operations of the lesser laws, some of them man-made, in order to bring about a better state of affairs.

Many human masters and adepts, of whom Jesus is the great Baconian exemplar, have demonstrated that this is possible. The

Building Paradise

Shakespeare play, *The Tempest*, specifically illustrates it, depicting a 'son of science' (Prospero) learning to work with the higher laws, and in particular with the law of mercy. But to do this effectively on a worldwide scale requires the willingness and concerted effort of all nations, all people—hence Bacon's desire that there should be a worldwide fraternity in learning and illumination who could help bring this about.

Bacon's Pyramid of Philosophy is in fact a tetrahedron: that is to say, it has a triangular base rather than a square base, with three sides joined together at the apex in a single point. In terms of Platonic solids it symbolises the element fire. Each side represents one of the three main aspects of truth to be researched, practised and known—divine, human and natural—which three correspond to the Hermetic description of the 'Three Heads'—God, Man and Cosmos.

> So there are these three: firstly, God, Father and the Supreme Good; secondly, the cosmos; thirdly, man.
>
> *The Corpus Hermeticum*, Bk 10, 14. [14]

> In Philosophy, the contemplations of man do either penetrate unto God, or are circumferred to Nature, or are reflected and reverted upon himself. Out of which several inquiries there do arise three knowledges, Divine Philosophy, Natural Philosophy, and Human Philosophy or Humanity. For all things are marked and stamped with this triple character of the power of God, the difference of Nature and the use of Man.
>
> Francis Bacon, *Advancement of Learning* (1605), Bk II.

Divine philosophy, human philosophy and natural philosophy are the three major aspects of philosophy, according to Bacon's scheme. Their operative counterparts, which should not be considered as separate from the speculative aspects, Bacon enumerates as ecclesiastical prudence, human prudence and natural prudence. Furthermore, in operative terms, each knowledge (divine, human and natural) can be put into action in three ways—experimental, mechanical and magical. Experimental speaks for itself; mechanical and magical relate to physical and metaphysical laws respectively. Most of modern science as we

The Great Instauration

know it is concerned with physical laws and so its resulting operations are mechanical; whereas Prospero's magic in *The Tempest* is an illustration of working with metaphysical laws in terms of all three philosophies—natural, human and divine.

The apex of the pyramid, which in Freemasonry and biblical teaching is known as the capstone or cornerstone that draws all the corners (and sides) together, represents the summary (or supreme) law of life, the law of love, which is divine charity or goodness—'the work which God maketh from the beginning to the end'.[15] By using this quotation from Solomon's *Ecclesiastes*, Bacon emphasises that this law is a 'work', a labour of love, not just some divine formula or idea. Were it not for Solomon pointing it out first, this is a revolutionary point of view concerning what a law of life actually is.

Besides the three philosophies—divine, human and natural—Bacon also includes a summary philosophy or universal science that embraces the other three and concerns the law or laws that are the source of the other three.

> But because the distributions and partitions of knowledge are not like several lines that meet in one angle, and so touch but in a point; but are like the branches of a tree that meet in a stem, which hath a dimension and quantity of entireness and continuance before it come to break itself into arms and boughs: therefore it is good, before we enter into the former distribution, to erect and constitute one universal science, by the name of *philosophia prima*, primitive or summary philosophy, as the main and common way, before we come to where the ways part and divide themselves...
>
> Therefore...my meaning touching this original or universal philosophy is thus, in a plain and gross description by negative: That it be a receptacle for all such profitable observations and axioms as fall not within the compass of any of the special parts of philosophy or sciences, but are more common and of a higher stage...
>
> Francis Bacon, *Advancement of Learning* (1605), Bk II.

Having described philosophy as a temple or pyramid, when it comes to the summary philosophy, which relates to the cap-

Building Paradise

stone of the pyramid, Bacon is forced to use another analogy, an image of a tree with three branches issuing from a trunk, to illustrate what this really means. In his *De Augmentis Scientiarum* of 1623 he further describes this summary philosophy or universal science as being the 'mother' of the rest.

Although Bacon foresaw that the development of an accurate and all-embracing philosophy was essential to the progress of humanity's evolution, yet at the same time he was always acutely aware of the limitations of human knowledge and warns us so.

> The true bounds and limitations whereby human knowledge is confined and circumscribed...are three: the first, that we do not so place our felicity in knowledge as we forget our mortality: the second, that we make application of our knowledge to give ourselves repose and contentment, and not distastes or repining: the third, that we do not presume by the contemplation of Nature to attain to the mysteries of God.
>
> Francis Bacon, *Advancement of Learning* (1605), Bk II.

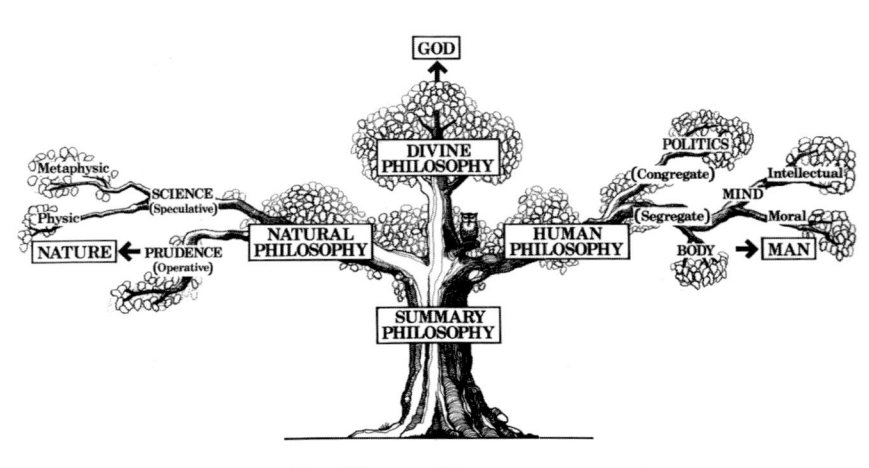

THE TREE OF PHILOSOPHY

The Great Instauration

PYRAMID OF DIVINITY

Philosophy, and the Pyramid of Philosophy, is not alone in Bacon's scheme. Philosophy is only one part of all knowledge. The other part is divinity or sacred knowledge, which knowledge is of an entirely different nature to philosophical knowledge. As Bacon puts it, all philosophical knowledge or human learning is informed by the light of nature, which consists of the notions of the mind and the reports of the senses; whereas divine or sacred knowledge is inspired by divine revelation, whether it be direct into the human heart, or by prophecy, or by way of the scriptures.

> The knowledge of man is as the waters, some descending from above, and some springing from beneath; the one informed by the light of nature, the other inspired by divine revelation. The light of nature consisteth in the notions of the mind and the reports of the senses... So then, according to these two differing illuminations or originals, knowledge is first of all divided into Divinity and Philosophy.
>
> Francis Bacon, *Advancement of Learning* (1605), Bk II.

> Knowledge is like waters: some waters descend from the heavens, some spring from the earth. So the primary partition of sciences is to be derived from their fountains: some are seated above, some are here beneath. For all knowledge proceeds from a two-fold information: either from divine inspiration, or from external sense... Wherefore we will divide sciences into Theology and Philosophy. By Theology we understand inspired or sacred Divinity, not natural, of which we are to speak anon.
>
> Francis Bacon, *Advancement of Learning* (1640), Bk III, i.

Natural divinity, to which Bacon refers in the above quote, is divine philosophy, one of the three aspects of the Pyramid of Philosophy. This Bacon defines as 'that knowledge or rudiment of knowledge concerning God, which may be obtained by the con-

Building Paradise

templation of His creatures' and which shows forth 'the omnipotency and wisdom of the Maker but not his image', just as 'all works do show forth the power and skill of the workman, but not his image'.[16] Sacred or inspired divinity, however, is not this, and we should not confuse the two; but nevertheless our reason is involved in divinity, although not in the same way as in philosophy. Religion is divinity.

> So then the doctrine of religion, as well moral as mystical, is not to be attained but by inspiration and revelation from God. The use, notwithstanding, of reason in spiritual things, and the latitude thereof, is very great and general: for it is not for nothing that the apostle calleth religion *our reasonable service of God*. [17]
>
> The use of human reason in religion is of two sorts: the former, in the conception and apprehension of the mysteries of God to us revealed; the other, in the inferring and deriving of doctrine and direction thereon.
>
> We ought not to attempt to draw down or submit the mysteries of God to our reason; but contrariwise to raise and advance our reason to the divine truth.
>
> Francis Bacon, *Advancement of Learning* (1605), Bk II.

Moreover, Bacon identifies divine learning (divinity) as having three parts that are analogous to the three parts of human learning (philosophy). That is to say, history, poesie and philosophy are paralleled in divine learning by the history of the church (divine history), parables and holy doctrine or precept, with prophecy being part of divine history.

> The parts of human learning have reference to the three parts of man's understanding, which is the seat of learning: history to his memory, poesie to his imagination, and philosophy to his reason. Divine learning receiveth the same distribution; for the spirit of man is the same, though the revelation of oracle and sense be diverse: so as theology consisteth also of the history of the church; of parables, which is divine poesie; and of holy doctrine or precept: for as for that part which seemeth

The Great Instauration

supernumerary, which is prophecy, it is but divine history; which hath that prerogative over human, as the narration may be before the fact as well as after.

Francis Bacon, *Advancement of Learning* (1605), Bk II.

THE TWO PYRAMIDS OR PILLARS OF KNOWLEDGE

The concern of philosophy is nature (divine, human and natural), which reveals the power of God. The concern of divinity is wisdom, the Will or Word of God. Bacon refers to the latter as the 'Book of God's Word' and the former as the 'Book of God's Works'. To reach enlightenment we need to earnestly study both books and practice what we learn.

> To conclude therefore, let no man upon a weak conceit of sobriety or an ill-applied moderation think or maintain, that a man can search too far, or be too well studied in the Book of God's Word, or in the Book of God's Works—Divinity or Philosophy. But rather, let men endeavour an endless progress or proficience in both; only let men beware that they apply both to charity and not to swelling [pride]; to use and not to ostentation; and again that they do not unwisely mingle or confound those learnings together.
>
> Francis Bacon, *Advancement of Learning,* Book I (1605).

These two knowledges, divinity and philosophy, can be pictured as two pyramids side by side. Their higher archetype is signified by the two 'A's of the double-A emblem used in headpieces of books published during Bacon's life-time, which denote Apollo and Athena (*i.e.* Wisdom and Intelligence), and the Alpha and Omega (*i.e.* Creation and Revelation—the Beginning and End). Wisdom creates and Intelligence reveals. Knowledge belongs to intelligence, being the revelation of truth: thus the two knowledges, divinity and philosophy, constitute the polarity or subdivision of intelligence. Whereas the 'A' is the spirit, the pyramid is the form or body of the spirit. Since the divine spirit is often

Building Paradise

described as being a 'fire', so the tetrahedral pyramid is the form of that fire.

The two pyramids of divinity and philosophy can likewise be envisioned as the twin pillars of Solomon's temple—divinity being the right-hand solar pillar and philosophy being the left-hand lunar pillar. The temple is the form of the spirit and therefore equated with intelligence, knowledge and the soul. Each of its aspects or pillars, divinity and philosophy, is also a temple

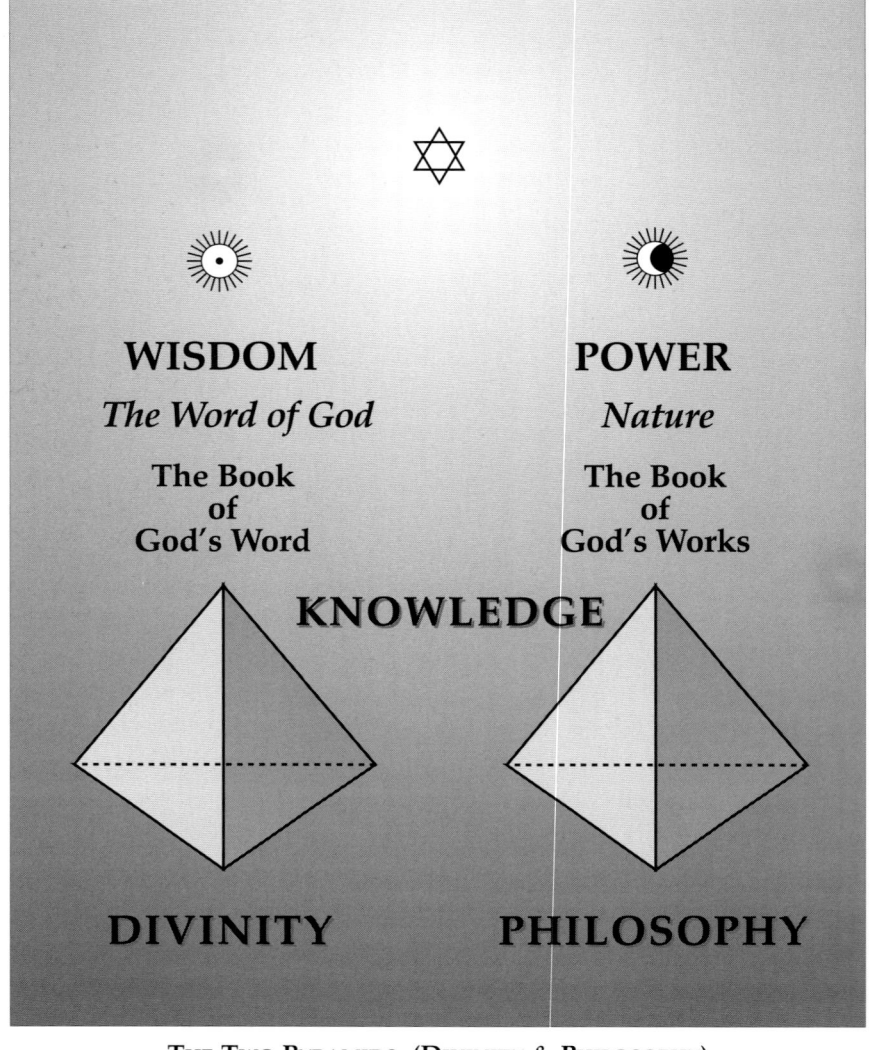

WISDOM

The Word of God

**The Book
of
God's Word**

POWER

Nature

**The Book
of
God's Works**

KNOWLEDGE

DIVINITY   **PHILOSOPHY**

THE TWO PYRAMIDS (DIVINITY & PHILOSOPHY)

The Great Instauration

(pyramid) in its own right and has, therefore, its own set of pillars. For instance, the title-page illustration to the 1640 edition of the *Advancement of Learning*, which depicts the six stages of the Great Instauration divided into two sets of three beneath the two pillars, represents the Pyramid of Philosophy. Bacon does not provide us with an illustration of the Pyramid of Divinity with its two pillars, since he purposely wrote little about this aspect of knowledge lest he be accused of heresy. However, since he particularly urged the translation of the Bible into as good an English version as possible, and since this was done under the auspices of King James I, the title-page of the *King James' Authorised Version of the Holy Bible*, published in 1611, in fact provides such an illustration. In this biblical title-page Moses, the prophet and law-giver, represents the right-hand pillar whilst Aaron, the priest and receiver-administrator of the law, symbolises the left-hand pillar. The whole picture, as in all the major Baconian-Rosicrucian illustrations, is Cabalistic. Since the 'AA' can also be written as 'AV' symbolically, so the 'Authorised Version' included in the title provides the same signal as the double-A headpiece.[18]

Bacon describes divinity and philosophy as the mistress and the handmaiden respectively. The role of the handmaiden is to serve her mistress.

> If one considers the matter rightly, Natural Philosophy is, after God's Word, the surest medicine for superstition, and also the most approved nourishment of Faith. And so she is rightly given to Religion as a most faithful handmaiden; the one manifesting the will of God, the other His power. Nor was he [the Saviour] wrong who said, *Ye do err, not knowing the Scriptures, nor the power of God*:[19] connecting and conjoining information as to His will with meditation on His power in indissoluble bonds.
>
> Francis Bacon, *Novum Organum* (1620), Bk I, Aph.89.

And if it be said, that the cure of men's minds belongeth to Sacred Divinity, it is most true: but yet Moral Philosophy may be preferred unto her as a wise servant and humble handmaid. For as the Psalm saith, *that the eyes of the handmaid look perpetually towards the mistress*,[20] and yet no doubt many things are left to the discretion of the handmaid, to discern of the mistress's

Building Paradise

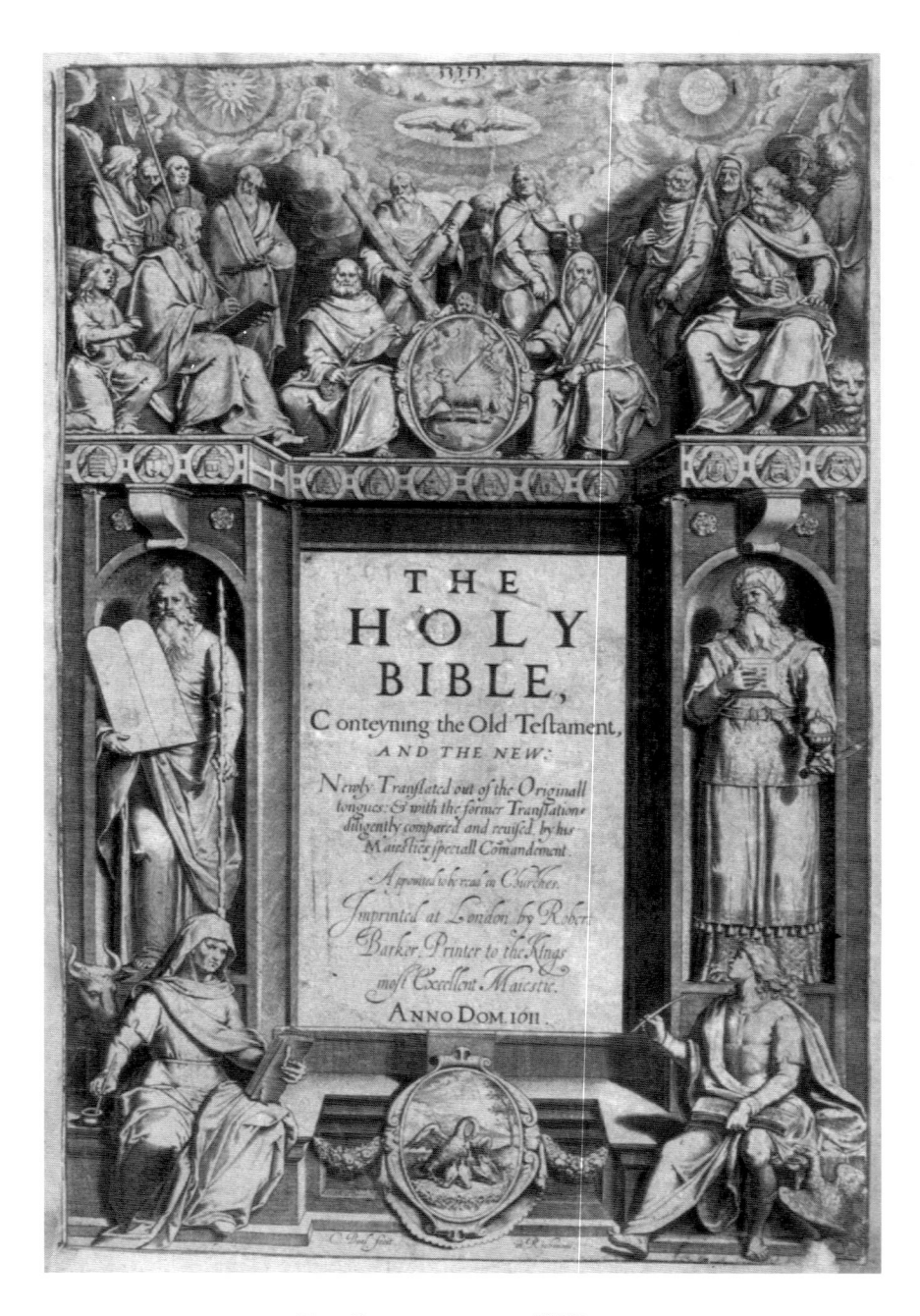

THE CABALA OF THE AV BIBLE
Title-page: King James' Authorised Version of the Holy Bible (1611).

will; so ought Moral Philosophy to give constant attention to the doctrines of Divinity, and yet so as it may yield of herself, within due limits, many sound and profitable directions.

Francis Bacon, *Advancement of Learning* (1605), Bk II.

Wherefore...let it be observed, that there be two principal duties and services, besides ornament and illustration, which Philosophy and human learning do perform to Faith and Religion. The one, because they are an effectual inducement to the exaltation of the glory of God: for as the Psalms and other Scriptures do often invite us to consider and magnify the great and wonderful works of God, so if we should rest only in the contemplation of the exterior of them, as they first offer themselves to our senses, we should do a like injury unto the Majesty of God, as if we should judge or construe of the store of some excellent jeweller, by that only which is set out toward the street in his shop. The other, because they minister a singular help and preservative against unbelief and error: for as our Saviour saith, *You err, not knowing the Scriptures, nor the Power of God*; laying before us two books or volumes to study, if we will be secured from error; first, the Scriptures, revealing the Will of God; and then the creatures expressing His Power; whereof the latter is a key unto the former: not only opening our understanding to conceive the true sense of the Scriptures, by the general notions of reason and rules of speech; but chiefly opening our belief, in drawing us into a due meditation of the omnipotency of God, which is chiefly signed and engraven upon His works.

Francis Bacon, *Advancement of Learning* (1605), Bk I.

Of the two knowledges (divinity and philosophy) Bacon is absolutely clear that divinity is the greater of the two; but nevertheless we need both in order to fulfil our purpose in life, which is to know ourselves and know God. Each helps the other to attain this joyful end.

But this inspired Theology...is the port and sabbath of all human contemplations.

Francis Bacon, *Advancement of Learning* (1640), Bk III, i.

Building Paradise

> God does not ignore man: He knows him fully, as God also wishes to be known. This is the salvation for man: knowledge of God.
>
> *The Corpus Hermeticum*, Bk 10, 15.

Bacon's writings are suffused with biblical references or quotes and his comments on them, to such an extent that his books seem almost to be expositions on the bible. The same applies to the Shakespeare plays. Bacon clearly practiced what he teaches.

PUBLICATION OF BACON'S PLAN

Francis Bacon first published the 'Plan of the Work' of his Great Instauration in 1620, printed as a prefix to his *New Method*. With the help of his 'good pens', the whole work was translated into and published in Latin, this being his declared intent for all those parts of the Great Instauration that he intended to supply and openly publish, which would describe his method and which he thought were sufficiently complete to do so.

Bacon's own description of his Plan of Work for the Great Instauration, outlining the six active parts of the Great Instauration, is given in the next chapter (Chapter 5). A commentary on these various parts is given in the following chapter (Chapter 6). The final chapter (Chapter 7) indicates how Bacon and his work is intimately connected with the Rosicrucians and Freemasons.

BACON'S PLAN OF WORK

Francis Bacon first published the 'Plan of the Work' ('Distributio Operis') of his Great Instauration ('Instauratio Magna') in 1620, printed as a preface to his *New Method* (*Novum Organum*). Both were translated into Latin.

The following 'Plan of Work', quoted in full, is the 'Distributio Operis' as translated into English by Robert Ellis and published in James Spedding's *Works of Francis Bacon* (1858), Vol. IV.

THE PLAN OF THE WORK

The work is in six Parts:-

1. *The Divisions of the Sciences.*

2. *The New Organon; or Directions concerning the Interpretation of Nature.*

3. *The Phenomena of the Universe; or a Natural and Experimental History for the foundation of Philosophy.*

4. *The Ladder of the Intellect.*

5. *The Forerunners; or Anticipations of the New Philosophy.*

6. *The New Philosophy; or Active Science.*

Building Paradise

THE ARGUMENTS OF THE SEVERAL PARTS

It being part of my design to set everything forth, as far as may be, plainly and perspicuously (for nakedness of the mind is still, as nakedness of the body once was, the companion of innocence and simplicity), let me first explain the order and plan of the work. I distribute it into six parts.

PART I

The first part exhibits a summary or general description of the knowledge which the human race at present possesses. For I thought it good to make some pause upon that which is received; that thereby the old may be more easily made perfect and the new more easily approached. And I hold the improvement of that which we have to be as much an object as the acquisition of more. Besides which it will make me the better listened to; for 'He that is ignorant (says the proverb) receives not the words of knowledge, unless thou first tell him that which is in his own heart.' We will therefore make a coasting voyage along the shores of the arts and sciences received; not without importing into them some useful things by the way.

In laying out the divisions of the sciences, however, I take into account not only things already invented and known, but likewise things omitted which ought to be there. For there are found in the intellectual as well as in the terrestrial globe waste regions as well as cultivated ones. It is no wonder therefore if I am sometimes obliged to depart from the ordinary divisions. For in adding to the total you necessarily alter the parts and sections; and the received divisions of the sciences are fitted only to the received sum of them as it stands now.

With regard to those things which I shall mark as omitted, I intend not merely to set down a simple title or a concise argument of that which is wanted. For as often as I have occasion to report anything as deficient, the nature of which is at all obscure, so that men may not perhaps easily understand what I mean or what the work is which I have in my head, I shall always (provided it be a matter of any worth) take care to subjoin either directions for the execution of such work, or else a portion of the work itself executed by myself as a sample of the whole: thus giving assistance in every case either by work or by counsel. For if it were for the sake of my own reputation only and other men's interests were not concerned in it, I would not have any man think that in such cases merely some light and vague notion as crossed my mind, and that the things which I desire and offer at are no better than wishes; when they are in fact things which men may certainly command if they will and of which I have formed in my own mind a clear and detailed conception. For I do not propose merely to survey these regions in my mind, like an augur taking auspices, but to enter them like a general who means to take possession. So much for the first part of the work.

PART II

Having thus coasted past the ancient arts, the next point is to equip the intellect for passing beyond. To the second part therefore belongs the doctrine concerning the better and more perfect use of human reason in the inquisition of things, and the true helps of the understanding: that thereby (as far as the condition of mortality and humanity allows) the intellect may be raised and exalted, and made capable of overcoming the difficulties and obscurities of nature. The art which I introduce with this view (which I call *Interpretation of Nature*) is a kind of logic, though the difference between it and the ordinary logic is great, indeed immense. For the ordinary logic professes to contrive and prepare helps and guards for the understanding, as mine does; and in this one point they agree. But mine differs from it in three points especially: viz. in the end aimed at, in the order of demonstration, and in the starting point of the inquiry.

For the end which this science of mine proposes is the invention not of arguments but of arts; not of things in accordance with principles, but of principles themselves; not of probable reasons, but of designations and directions for works. And as the intention is different, so accordingly is the effect;

the effect of the one being to overcome an opponent in argument, of the other to command nature in action.

In accordance with this end is also the nature and order of the demonstrations. For in the ordinary logic almost all the work is spent about the syllogism. Of induction the logicians seem hardly to have taken any serious thought, but they pass it by with a slight notice, and hasten on to the formulae of disputation. I on the contrary reject demonstration by syllogism, as acting too confusedly, and letting nature slip out of its hands. For although no one can doubt that things which agree in a middle term agree with one another (which is a proposition of mathematical certainty), yet it leaves an opening for deception; which is this. The syllogism consists of propositions; propositions of words; and words are the tokens and signs of notions. Now if the very notions of the mind (which are as the soul of words and the basis of the whole structure) be improperly and over-hastily abstracted from facts, vague, not sufficiently definite, faulty in short in many ways, the whole edifice tumbles. I therefore reject the syllogism; and that not only as regards principles (for to principles the logicians themselves do not apply it) but also as regards middle propositions;; which, though obtainable no doubt by the syllogism, are, when so obtained, barren of works, remote from practice, and altogether unavailable for the active department of the sciences. Although therefore I leave to the syllogism and these famous and boasted modes of demonstration their jurisdiction over popular arts and such as are matter of opinion (in which department I leave all as it is), yet in dealing the nature of things I use induction throughout, and that in the minor propositions as well as the major. For I consider induction to be that form of demonstration which upholds the sense, and closes with nature, and comes to the very brink of operation, if it does not actually deal with it.

Hence it follows that the order of demonstration is likewise inverted. For hitherto the proceeding has been to fly at once from the sense and particulars up to the most general propositions, as certain fixed poles for the argument to turn upon, and from these to derive the rest by middle terms; a short way, no doubt, but precipitate; and one which will never lead to nature, thought it offers and easy and ready way to disputation. Now my plan is to proceed regularly and gradually from one axiom to another, so that the most general are not reached till the last; but then when you do come to them you find them to be not empty notions, but well defined, and such as nature would really recognise as her first principles, and such as lie at the heart and marrow of things.

But the greatest change I introduce is in the form itself of induction and the judgement made thereby. For the induction of which the logicians speak, which proceeds by simple enumeration, is a puerile thing, concludes at hazard, is always liable to be upset by a contradictory instance, takes into account only what is known and ordinary, and leads to no result.

Now what the sciences stand in need of is a form of induction which shall analyse experience and take it to pieces, and by a due process of exclusion and rejection lead to an inevitable conclusion. And if that ordinary mode of judgement practised by the logicians was so laborious, and found exercise for such great wits, how much more labour must we be prepared to bestow upon this other, which is extracted not merely out of the depths of the mind, but out of the very bowels of nature.

Nor is this all. For I also sink the foundations of the sciences deeper and firmer; and I begin the inquiry nearer the source than men have done heretofore; submitting to examination those things which the common logic takes on trust. For first, the logicians borrow the principles of each science from the science itself; secondly, they hold in reverence the first notions of the mind; and lastly, they receive as conclusive the immediate informations of the sense, when well disposed. Now upon the first point, I hold that true logic ought to enter the several provinces of science armed with a higher authority than belongs to the principles of those sciences themselves, and ought to call those putative principles to account until they are fully established. Then with regard to the first notions of the intellect; there is not one of the impressions taken by the intellect when left to go its own way, but I hold it for suspected, and no way established, until it has submitted to a new trial and a fresh judgment has been thereupon pronounced. And lastly,

Building Paradise

the information of the sense itself I sift and examine in many ways. For certain it is that the senses deceive; but then at the same time they supply the means of discovering their own errors; only the errors are here, the means of discovery are to seek.

The sense fails in two ways. Sometimes it gives no information, sometimes it gives false information. For first, there are very many things which escape the sense, even when best disposed and no way obstructed; by reason either of the subtlety of the whole body, or the minuteness of the parts, or distance of place, or slowness or else swiftness of motion, or familiarity of the object, or other causes. And again when the sense does apprehend a thing its apprehension is not much to be relied upon. For the testimony and information of the sense has reference always to man, not to the universe; and it is a great error to assert that the sense is the measure of things.

To meet these difficulties, I have sought on all sides diligently and faithfully to provide helps for the sense—substitutes to supply its failures, rectifications to correct its errors; and this I endeavour to accomplish not so much by instruments as by experiments. For the subtlety of experiments is far greater than that of the sense itself, even when assisted by exquisite instruments; such experiments, I mean, as are skilfully and artificially devised for the express purpose of determining the point in question. To the immediate and proper perception of the sense therefore I do not give much weight; but I contrive that the office of the sense shall be only to judge of the experiment, and that the experiment itself shall judge of the thing. And thus I conceive that I perform the office of a true priest of the sense (from which all knowledge in nature must be sought, unless men mean to go mad) and a not unskilful interpreter of its oracles; and that while others only profess to uphold and cultivate the sense, I do so in fact. Such then are the provisions I make for finding the genuine light of nature and kindling and bringing it to bear. And they would be sufficient of themselves, if the human intellect were even, and like a fair sheet of paper with no writing on it. But since the minds of men are strangely possessed and beset, so that there is no true and even surface left to reflect the genuine rays of things, it is necessary to seek a remedy for this also.

Now the idols, or phantoms, by which the mind is occupied are either adventitious or innate. The adventitious come into the mind from without; namely, either from the doctrines and sects of philosophers, or from perverse rules of demonstration. But the innate are inherent in the very nature of the intellect, which is far more prone to error than the sense is. For let men please themselves as they will in admiring and almost adoring the human mind, this is certain; that as an uneven mirror distorts the rays of objects according to its own figure and section, so the mind, when it receives impressions of objects through the sense, cannot be trusted to report them truly, but in forming its notions mixes up its own nature with the nature of things.

And as the first two kinds of idols are hard to eradicate, so idols of this last kind cannot be eradicated at all. All that can be done is to point them out, so that this insidious action of the mind may be marked and reproved (else as fast as old errors are destroyed new ones will spring up out of the ill complexion of the mind itself, and so we shall have but a change of errors, and not a clearance); and to lay it down once for all as a fixed and established maxim, that the intellect is not qualified to judge except by means of induction, and induction in its legitimate form. This doctrine then of the expurgation of the intellect to qualify it for dealing with truth, is comprised in three refutations; the refutation of the Philosophies; the refutation of the Demonstrations; and the refutation of the Natural Human Reason. The explanation of which things, and of the true relation between the nature of things and the nature of the mind, is as the strewing and decoration of the bridal chamber of the Mind and Universe, the Divine Goodness assisting; out of which marriage let us hope (and be this the prayer of the bridal song) there may spring helps to man, and a line and race of inventions that may in some degree subdue and overcome the necessities and miseries of humanity. This is the second part of the work.

Building Paradise

Part III

But I design not only to indicate and mark out the ways, but also to enter them. And therefore the third part of the work embraces the Phenomena of the Universe; that is to say, experience of every kind, and such a natural history as may serve for a foundation to build philosophy upon. For a good method of demonstration or form of interpreting nature may keep the mind from going astray or stumbling, but it is not any excellence of method that can supply it with the material of knowledge. Those however who aspire not to guess and divine, but to discover and know; who propose not to devise mimic and fabulous worlds of their own, but to examine and dissect the nature of this very world itself; must go to facts themselves for everything. Nor can the place of this labour and search and worldwide perambulation be supplied by any genius or meditation or argumentation; no, not if all men's wits could meet in one. This therefore we must have, or the business must be fore ever abandoned. But up to this day such has been the condition of men in this matter, that it is no wonder if nature will not give herself into their hands.

For first, the information of the sense itself, sometimes failing, sometimes false; observation, careless, irregular, and led by chance; tradition, vain and fed on rumour; practice, slavishly bent upon its work; experiment, blind stupid, vague, and prematurely broken off; lastly, natural history trivial and poor;—all these have contributed to supply the understanding with very bad materials for philosophy and the sciences.

Then an attempt is made to mend the matter by a preposterous subtlety and winnowing of argument. But this comes too late, the case being already past remedy; and is far from setting the business right or sifting away the errors. The only hope therefore of any greater increase or progress lies in a reconstruction of the sciences.

Of this reconstruction the foundation must be laid in natural history, and that of a new kind and gathered on a new principle. For it is in vain that you polish the mirror if there are no images to be reflected; and it is as necessary that the intellect should be supplied with fit matter to work upon as with safeguards to guide its working. But my history differs from that in use (as my logic does) in many things,—in end and office, in mass and composition, in subtlety, in selection also and setting forth, with a view to the operations which as to follow.

For first, the object of the natural history which I propose is not so much to delight with variety of matter or to help with present use of experiments, as to give light to the discovery of causes and supply a suckling philosophy with its first food. For though it be true that I am principally in pursuit of works and the active department of the sciences, yet I wait for harvest-time, and do not attempt to mow the moss or to reap the green corn For I well know that axioms once rightly discovered will carry whole troops of works along with them, and produce them, not here and there one, but in clusters. And that unseasonable and puerile hurry to snatch by way of earnest at the first works which come within reach, I utterly condemn and reject, as an Atalanta's apple that hinders the race. Such then is the office of this natural history of mine.

Next, with regard to the mass and composition of it: I mean it to be a history not only of nature free and at large (when she is left to her own course and does her work her own way),—such as that of the heavenly bodies, meteors, earth and sea, minerals, plants, animals,—but much more of nature under constraint and vexed; that is to say, when by art and the hand of man she is forced out of her natural state, and squeezed and moulded. Therefore I set down at length all experiments of the mechanical arts, of the operative part of the liberal arts, of the many crafts which have not yet grown into arts properly so called, so far as I have been able to examine them and as they conduce to the end in view. Nay (to say the plain truth) I do in fact (low and vulgar as men may think it) count more upon this part both for helps and safeguards than upon the other; seeing that the nature of things betrays itself more readily under the vexations of art than in its natural freedom.

Nor do I confine the history to Bodies; but I have thought it my duty besides to make a separate history of such Virtues as may be considered cardinal in nature. I mean those original passions or desires of matter which constitute the primary elements of nature; such as Dense and Rare, Hot and Cold, Solid and Fluid, Heavy and Light, and several others.

Then again, to speak of subtlety: I seek out and get together a kind of experiments much subtler and simpler than those which occur accidentally. For I drag into light many things which no one who was not proceeding by a regular and certain way to the discovery of causes would have thought of inquiring after; being indeed in themselves of no great use; which shows that they were not sought for on their own account; but having just the same relation to things and works which the letters of the alphabet have to speech and words—which, though in themselves useless, are the elements of which all discourse is made up.

Further, in the selection of the relations and experiments I conceive I have been a more cautious purveyor than those who have hitherto dealt with natural history. For I admit nothing but on the faith of the eyes, or at least of careful and severe examination; so that nothing is exaggerated for wonder's sake, but what I state is sound and without mixture of fables or vanity. All received or current falsehoods also (which by strange negligence have been allowed for many ages to prevail and become established) I proscribe and brand by name; that the sciences may be no more troubled with them. For it has been well observed that the fables and superstitions and follies which nurses instil into children do serious injury to their minds; and the same consideration makes me anxious, having the management of the childhood as it were of philosophy in its course of natural history, not to let it accustom itself in the beginning to any vanity. Moreover, whenever I come to a new experiment of any subtlety (though it be in my own opinion certain and approved), I nevertheless subjoin a clear account of the manner in which I made it; that men knowing exactly how each point was made out, may see whether there be any error connected with it, and may arouse themselves to devise proofs more trustworthy and exquisite, if such can be found; and finally, I interpose everywhere admonitions and scruples and cautions, with a religious care to eject, repress, and as it were exorcise every kind of phantasm.

Lastly, knowing how much the sight of man's mind is distracted by experience and history, and how hard it is at the first (especially for minds either tender or preoccupied) to become familiar with nature, I not unfrequently subjoin observations of my own, being as the first offers, inclinations, and as it were glances of history towards philosophy; both by way of an assurance to men that they will not be kept for ever tossing on the waves of experience, and also that when the time comes for the intellect to begin its work, it may find everything the more ready. By such a natural history then as I have described, I conceive that a safe and convenient approach may be made to nature, and matter supplied of good quality and well prepared for the understanding to work upon.

Part IV

And now that we have surrounded the intellect with faithful helps and guards, and got together with most careful selection a regular army of divine works, it may seem that we have no more to do but to proceed to philosophy itself. And yet in a matter so difficult and doubtful there are still some things which it seems necessary to premise, partly for convenience of explanation, partly for present use.

Of these the first is to set forth examples of inquiry and invention according to my method, exhibited by anticipation in some particular subjects; choosing such subjects as are at once the most noble in themselves among those under enquiry, and most different one from another; that there may be an example in every kind. I do not speak of those examples which are joined to the several precepts and rules by way of illustration (for of these I have given plenty in the second part of the work); but I mean actual types and models, by which the entire process of the mind and the whole fabric and order of invention from the beginning to the end, in certain subjects, and those various and remarkable, should be set as it were before the eyes. For I remember that in the mathematics it is easy to follow the demonstration when you have a machine beside you; whereas without that help all appears involved and more subtle than it really is. To examples of this kind—

being in fact nothing more than an application of the second part in detail and at large,—the fourth part of the work is devoted.

Part V

The fifth part is for temporary use only, pending the completion of the rest; like interest payable from time to time until the principal be forthcoming. For I do not make so blindly for the end of my journey, as to neglect anything useful that may turn up by the way. And therefore I include in this fifth part such thins as I have myself discovered, proved, or added,—not however according to the true rules and methods of interpretation, but by the ordinary use of the understanding in inquiring and discovering. For besides that I hope my speculations may in virtue of my continual conversancy with nature have a value beyond the pretensions of my wit, they will serve in the meantime for wayside inns, in which the mind may rest and refresh itself on its journey to more certain conclusions. Nevertheless I wish it to be understood in the meantime that they are conclusions by which (as not being discovered and proved by the true form of interpretation) I do not at all mean to bind myself. Nor need any one be alarmed at such suspension of judgment, in one who maintains so simply that nothing can be known, but only that nothing can be known except in a certain course and way; and yet establishes provisionally certain degrees of assurance, for use and relief until the mind shall arrive at a knowledge of causes in which it can rest. For even those schools of philosophy which held the absolute impossibility of knowing anything were not inferior to those which took upon them to pronounce. But then they did not provide helps for the sense and understanding, as I have done, but simply took away all their authority: which is quite a different thing—almost the reverse.

Bacon's Plan of Work

PART VI

The sixth part of my work (to which the rest is subservient and ministrant) discloses and sets forth that philosophy which by the legitimate, chaste, and severe course of inquiry which I have explained and provided is at length developed and established. The completion however of this last part is a thing both above my strength and beyond my hopes. I have made a beginning of the work—a beginning, as I hope, not unimportant:—the fortune of the human race will give the issue:—such an issue, it may be, as in the present condition of things and men's minds cannot easily be conceived or imaged. For the matter in hand is no mere felicity of speculation, but the real business and fortunes of the human race, and all power of operation. For man is but the servant and interpreter of nature: what he does and what he knows is only what he has observed of nature's order in fact or in thought; beyond this he knows nothing and can do nothing. For the chain of causes cannot by any force be loosed or broken, nor can nature be commanded except by being obeyed. And so those twin objects, human Knowledge and human Power, do really meet in one; and it is from ignorance of causes that operation fails.

And all depends on keeping the eye steadily fixed upon the facts of nature and so receiving their images simply as they are. For God forbid that we should give out a dream of our own imagination for a pattern of the world; rather may he graciously grant to us to write an apocalypse or true vision of the footsteps of the Creator imprinted on his creatures.

Therefore do Thou, O Father, who gavest the visible light as the first fruits of creation, and didst breath into the face of man the intellectual light as the crown and consummation thereof, guard and protect this work, which coming from Thy goodness returneth to Thy glory. Thou when Thou turnedst to look upon the works which Thy hands had made, sawest that all was very good, and didst rest from Thy labours. But man, when he turned to look upon the work which his hands had made, saw that all was vanity and vexation of spirit, and could find no rest therein. Wherefore if we labour in Thy works with the sweat of our brows Thou wilt make us partakers of Thy

Building Paradise

vision and Thy sabbath. Humbly we pray that this mind may be steadfast in us, and that through these our hands, and the hands of others to whom Thou shalt give the same spirit, Thou wilt vouchsafe to endow the human family with new mercies.

Francis Bacon, 'Plan of the Work', *The Great Instauration* (1620).

COMMENTARY ON THE PLAN OF WORK

PART I

THE ADVANCEMENT AND PROFICIENCE OF LEARNING

The first part of the Great Instauration is to contain a general survey of the existing state of human knowledge. This survey can also act as a plan for action, as it will identify those areas of human knowledge that are well covered and those in which mankind is deficient. The idea is not only to advance knowledge in all areas, but in particular to make up deficiencies in knowledge, so that there might be a harmonious balance in proceedings. Bacon, who early on declared that he took all knowledge as his province, acknowledged that all areas of knowledge are interconnected, and that there can be no satisfactory advancement of knowledge in some areas whilst neglecting others.

Bacon provided his example of the first part of the Great Instauration in his nine-book version of *The Advancement and Proficience of Learning*, translated into Latin as the *De Dignitate et Augmentis Scientiarum* and published in 1623. This was a greatly expanded version of the first two-book version that was printed in English in 1605. Published as an example to give 'light' to future ages, Bacon undoubtedly hoped that his survey of the state of knowledge in his day would be imitated by his philosophical successors, by their carrying out new surveys periodically.

Bacon's approach is not only like that of a navigator charting the seas and continents of the world, but also like that of an architect who must first survey the ground on which the proposed building is to be erected, seeing what is needed and what is already provided for, what are the strengths and weaknesses, what possibilities there are, and generally envisioning the sort of design that the building might take. In Bacon's case he already has a vision of the building, which is to be a three-sided temple or pyramid of philosophy, having a triangular base and with its sides meeting at a point at its summit. Each side represents scientific knowledge concerning one of the three great areas of life—divine, human and natural. Based on grounded observation and experience, yet infused with divine inspiration and guidance, it is to rise from earth to heaven, from physical to metaphysical truths, like Jacob's ladder.

Although Bacon states clearly and categorically that the advancement of learning (and proficiency in its use) is to embrace all three worlds of divinity, humanity and nature, in order to discover the nature and laws of each at every level of life, he in fact only deals at length with the natural world. He touches but briefly on the human sphere and even less on the divine sphere. Yet he definitely states that his intention is to build a temple of natural, human and divine philosophy. This occulting of knowledge and his method of approach concerning divine and human nature is entirely in keeping with a Cabalistic scheme, as pointed out in Chapter 4.

PART II

THE NEW METHOD; OR A TRUE GUIDE TO THE INTERPRETATION OF NATURE

Francis Bacon carefully chose the name of the second part of the Great Instauration so that we could easily make the inference that the New Method (*Novum Organum*) is to Aristotle's Method (*Organum*) as the New Atlantis is to the original Atlantis, the latter having become full of corruption and errors which led to its demise by war and flood, and the former being intended to be guarded against corruption and error and therefore capable of manifesting paradise on earth. This New Method Bacon also calls 'the Art of Interpretation', and he saw it as the principal gift he

Commentary on the Plan of Work

had to give to mankind. He refers to it as being a special form of induction by means of which the 'enchanted glass' of the human mind might be purged of its erroneous habits and misconceptions, be guarded against erecting any new 'idols' or false conceptions, and be led step by step to a discovery of real truth. Recognising his own limitations and that of the state of knowledge in his time, Bacon also pointed out that his vision and definition of the Art of Interpretation should not be taken as a dogma but only as a starting point, and should be able to adapt, grow and evolve as new discoveries are made.

Bacon's plan is to start with information derived from the senses and then, by means of a 'true induction', to discover axioms and then the various laws ('Forms') of the universe, from physical laws (physics) to the summary metaphysical laws, and ultimately the supreme law of all, referred to in Ecclesiastes as 'the work which God worketh from the beginning to the end'[1]—this work being the divine act of love. In respect of the supreme law Bacon acknowledged that 'we know not whether man's enquiry can attain unto it', but that if we imitated the Creator and practised charity then we might come to know it and thereby work as God works—divinely. It is how to act both individually and as a human race in ways that are truly useful and charitable to all creatures—mankind and nature—which is the difficult problem.

The method which Bacon proposed is to start by collecting histories (*i.e.* records) of particular examples drawn from life concerning the behaviour, design and nature of things (including human beings as well as the rest of nature), using information gleaned from books, men of repute and one's own observations, experience and experiments. These histories are then to be made into various tables of 'well ordered and digested experience' made ready for 'presentation to the intellect'. The making of these tables is a step by step affair, involving a careful scrutiny of each table and the forming of axioms (*i.e.* informed ideas or proposals based on experience) about them; then, with the help of further experiments, leading on to the creation of the next table. In this way the experimenter-interpreter is to ascend as if on a ladder from lesser to middle to higher and more general axioms, culminating with a final table called 'the Ascending and Descending Ladder of Axioms or Tables of Invention' from which a true philosophy

Building Paradise

regarding the laws of nature—divine, human and natural—can be derived. This philosophy is then to be put into action and, if true, its results will be good and stand the test of time as being truly good, for God is Good. Bacon summed it up in three words: 'Truth prints goodness'.

Only two out of three books of the *Novum Organum* were actually published—*Aphorisms on the Interpretation of Nature and the Realm of Man* (Book I) and *Aphorisms of the Interpretation of Nature or the Reign of Man* (Book II). For some reason the third and final book, *Remaining Helps or Ministrations to the Intellect*, was never published, and so the general opinion on this is that Bacon never completed writing it. This does not mean, however, that he never taught these helps to his 'sons of the sciences' or 'sons of wisdom', thereby reserving a knowledge of the full working of the New Method for a 'private succession', or for 'future ages' to discover using their own wits; for there is no doubt that Bacon knew exactly what his method was, and had both practised and tested it out himself to his complete satisfaction before he even attempted to write it down for general publication. As already pointed out, this habit of publishing part and reserving part is entirely in keeping with his whole Cabalistic method and approach to life, and there may indeed be philanthropic people living now who both know and practice Bacon's method in its entirety. There may also be many others who would like to if only they could discover what the method really is and how to apply it.

Not surprisingly for a lawyer and Lord Chancellor, Bacon's form of induction has a close similarity to the conduct of a lawsuit. In fact, his philosophical enquiry into the nature of the world and universe has much in common with his scheme for a new or reformed science of law: for Bacon saw the laws of heaven and earth, and of nature and man, as being (ideally) connected.[2] In addition, Bacon was a great poet, although concealed under a pseudonym, and this is another (hidden) clue as to the design and working of his Great Instauration. A third clue is that he was a master of Cabala and Hermeticism, well-versed in the Western Wisdom traditions and following the path of the Ancients, as he put it.

As already pointed out in Chapter 4, in the first Rosicrucian manifesto, *Fama Fraternitatis*, Bacon's scheme to reform philosophy is described as a 'philosophical *Bibliotheca*, amongst which our

Commentary on the Plan of Work

Axiomata was held for the chiefest, *Rota Mundi* for the most artificial, and *Protheus* the most profitable'. *Protheus* refers to Matter, and so the Book of Protheus is none other than the Natural History, referred to also as the *'Librum Naturae'* ('Book of Nature') or 'Book M' (*i.e. Librum Mundi* or 'Book of the World') in the *Fama*.

THE UNIVERSAL & GENERAL REFORMATION OF THE WHOLE WIDE WORLD *through the renewal of all arts and sciences*	
BACONIAN--ROSICRUCIAN	
Pyramid of Philosophy *Temple of Light*	House Sanctus Spiritus *Philosophical Bibliotheca*
ACTIVE SCIENCE Second Philosophy	**AXIOMATA (2)** Final
ANTICIPATIONS Speculations	**AXIOMATA (1)** Temporary
LADDER OF THE INTELLECT	**ROTA MUNDI** Wheel of the World
NATURAL HISTORY	**PROTEUS (Matter)**
NEW METHOD of all arts	**PERFECT METHOD** of all arts
The Advancement and Proficience of Learning	The Renewal of all Arts and Sciences

TEMPLE OF PHILOSOPHIA

Building Paradise

This is indeed the most profitable, as it is the basis of all the rest as well as the world of operations. *Rota Mundi* ('Wheel of the World') refers to the working of Bacon's method, which is an art (the Art of Interpretation). The *Axiomata* are the axioms or philosophy derived from the method, which is the 'Second Philosophy' of Bacon's scheme and the chief part or purpose of the work.

PART III

THE PHENOMENA OF THE UNIVERSE, OR NATURAL AND EXPERIMENTAL HISTORY FOR CONSTRUCTING PHILOSOPHY

The third part of the Great Instauration forms the foundation of Bacon's Pyramid of Philosophy and consists of a natural and experimental history concerning the phenomena of the universe. Bacon perceived that without such a history, made up of carefully recorded observations of various facets of life, human and natural, and including observations of divine operations in the lives of people and the rest of nature (*e.g.* miracles, visions, dreams, inspirations), there could be no true philosophy and knowledge of life. Bacon's proposal is to make and collect histories in a disciplined way on as wide and varied subject matter as possible, using information gleaned from books, men of repute and the historian's own observations, experience and experiments. He particularly urges us to study and collect information on the desires and passions of all things—of matter, nature and humanity—as therein will lie the key to understanding the summary laws of the universe, the chief of which is God's will or desire, which is love. Once collected, the histories are to be put into suitable order and made into three 'Tables of First Presentation' by means of which they may be more easily worked upon by the understanding—a 'Table of Essence and Presence', a 'Table of Deviation' and a 'Table of Degrees'.

It is important to understand that Bacon set to work to develop divine and human philosophy as well as a natural philosophy, for he is normally only known for the latter. But it is absolutely clear that he included all three in his scheme, and understood that a true philosophy about the summary laws could not be made with-

Commentary on the Plan of Work

out all three departments of philosophy being included and developed together. The fact that he mostly wrote about and gave examples in natural philosophy, and urged a natural history to be written, is because he veiled to some extent the other two, they being delicate matters to publicise. Bacon's 'Natural History' actually signifies a history of the nature of things—divine, human and natural; and he urges us to construct a history of human emotions, thoughts and civil affairs, just as much as of cold, heat, light, vegetation, and such-like natural phenomena.

> It may also be asked…whether I speak of natural philosophy only, or whether I mean that the other sciences, logic, ethics, and politics, should be carried on by this method. Now I certainly mean what I have said to be understood of them all; and as the common logic, which govern by the syllogism, extends not only to natural but to all sciences; so does mine also, which proceeds by induction, embrace everything. For I form a history and tables of discovery for anger, fear, shame, and the like; for matters political; and again for the mental operations of memory, composition and division, judgment and the rest; not less for heat and cold, or light, or vegetation, or the like.
>
> Francis Bacon, *Novum Organum,* Bk I, Aph 127 (1620).[3]

> And not only should the characters of dispositions which are impressed by nature be received into this treatise, but those which are imposed on the mind by sex, by age, by region, by health and sickness, by beauty and deformity, and the like; and again, those which are caused by fortune, as sovereignty, nobility, obscure birth, riches, want, magistracy, privateness, prosperity, adversity and the like.
>
> Francis Bacon, *De Augmentis Scientiarum* (1623), Bk VII, Ch 3 (1623).[4]

Bacon went to great lengths to get such a history started, because without it a true philosophy could not be developed. Because he knew it was not possible for one person alone to do such a gigantic work, but that it would need the labour of many people over a long period of time, he constantly urged others to

Building Paradise

become involved—and many people eventually did. Besides the small group of friends who worked directly with him, through his own Baconian writings, the Rosicrucian manifestos, and various groups and societies,[5] he inspired and organised a sufficient number of people to begin the work—a work which is now being carried out on a large, international scale in respect of a science concerning mainly physical laws, and taken for granted by society as if it had always been the case. The only pity is that our worldwide science lacks in far too many instances the ethical and philanthropic purpose of Bacon's scheme, and is principally driven by the desire for material riches. Neither is our present-day science initiative, as Bacon intended, except in terms of State or corporation secrets wherein the moral ethos is often dubious. Bacon's plan was that the State would sponsor scientific research, which would be developed and used entirely for good and useful (*i.e.* charitable) purposes.

Bacon published several treatises as examples for this third part of the Great Instauration. The principal example is a suitably title-paged volume entitled *Sylva Sylvarum or A Natural History*, which was first published towards the end of 1626, immediately after Bacon's death, by Bacon's chaplain, confidante and secretary, Dr. William Rawley, to whom Bacon left most of his papers together with instructions. The other treatises were the *Parasceve ad Historiam et Naturalem* ('Preparative towards a Natural and Experimental History'), published in 1620, and a special collection of six natural histories that he wrote during 1622-3. Bacon began to publish these under the title of *Historia Naturalis* ('Natural History'). The first to be published was the *Historia Ventorum* ('History of Winds') in 1622, followed by the *Historia Vitae et Mortis* ('History of Life and Death') in 1623. A third, the *Historia Densi et Rari* ('History of Density and Rarity'), was not published until 1658. The remaining three of the set were mentioned in his introduction and written in 1623, but not published. These were the *Historia Gravis et Levis* ('History of Gravity and Levity'), *History of the Sympathy and Antipathy of Things* and *History of Sulphur, Salt and Mercury*. Bacon also began a civil history as part of a study of human nature, which also belongs to the third part of the Great Instauration. However, he only managed to complete one of these histories, the *History of the Reign of King Henry VII*, which

Commentary on the Plan of Work

was published in 1622. The Latin version of this, *Historiam Regni Henrici VII, Regis Angliae*, completed in 1625, was not published until 1665. Bacon also made a start in 1625 on the *History of the Reign of King Henry VIII*, but this remained unfinished.

THE SECOND VINTAGE (The New Philosophy) *Higher Axioms*	Active Science ("*Truth prints Goodness*")	
THE FIRST VINTAGE (The beginning of interpretation) *Middle Axioms*	Definitions of the middle axioms	Table of Differences (Defining characteristics)
		Conjectures about middle axioms
[PRELIMINARIES] *Lesser Axioms*	Table of Affirmations (Lesser Axioms)	Table of Rejection or Exclusion
3 TABLES OF FIRST PRESENTATION *History*	Table of Degrees	Table of Deviation
		Table of Essence & Presence

BACON'S METHOD

Building Paradise

Part IV

The Ladder of the Intellect

The fourth part of the Great Instauration comprises the actual application of the second part (the New Method), which Bacon calls a process of 'true induction'. Besides 'The Ladder of the Intellect' Bacon also titles this part 'The Thread of the Labyrinth,' or 'The Method of the Mind in the Comprehension of Things Exemplified,' or 'The Intellectual Sphere Rectified to the Globe'. However, the first title is probably the most comprehensible.

Having compiled suitable histories in the third part of the Great Instauration and made them ready for the understanding to work upon (*i.e.* by organising them into the three Tables of First Presentation), the New Method can be applied in this fourth part. This method involves a careful scrutiny of each table, coupled with the forming of preliminary axioms and the invention of new experiments to test out the axioms. From the new experiments a fresh or revised history can be made and the process repeated with the creation of new tables, further scrutiny, better or more advanced axioms, and so on. In other words the 'Interpreter' is to ascend as if on a ladder from lesser to middle to higher axioms.

The first step is to produce a 'Table of Rejection or Exclusion', resulting in conjectures as to the 'Form' or law which produces the phenomena under consideration, which conjectures Bacon refers to as the 'lesser axioms'. Having organised these into a 'Table of Affirmations' (*i.e.* of that which has so far passed the various tests of verification), the next step is to produce 'the First Vintage', which Bacon notes as being the 'beginning of interpretation'. This commences with conjectures about the 'middle axioms', noting the various 'differences' or defining characteristics, followed by a process of verification and refining of these conjectures that will culminate in a definition of the middle axioms. At this point Bacon does not tell us openly, in writing, how to proceed further; but from the second step (which produced the middle axioms) a further third step is required to produce the higher axioms concerning the 'summary laws of nature'.

Commentary on the Plan of Work

To assist this three-step process Bacon states that he has defined nine 'Helps' or techniques; but of these nine only the first one ('Prerogative Instances') is published in Book II of his *Novum Organum*. The other eight belong to Book III, *The Remaining Helps or Ministration to the Intellect*, which he never published. These nine Helps culminate with a table called 'the Ascending and Descending Ladder of Axioms or Tables of Invention'.

In the examples which Bacon gives in his *Novum Organum*, which are concerned primarily with natural phenomena rather than human or divine matters, the lesser axioms appear to deal with the physical laws, the middle axioms with metaphysical laws, and the final or higher axioms with the summary or spiritual laws. Bacon explains that he chose these examples specifically to give us 'light' rather than for any other purpose, and so like parables they can teach us by analogy, allusion and symbolism the full scope of interpretation intended. This is nothing less than to discover the physical, metaphysical and summary (or spiritual) laws concerning divinity, humanity and nature in the phenomenal universe. In other words Bacon defines three departments of life (natural, human and divine) and three levels of law (physical, metaphysical and summary) to research, and three steps or degrees by which to proceed in his method. The three levels relate to the natural, celestial and spiritual worlds of Neoplatonic and Cabalistic philosophy.

For the purpose of developing an accurate natural philosophy, which is only one third of the whole philosophy to be developed in Bacon's scheme, one can imagine perhaps a vast laboratory or series of laboratories such as Bacon describes as laid out in the landscape of Bensalem in his *New Atlantis*. But for the human and divine philosophies something else is obviously needed. A possible key to this is that Bacon always referred to the eye of the mind as the imagination. Moreover, he states in his *Advancement of Learning* that it is the work of the imagination to receive information from the senses so as to present it to the reason; and then, when the reason has made its judgement and decision, to convey that 'decree' to the will, which puts the decree into action. This is certainly an outline of the natural law or process upon which Bacon's method is based, and which he must have verified for himself when developing and testing his method.

Building Paradise

Then, human philosophy is inevitably involved with human passions and thoughts as well as behaviour, and hence with ethics. Human philosophy, therefore, naturally includes a philosophy of ethics, the highest ethic of all being goodness, or charitableness, or philanthropy, as Bacon defined it. Such a philosophy of ethics is the *Philosophia Moralis* mentioned in the Rosicrucian manifesto, *Fama Fraternitatis*, which was to be amended by the [Baconian] reformation of philosophy. The further fact that the Rosicrucian manifestos were described as 'jests' or poetic fictions masking real truths, and that 'Invention' (such as in 'Tables of Invention') referred not only to inventions as we understand it today but also to poetry and stage-plays, gives us another clue. Couple this with the fact that Bacon defines poetry as a work or play of the imagination, and attaches to poetry a great importance in matters of ethics, and that he was described as renovating philosophy in the 'socks of Comedy' and 'buskin of Tragedy' (Elegy 4, *Manes Verulamiani*), then it is not hard to discover Bacon's example of his method at work in a suitable 'laboratory' in respect of human and divine philosophy.

> Plato saith elegantly: 'That virtue if she could be seen would move great love and affection'... Rhetoric paints our virtue and goodness to the life, and makes them in a sort conspicuous... Shew them to the imagination so as maybe in a lively Representation.
>
> Francis Bacon, *Advancement of Learning* (1605), Bk 2.

> For I form a history and tables of discovery for anger, fear, shame and the like.
>
> Francis Bacon, *Novum Organum*, Aphorism CXXVII.

> Men generally taste well knowledges drenched in flesh and blood, civil history, morality, policy, about which men's affections, praises, fortunes do turn, and are conversant'.
>
> Francis Bacon, *Advancement of Learning* (1605), Bk 2.

> Because true History reports the successes of business, not proportionable to the merit of virtues and vices; Poesie corrects it, and presents events and fortunes according to desert, and acc-

Commentary on the Plan of Work

ording to the law of Providence: because true History, through the frequent satiety and similitude of things, works a distaste and misprision in the mind of man; Poesie cheereth and refresheth the soul, chanting things rare, and various, and full of vicissitudes. So as Poesie serveth and conferreth to delectation, magnanimity, and morality; and therefore it may seem deservedly to have some participation of divineness; because it doth raise the mind, and exalt the spirit with high raptures, by proportioning the shews of things to the desires of the mind; and not submitting the mind to things, as Reason and History do...

Dramatical, or Representative Poetry, which brings the world upon the stage, is of excellent use... The care of the Ancients was that it should instruct the minds of men unto virtue. Nay, wise men and great philosophers have accounted it as the archet or musical bow of the mind. And certainly it is most true, and as it were a secret of nature, that the minds of men are more patent to affections and impressions, congregate, than solitary.

But Poesie Allusive, or Parabolical, exceeds all the rest, and seemeth to be a sacred and venerable thing, especially seeing Religion itself hath allowed it a work of that nature, and by it traffics divine commodities with men.

Francis Bacon, *Advancement of Learning* (1640), Bk. II, ch xiii.

That Bacon intends poetry to form the fourth part of the Great Instauration, at least in relationship to human and divine matters, is further confirmed by his description of the three parts of human learning as history, poesie and philosophy, with these three relating to the human faculties of memory, imagination and reason. History constitutes the third part of the Great Instauration, whilst the new philosophy forms the sixth part. The fifth part is a temporary philosophy only and therefore is included in the Pyramid of Philosophy purely on a temporary basis. The first and second parts of the Great Instauration deal with an outline of the plan and a description of the method, so do not form part of the Pyramid of Philosophy. This leaves poesie as the means by which one moves from history to philosophy, and as such it is an integral part of the Pyramid of Philosophy, the temple of human learning.

Building Paradise

Moreover, since Bacon perceived the summary laws as being laws of love, then the third stage of this fourth part of the Great Instauration (which would appear to deal with the making of the higher axioms concerning the summary laws of nature) is actually dealing with desires. Whether they be the desires of matter, or of human beings, or of divinity, at this high or summary level they are all one, summed up by Bacon under the name of Cupid, or Love, and described in his various writings on Cupid and Coelum, and Cupid and the Atom.

> It has been said then that the primitive essence, force and desire of things has no cause. How it proceeded, having no cause, is now to be considered. Now the manner is itself also very obscure: and of this we are warned by the parable, where Cupid is elegantly feigned to come of an egg which was laid by Nox. Certainly the divine philosopher declares that 'God hath made everything beautiful in its season, also he hath given the world to their disputes; yet so that man cannot find out the work that God worketh from the beginning to the end'.[6] For the summary law of being and nature, which penetrates and runs through the vicissitudes of things (the same which is described in the phrase, "the work which God worketh from the beginning to the end"), that is, the force implanted by God in these first particles, from the multiplication whereof all the variety of things proceeds and is made up, is a thing which the thoughts of man may offer at but can hardly take in...
>
> Francis Bacon, *On Principles and Origins according to the fables of Cupid and Coelum.*

They say then that Love was the most ancient of all the gods; the most ancient therefore of all things whatever, except Chaos, which was said to have been coeval with him; and Chaos is never distinguished by the ancients with divine honour or the name of a god. This Love is introduced without any parent at all; only that some say he was an egg of Night. And himself out of Chaos begot all things, the gods included...

...This Love I understand to be the appetite or instinct of primal matter; or to speak more plainly, the natural motion of the atom; which is indeed the original and unique force that

Commentary on the Plan of Work

> constitutes and fashions all things out of matter... To know it by way of cause is not possible; it being, next to God, the cause of causes—itself without cause...
>
> For the summary law of nature, that impulse of desire impressed by God upon the primary particles of matter which makes them come together, and which by repetition and multiplication produces all the variety of nature, is a thing which mortal thought may glance at, but can hardly take in...
>
> For beyond all doubt there is a single and summary law in which nature centres and which is subject and subordinate to God; the same in fact which in the text just quoted is meant by the words, *The work which God worketh from the beginning to the end.*
>
> Francis Bacon, *Wisdom of the Ancients,* 'Cupid or the Atom.'

Nowadays, largely due to philosophical influences stemming from Eastern wisdom teachings coupled with orthodox Church teachings, there is a tendency to consider all desire as something base that should be banished or transcended. This may of course be a misunderstanding of what is meant by desire, but the Western wisdom tradition does not relegate all desire to something that is unworthy—as neither do the ancient Tantric teachings of the Indian tradition. On the contrary, from the ancient Egyptians onwards, desire was understood to be, in its primal sense, that which brings everything into being. Both the ancient Egyptians and the Hebrew Cabalists spoke of God desiring to be (*i.e.* to be manifest), which desire brought the universe into being, and of God desiring to know God, which self-knowledge is the purpose of creation and evolution. This desire is the primal will, the divine will, which is pure and holy. Such desire is love. The ancient Greeks also saw it this way, and expressed their understanding of this creative desire in the myth of Eros (Cupid), who is also equated with the Logos or Word: for in love is all wisdom.

Bacon follows and adopts this perception of truth, further equating desire with movement: for desire is an emotion, a word which itself expresses the idea of motion. This motion is the Holy Spirit that moves upon the face of the waters, sounding the Word and thereby creating light.[7] Bacon refers to this movement or desire as being 'impressed' upon matter, making the 'atoms' of matter come together and give birth to light and all the forms of creation. He also speaks of how the desire is not separate from primal matter, but is matter's natural 'appetite', 'instinct' or 'motion'—its spirit, in other words. Such a description seems to owe a great deal to a knowledge of Cabala. Elsewhere Bacon refers to Cupid or Logos as Mercury (*i.e.* the Divine Mercury), which again demonstrates his intimate knowledge and understanding of the subject from the Hermetic point of view.[8]

From what Bacon says concerning poesie, it is only by means of poesie that the human mind can be sufficiently stirred with emotion and raised in consciousness to grasp the higher laws of life, which are laws of emotion and love, and which include the laws of ethics or morality. We need to feel, hear and see emotion, and what it does, in order to recognise and comprehend the higher laws. The theatre makes a perfect laboratory for this—a laboratory to investigate the wide panorama of human desires, with their resulting thoughts and actions, together with the effect of divine inspiration and intervention, the cycles of life and the redeeming power of love.

Bacon identifies three types of poesie—heroic, dramatic and parabolic (see Appendix D)—and uses all three in the Shakespeare plays. The 1623 Shakespeare Folio of plays, entitled *Mr. William Shakespeares Comedies, Histories, & Tragedies*, is Bacon's prime published example of this fourth part of the Great Instauration. But it is not the only example, for Freemasonry in its rituals, symbols, allegories and legends also consists of the three types of poesie and forms a magnificent 'initiative' laboratory of human emotion, thought and ethics dedicated to charity. It was not for nothing that Francis Bacon formed (or reformed) Freemasonry in England, gave it its new constitution and became its first Grand Master: this being another 'secret' of authorship which he carefully hid, but only so that it could be discovered using his method.

Part V

Forerunners, or Anticipations of the Second Philosophy

The fifth part of the Great Instauration comprises a storehouse for useful conclusions or axioms, but which are not yet proved by the

Commentary on the Plan of Work

New Method. Bacon included in this part such things as he had himself discovered, proved or added—'not however according to the true rules and methods of interpretation, but by the ordinary use of the understanding in inquiring and discovering'. He speaks of this part as being 'for temporary use only, pending the completion of the rest', and hopes that his speculations might 'serve in the meantime for wayside inns, in which the mind may rest and refresh itself on its journey to more certain conclusions'.

It may be that Bacon's *Essays* and *Wisdom of Ancients* constitute his published example of such speculations. Because the fifth part of the Great Instauration belongs, together with the fourth and sixth parts, to the left-hand 'dark' or 'veiled' pillar of the temple of philosophy, then Bacon is not likely to inform us openly that this is so. But his essays and interpretations of the wisdom of the ancients are certainly his speculations, which he almost blatantly uses in the Shakespeare plays for instance; but it is in the laboratory of the theatre where such speculations might eventually be proved, or else reveal in the process a truer or greater law when seen and experienced and tested by Bacon's 'sons of science'. Francis Bacon spent a great deal of time and effort on his essays, adopting a highly disciplined and polished style, and refining them further and further with each new publication.

Following his example, this is the section in the Great Instauration where anyone else's useful speculations would also be placed, pending scrutiny and proving by means of the new method.

Part VI

The New or Second Philosophy

The sixth part of the Great Instauration 'discloses and sets forth that philosophy which by the legitimate, chaste, and severe course of inquiry…is at length developed and established'. This is the jewel, the temple of true philosophy that stands upon a solid and well-examined base of experience. It is comprised of all the fully proven axioms concerning the laws of the universe—divine, human and natural, and the 'Summary Philosophy' or universal

Building Paradise

science from which the separate divine, human and natural philosophies stem.

Besides the *New* or *Second Philosophy*, Bacon also referred to this culminating part of the Great Instauration as the *Scientia Activa* ('Active Science'). Sometimes this is translated as 'Practical Science'. However, the 1640 *Advancement of Learning*, which is the first English translation of the 1623 *De Augmentis Scientiarum*, made whilst Bacon's confidantes and executors were still alive to endorse it, lists the titles of the six parts of the Great Instauration and names the sixth part as '*Secunda Philosophia*, or Active Philosophy, from intimate Converse with Nature'.

The distinction between Active Science and Practical Science is important. There is no doubt that the Second Philosophy is a practical science, as it is founded on practical experience and has practical uses; but it is more than just this. Bacon takes great care to emphasise that when the true and summary laws of the universe are discovered, they will be found to be laws of love—and this love is an active, creative love, called in the Bible 'the work which God worketh from the beginning to the end'.[9] It will, therefore, be impossible to separate knowledge of these laws from the practice of them, for the two go together hand in hand. Love in action is light, and light is love in action. Light is wisdom, or divine knowledge. Human knowledge of this is, therefore, an active, living experience. Charity (*i.e.* love in action) is illumination, and illumination is charity.

The Active Science that Bacon is talking about is nothing else but charity. His temple of philosophy is a temple of light, a temple of active, creative love. This is why it is referred to in the Rosicrucian manifestos as 'his new building, called *Sancti Spiritus*' (*i.e.* the House of the Holy Spirit), and in modern Freemasonry as the rebuilt or second Temple of Solomon, the Temple of Light. It is also the College of the Six Days' Work, which Work is 'the work which God worketh from the beginning to the end'.

> In sum, I would advise all in general, that they would take into serious consideration the true and genuine ends of knowledge; that they seek it not either for pleasure, or contention, or contempt of others, or for profit, or fame, or for honour and promotion, or such like adulterate or inferior ends; but for the

Commentary on the Plan of Work

merit and emolument of life; and that they regulate and perfect the same in charity. For the desire of power was the fall of angels, the desire of knowledge the fall of man; but in charity there is no excess, neither man nor angels ever incurred danger by it.

Francis Bacon, *Advancement of Learning,* The Preface (1640).

…the essential form of knowledge…is nothing but a representation of truth: for the truth of being and the truth of knowing are one, differing no more than the direct beam and the beam reflected.

Francis Bacon, *Advancement of Learning*, Bk I (1605).

But this is that which will dignify and exalt knowledge: if contemplation and action be more nearly and straitly conjoined and united together than they have been: a conjunction like unto that of the highest planets, Saturn, the planet of rest and contemplation, and Jupiter, the planet of civil society and action.

Francis Bacon, *Advancement of Learning*, Bk II (1605).

In Cabalistic lore, when there is a conjunction of Saturn and Jupiter, the Messiah is said to appear. The Messiah is the light of love.

Bacon's working example of this part of the Great Instauration (about which he claimed: 'I have made a beginning of the work—a beginning, as I hope, not unimportant') may well have been enshrined in his 'Invisible' or Rosicrucian College of the Six Days' Work, which both generated and inspired various fraternities in learning and illumination, including especially modern speculative Freemasonry. The wisdom teachings or 'landmarks' of Freemasonry undoubtedly derive from (or belong to) this part of the Great Instauration, and the actual practice of charity—the purpose of Freemasonry as well as Christianity—is a working example of this part.

In terms of a published volume or book that represents the sixth part of the Great Instauration, it is possible that Bacon's *New Atlantis* fills the spot. This book, although it was never named by Francis Bacon as being intended to form his example in writing of

NEVV ATLANTIS.

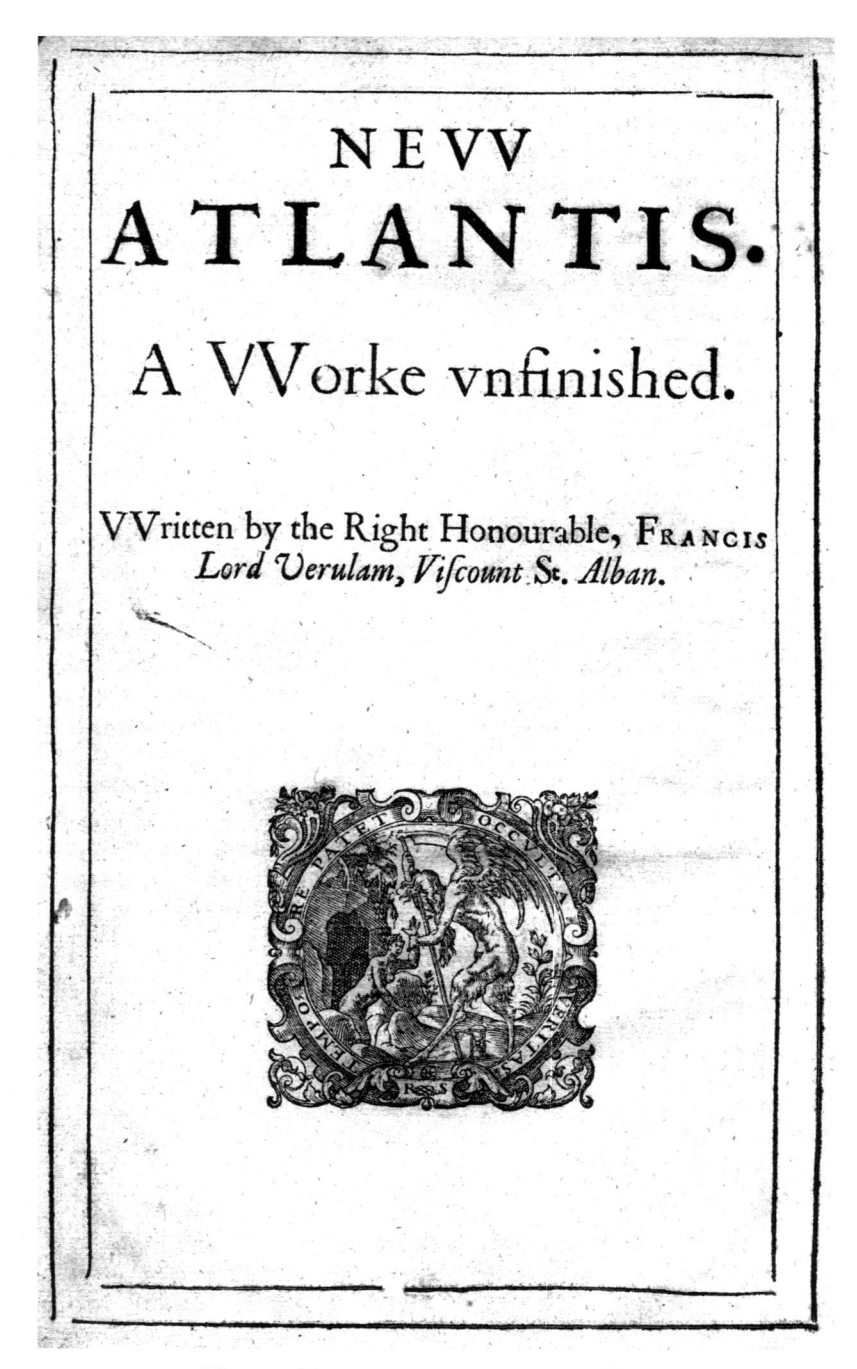

A VVorke vnfinished.

VVritten by the Right Honourable, Francis Lord Verulam, Viscount St. Alban.

Hidden Truth brought forth by Time
Title-page: Francis Bacon's *New Atlantis*—
included as an appendix to the first edition of *Sylva Sylvarum* (1626).

the sixth part of the Great Instauration, nevertheless points the way. It was clearly seen as important enough by Bacon's chaplain and guardian of Bacon's unpublished papers, William Rawley, to publish immediately after Bacon's death in conjunction with Bacon's *Sylva Sylvarum or A Natural History*. This in itself is an indication that it is representative of the sixth part of the Great Instauration, Bacon's Active Science, since Part 3 (A Natural History) and Part 6 (The Second Philosophy or Active Science) are twinned together in Bacon's 'twin pillars' scheme. This compares well with the twinned publication of the *De Augmentis Scientiarum* and Shakespeare Folio in 1623, depicting respectively Parts 1 and 4.

Although the story of *New Atlantis* is an allegory, it depicts an illumined, charitable society living in truth and seeking truth according to Bacon's method, and as such it points the way to discovering Bacon's real example—his own life and those of his devoted friends, who together formed the exemplar Rosicrucian College of Six Days' Work.

PART VII

THE JOY

The seventh part of Bacon's Great Instauration can be easily inferred from the fact that he modelled his work on the divine Creation, in which there are six 'days' of creative work and one 'day' of rest, or peace. He does not, however, mention this final part as such in any of his published writings, although he does refer to 'the sabbath or port' of human endeavour, which he describes as a time of enlightenment and joy. However, in the frontispiece illustration to the 1640 edition of his *Advancement of Learning*, this seventh part is clearly shown, as a seventh book in his 'library'. This book is depicted open on the writing desk in front of Bacon, and in it he is writing.

On the left-hand page of the open book in this illustration are written two words, *'Mundus'* and *'Mens'* (*i.e.* 'World' and 'Mind'), whilst on the right-hand page Bacon has just completed writing

Building Paradise

THE SABBATH BOOK
Detail: Frontispiece: Francis Bacon's
Of the Advancement and Proficiency of Learning
(1640)

Commentary on the Plan of Work

the phrase, *'Conubio jungam stabili'* (*i.e.* 'The connection made firm by marriage'). This is a reference to the major concern of Bacon's, that there should be a marriage between the rational and the empirical, between thought and action, between heaven (the mind or sphere of thought) and earth (the world or sphere of action), echoing and explaining the famous 'As above, so below' statement of Hermes Trismegistus:-

> It is most true, it is without error, it is the sum of verity: That which is beneath is like that which is above, and that which is above is like that which is below, for the performance of the wonders of one thing.
>
> The Emerald Tablet of Hermes.

> By this means we presume we have established for ever, a true and legitimate marriage between the Empirical and Rational faculty; whose fastidious and unfortunate divorce and separation hath troubled and disordered the whole race and generation of mankind.
>
> Francis Bacon, Advancement of Learning, Preface (1640).

> If there be any one on whose ear my frequent praise of practical activities has a harsh and unpleasing sound because he is wholly devoted to contemplative philosophy, let me assure him that he is the enemy of his own desires. In natural philosophy practical results are not only the means to improve human well-being. They are also the guarantee of truth. There is a true rule in religion, that a man must show his faith by his works. The same rule holds good in natural philosophy. Science too must be known by its works. It is by the witness of works rather than by logic or even observation that truth is revealed and established. It follows from this that the improvement of man's lot and the improvement of man's mind are one and the same thing.
>
> Francis Bacon, Cogittata et Visa ('Thoughts and Conclusions', transl.)

The understanding of man and his will are twins by birth as it were; for the purity of illumination and the liberty of will

Building Paradise

began together. Nor is there in the universal nature of things so intimate a sympathy as that of truth and goodness.

Francis Bacon, *Advancement of Learning*, Bk V (1640).

Nay, further, in general and in sum, certain it is that *Veritas* and *Bonitas* differ but as the seal and the print: for Truth prints Goodness...

Francis Bacon, *Advancement of Learning*, Bk 2 (1605).

The knowledge of truth that comes from doing something good and useful is a great joy. This joy is an illumination. It lights up the face and eyes, and shines to others, lighting them up also. Joy is infectious: it is creative. If we have joy, we give joy to others. If we enjoy each other, we give joy to each other. To do this we have to love. This is truth, and it is peace. How to do this in the most perfect, consistent and exquisite way, and be gardeners and caretakers of the world at the same time, is the purpose of Bacon's Great Instauration.

BACONIAN REVELATION

A wonderful summary and revelation in picture form of Bacon's method and Great Instauration was published in 1645, in Leyden, Holland. This is the title-page to the first continental edition of Francis Bacon's *De Dignitate & Augmentis Scientiarum*. Of all the Baconian illustrations this title-page engraving shows Francis Bacon most clearly as a philosopher-poet and secret dramatist. It also portrays symbolically the whole scheme of Bacon's Great Instauration and forms an important member of the special group of engraved title-pages and frontispieces, produced in the early 1640's after Bacon's death, that visually help to explain his grand project.

In this title-page illustration Bacon is shown seated on a similar chair as in the 1640 *Advancement of Learning* frontispiece, hatted and robed as the Lord Chancellor. A large folio book lies open on the table in front of him (presumably the *De Augmentis*), to a line or word of which he is pointing with the first finger of his

Commentary on the Plan of Work

right hand. Beneath this book is another book, on which the open book is supported. The open folio book, together with Bacon's right hand and arm, is illuminated and therefore 'in the light'.

By contrast Bacon's left arm and hand is 'in the shadow', and is supporting and pushing the figure of a wildly dressed man up a rocky hill, on top of which is a temple, also in shadow. The figure is clothed in a tunic of fawn or goatskin and has an out-sized face with an unusual nose that looks like a mask, all of which identifies him as a bacchant, a performer of the rites of Bacchus, the god of drama.

Held out in front of the bacchant, in both his hands, is a clasped book with the symbol of a mirror on its cover. Above the actor, on the crown of the rocky hill, is a temple, symbolic of the Temple of Philosophy that Bacon's method can build.

The picture is beautifully made, with every detail carefully thought out and executed. Just to demonstrate absolutely that this is so, look carefully at the cloak that is draped over Bacon's legs, hanging just beneath the large folio book and his right hand. Near the hem of the cloak you should be able to see the face that is picked out in dots upon the cloth—a face that appears to be that of the sun god, Apollo, crowned with solar rays.

This title-page illustration depicts the whole of Bacon's scheme and complements the title-page illustration of the 1640 *Advancement of Learning* with great skill. For instance, the depiction of the *De Augmentis Scientiarum* (Advancement of Learning) book at Bacon's right hand is a straightforward pictorial illustration of Part 1 of the Great Instauration. Part 2 (the New Method) seems to be represented by the half-concealed book that lies beneath the large folio of the *De Augmentis*. Part 3 (a Natural History) is more subtly but neatly represented by the Apollonian sun face on Bacon's cloak that is draped over his right leg, which is a fine symbol of the light of nature—*i.e.* the veil or cloak of nature in which is hidden the divine light. In the 1640 *Advancement of Learning* title-page illustration these first three parts of the Great Instauration are shown as three books stacked on top of each other and supporting the right-hand solar pillar, which is 'in the light'. In complementary polarity to this, in the same 1640 illustration Parts 4-6 are similarly represented by three further books stacked on top of each other, but supporting the

Building Paradise

left-hand lunar pillar that is 'in the shadow'. Matching this, the 1645 *De Augmentis* illustration places its own explanatory symbols for these three parts of the Great Instauration at Bacon's left hand side—the actor held by Bacon, the book held by the actor, and the temple on the hill, symbolising Parts 4, 5 and 6 respectively.

The classical rites of Bacchus involved a mixture of comedy and tragedy, reflecting the nature of life and the universal principle of strife and friendship as taught in the Orphic Mystery schools. When clothed in a fawn skin the bacchant (or female bacchante) wore soft sandals made of fawn skin, the original of the socks of comedy. The tragic actor or bacchant, by contrast, wore high-soled hunting boots made of goatskin, known as buskins, and a goatskin tunic. The bacchant in this picture is not wearing buskins, therefore the deduction is that the bacchant is clothed in fawn skin and is performing comedy. Comedy, which has a happy or joyful result, is a drama in which the characters are taken through sequential stages of initiation, undergo psychological death and rebirth, and finally achieve a marriage and illumination of some kind—a goal symbolised by the temple on the hill.

The mask was used in the Dionysian masquerades to represent the way the incarnate god functioned. Just as the mask veiled the bacchant whilst he played his role on the stage, so the bacchant or tragi-comic actor was himself the mask or earthly representative of the god Bacchus on the stage of the world.

Quite clearly the picture is showing that the actor is the mask of the poet-dramatist Bacon, the Italianate form of whose name is Bacco, the same as that of Bacchus. Just as the actor in the picture wears his own mask, so Bacon in his chair holds his human mask, the actor, who looks back to Bacon, the author, for his words or instructions. Bacon's particular actor-mask was Will Shakspere.

The book with the symbol of a mirror on its cover is like a notebook, whilst the mirror is representative of the mind and of reflections. A notebook is a book of reflections and, since the actor is carrying it, it is presumably for the noting down of ideas or observations drawn from the experience of acting out the mysteries of life in the laboratory of the theatre. This seems to illustrate nicely the meaning of Bacon's fifth part of the Great Instauration, which follows on from the theatrical fourth part.

Commentary on the Plan of Work

BACON, THE PHILOSOPHER-POET
Title-page: Francis Bacon's
De Dignitate et Augmentis Scientiarum
(1645).

Building Paradise

Above the actor, on the crown of the rocky hill, is a temple, symbolic of the Temple of Philosophy. But there is more to it than this, for the depiction of this precipitously rocky, flat-topped hill with the temple on it shows that it is an acropolis—the most famous and fitting one for this Bacon-Shakespeare story being the acropolis of Athens, home of the spear-shaking goddess Athena, patroness of philosophers and poets.

However, the temple shown in the picture is circular, covered with a dome and having arches between its columns. There were not many circular temples built by either the Greeks or Romans in classical times. There was certainly not one on the acropolis of Athens, and the Greeks did not use domes or arches in their temple architecture. However, the Romans did, but they did not have a steep-sided rocky acropolis like Athens. Their famous round temple was the Temple of Vesta in Rome, the most sacred shrine in the imperial city where the vestal fire, representing the fire of the hearth or heart, was kept continually burning by the vestal virgins. The Baconian temple in the picture would appear, therefore, to represent an entirely new temple built on ancient principles and foundations, fusing together the best and most sacred elements of the martial Romans and sensual Greeks—of Mars and Venus—being a temple of the virgin goddess, the buskined Diana, sister of Apollo, great goddess of nature and guardian of the flame of love. Such symbolism beautifully encapsulates the sixth part of the Great Instauration.

SOLOMON'S HOUSE

THE COLLEGE OF THE SIX DAYS' WORK

Francis Bacon wrote his vision of how he hoped his Great Instauration might be accomplished in political and cultural terms as an allegory modelled on that of Plato's *Atlantis* and Sir Thomas More's *Utopia*. Like Plato, Bacon did not complete his story—or did not publish it all. Dr. Rawley, who published the work after Bacon's death as an appendix to the 1626 *Sylva Sylvarum or Natural History*, explained that the *New Atlantis* was a work unfinished because his lordship's attentions were called to more serious matters, namely the compiling and publishing of a Natural History. This may or may not be true, for reasons already given (see Chapter 4: The Great Instauration). In 1660 a continuation of the *New Atlantis* was published, written by an anonymous R. H. Esquire as an attempt to complete Bacon's story. Two years later, in 1662, John Heydon, a well-known writer on Rosicrucianism, published a curious work called *The Holy Guide*, which was prefaced by an almost verbatim reprint of Bacon's *New Atlantis*. Remarkably, Heydon does not credit Bacon with the authorship, but he inserts direct references to the Rosicrucians so as to imply that Bacon's story is about the Fraternity of the Rosy Cross.

The story of *New Atlantis* is, as Rawley described it in his preface to the work, a 'fable my lord devised, to the end that he might exhibit therein a model or description of a college, instituted for the interpretation of nature, and the producing of great and marvellous works for the benefit of man, under the name of Solomon's House, or the College of the Six Days' Work'.

Building Paradise

The work contains Bacon's vision of a future civilisation, living in peace, friendship and charity in the island of Bensalem (*Bensalem* means 'Son of Peace') and having as its 'lantern' an order or society of philosophers formed into a college 'dedicated to the study of the works and creatures of God', and for the 'finding out of the true nature of all things, whereby God might have the more glory in the workmanship of them, and men the more fruit in the use of them'. Their emissaries, bound by laws of secrecy, are sent to all parts of the world to collect and trade in 'light'.

From the name of the college and Bacon's other writings we know that the goal of these philosophers is to understand and imitate (as far as human beings may) the divine Creation or Six Days' Work, including the illumination of mankind, which work Bacon pointed out was, and continues to be, a creative act of perfect, boundless love. This is summed up in the fable by a 'father' of Solomon's House, who declares that 'the end of our foundation is the knowledge of causes and secret motions of things, and the enlarging of the bounds of human empire, to the effecting of all things possible'.

In the *New Atlantis* the college, order or society of Solomon's House had been founded by a king called Solamona, who likened himself to the Hebrew King Solomon and who instituted laws based on Moses' secret Cabala. Later the society became Christian through 'the apostolical and miraculous evangelism of St. Bartholomew', being given all the canonical books of the Old and New Testaments plus the Apocalypse and, significantly, 'some other books of the New Testament which were not at that time written'.

Bartholomew, the miraculous founder of the New Atlanteans' Christian mode of life, was the apostle whom Jesus found sitting under a fig tree and meditating upon Jacob's Ladder. The fig tree is symbolic of the Tree of Knowledge, an integral part of the Tree of Life that is the basic glyph and secret of the Cabala. Jacob's ladder is a symbol for the various levels or heavens of consciousness which knowledge of the Tree of Life helps a cabalist explore. According to the apocryphal Gospel of Bartholomew the apostle was the one who carefully questioned Jesus after his resurrection, and it was to Bartholomew that Jesus revealed the knowledge of the angels and of Satan—the greatest Cabalistic mystery of all.

Solomon's House

From then on Bartholomew became known as 'the Depository of the Mysteries of the Son', which is virtually what the word 'Cabala' means.

In the *New Atlantis* the philosophers of Solomon's House are clearly Rosicrucians, whose emblem is a red cross on a white background and whose aims are identical to those announced in the Rosicrucian manifestos in the second decade of the 17th century. The 17th century Rosicrucians were known as the 'Invisible Brethren', whose work was that of the 'Six Days'.

New Atlantis is a utopia, but historians tend to use the term to also imply that what the story describes never happened and never will happen. However, there is more than enough evidence to indicate that Bacon did establish such a college, but privately and secretly; even though his writings suggest that he hoped his ideal college might become the model for a state institution.

With regard to this it is interesting to note that in 1617, the year in which Bacon became the Lord Keeper of the Great Seal and the year after the reputed founding of the 'Invisible College', the poet Edmund Bolton, a barrister of the Inner Temple, friend of Bacon and kinsman of the Duke of Buckingham, proposed to King James I a design for a Royal Academy or College, complete with a Senate of Honour, for the advancement of learning. It was to consist of three classes of persons called Tutelaires, Auxiliares and Essentials, and its members were to 'love, honour and serve each other according to the spirit of St. John'. This was Bacon's project, details of which can be found in the *Commentaries* or *Transportata* among Bacon's manuscripts in the British Museum. The official proposal was for the College to be held at Windsor. In 1624 the details of this scheme were laid before the Lords by Buckingham and finally settled, but it was not given the support it needed by Parliament. The Government then abandoned the scheme and it shortly afterwards collapsed. However, Bacon's private 'Invisible College' already existed and carried on existing. Eventually, it brought about in Charles II's reign the foundation of the Royal Society, whose 'Instaurator' was declared to be Francis Bacon. It also led to the foundation of colleges and societies of various kinds in many countries, including the Académie des Sciences in France, all following Bacon's design as far as they understood it.

Building Paradise

According to Michael Maier (1568-1622) the 'Invisible' or Rosicrucian College of the Six Days' Work was the regenerated form in Europe of the ancient Society of Magians or Wise Men—the western branch of the planetary Brotherhood of Light. Maier wrote that the Society of the ancient Brother Magians or Wise Men was revived in 1570 under the denomination of 'Brothers of the Golden Rose-Croix' and was ruled by a 'President'. It is unlikely that Francis Bacon was its first President in 1570, since he would have been only nine years old; but Francis grew up under the tutelage of Sir Nicholas Bacon and, after obtaining his vision in 1573-4 of his life's work, proceeded to develop Sir Nicholas' ideas for the advancement of learning and training of statesmen into something much greater.

Sir Nicholas' scheme, which he had partly derived from the earlier example of Sir Thomas More, was the establishment of a special academy in London for the education of the wealthier of the crown wards, to train them for royal service. This involved not only special instruction in French, Latin and Greek, and in both common and civil law, but also in the necessary courtly arts of music and dancing. In addition, practical experience would be obtained by accompanying ambassadors on overseas missions. His ideas were not adopted officially, but at the behest of the Queen he did establish a special academy (a Platonic Academy) at Gorhambury, St. Albans, and teamed up with Sir Francis Walsingham to provide a centre in London for the training of suitable people for diplomatic and intelligence-gathering missions overseas. In addition, the lawyers' Inns of Court, and especially Sir Nicholas Bacon's Inn, Gray's Inn, were encouraged to develop accordingly as such training centres. Francis Bacon was a particular beneficiary and example of the special training, as also was his brother Anthony.

Roger Asham (1515-68), the Queen's tutor and greatest scholar of his time, was an important influence. The Queen specially commissioned his book, *The Schoolmaster*, concerning the education of the children of aristocrats and princes, and Sir Nicholas Bacon naturally took note of its principles. Sir Nicholas' father-in-law, the great humanist scholar Sir Anthony Cooke, who had been tutor to Edward VI, was also deeply involved. Sir Anthony's daughters were considered to be the most highly educated and accomplished

Solomon's House

women in England. Two of the five, Anne and Mildred, were married to the two chief ministers of the Queen—the Lord Keeper Sir Nicholas Bacon (who was also Lord Chancellor in all but name) and the Principal Secretary of State Sir William Cecil, who later became Lord Burghley, the Lord Treasurer.

Besides the special education that Francis Bacon received in England, there were also strong continental influences adopted by him in the formation and development of his work and society. These influences may well have been associated with an esoteric transmission amongst the Society of Wise Men. For instance, it is claimed that there have been a succession of leaders or international 'Imperators' and national 'Grand Masters' of this society, through whom the torch of initiation and illumination has been passed on—even though the members of this society were mostly linked not so much by any specific earthly organisation but rather by a common humanity and desire to search for truth.[1] An example of one of these members is the Abbot Johann Trithemius of Spondheim, who lived in the late 15th and early 16th century. He was made particularly famous in the public eye by the printing of his *Steganographia* in 1499, the first great cipher book ever to be published. Much if not all of it was Cabalistic in nature. Francis Bacon, with his love and use of cipher, adopted and adapted several of Trithemius' systems, as well as inventing new ones of his own. The great cipher compendium, *Cryptomenytices et Cryptographiae*, which was published in Germany in 1624, contained many of Francis' and Trithemius' ciphers together with occult teachings, and was well timed to coincide with the publication of the Shakespeare Folio and the *De Augmentis Scientiarum*, which employ some of the cipher.

Trithemius is said to have taught Cornelius Agrippa von Nettesheim (1486-1531), the next leader, who was styled the Imperator of Sodalitium, a 'Community' that he founded at Paris in 1507. Agrippa then proceeded to establish a section of his community in London in 1510, perhaps with Sir Thomas More at its head. Sir Thomas More (1478-1535) was one of the outstanding English humanists of his time, amongst whose friends were Erasmus, who visited More in England twice (1499 and 1509-14), and John Colet, the theologian and founder of St. Paul's School in London, who was, together with More, one of the chief Tudor humanists. More's

Building Paradise

Utopia (1516), like Plato's *Timaeus* and *Critias* that describe Atlantis, had a strong influence on Bacon's *New Atlantis*.

Likewise, Trithemius is said to have taught Paracelsus (Theophrastus von Hohenheim, 1493-1541), who also became the reputed leader of the Magi after Agrippa. Paracelsus had a very important influence on the Rosicrucians but was not a member of the Fraternity of the Rosy Cross (which the Rosicrucian manifesto *Fama Fraternitatis* is careful to point out), because the Rosicrucian Fraternity was not founded until 1570, almost thirty years after Paracelsus' death. However, the *Fama* refers to the 'Father C.R.C.' of the Rosicrucians as 'the Theophrastian Master', thereby emphasising the link with Paracelsus. Paracelsus was known as the reorganiser and 'Monarcha Secretorium' of the Order (of Magi), and his writings were marked with the letter 'R' or a rose.

These wise men were, above all, associated with the Renaissance and the Hermetic-Neoplatonic-Cabalistic undercurrent of Humanism that originated in Italy in the 15th century, primarily from the Platonic Academy of Marsilio Ficino in Florence. (Ficino was known as the Second Plato; Francis Bacon was called the Third Plato.) It carried, therefore, the Western wisdom tradition derived from Hermes (Ancient Egypt), Zoroaster and the Magi (Mesopotamia/Persia), Moses and Jesus (Israel), and Orpheus, Pythagoras and Plato (Greece). The Elizabethans added to this the Celtic-Druidic tradition.

According to the Rosicrucian manifestos and other literature, the Rosicrucian Fraternity was particularly marked by its Protestantism and antipathy towards popery. Its symbolism, although found elsewhere, is peculiarly English, for the emblems of the rose and the red cross are in particular associated with England and England's patron saint, St. George. The Red Cross on a white field is also the specific emblem of King Arthur and England's archangel, Michael. Since red is the heraldic colour of gold, the Red Cross is sometimes known as the Golden Cross—the Cross of Light or Cross of Truth. The rose is also a special attribute of the Virgin Mary, whose land or 'dowry' England is—and Elizabeth I, Queen of England, was deliberately associated with the Virgin.[2]

The Knights Templar, who used a form of the Red Cross and who some equate with the Rosicrucians, had their English head-

Solomon's House

quarters at the Temple in London, the site of which became the Inns of Court, the residence of the lawyers in Queen Elizabeth's reign. Gray's Inn, the Inn of Court of Sir Nicholas Bacon and his sons, is twinned with the Inner Temple. Leicester House, later Essex House, was on the site of the Templars' Outer Temple, and it was there that the English Areopagus of poets met under the patronage of the Earl of Leicester, and there that Anthony Bacon later set up his intelligence headquarters and scrivenery of secretaries, cryptographers, writers and translators whilst working for Leicester's stepson, Robert Devereux, the Earl of Essex.

It is possible that Sir Nicholas Bacon headed the new Order of the Rosy Cross in its initial years, since Francis Bacon's version of it, as a society dedicated to the advancement of learning, clearly grew out of what Sir Nicholas began. Sir Nicholas Bacon (1510-79) was far wiser than most people realised (as Francis himself pointed out), and had great power and influence. Not only was he the principal judge of the land and the Queen's friend and 'royal conscience', he was also the one who had the vitally important task of stage-managing the acts of uniformity and supremacy for the settlement of religion in 1559, in which the English Church was once more reformed according to the Protestant model.

Dr. John Dee (1577-1608), the Queen's astrologer and mage, who possessed one of the greatest libraries in the kingdom, was also deeply involved, as too was Robert Dudley, the Earl of Leicester (1532-88), unofficial consort of the Queen and enthusiastic patron of philosophers, poet-lawyers, artists and actors, and of the English Areopagus led by his protégé, Sir Philip Sydney. It is even conceivable that Leicester was the head of the Rosicrucian Order, or co-head (for there were three principals); for, interestingly, it is immediately after Leicester's death in 1588 that Francis Bacon began work on his *New Method* and commenced writing the Shakespeare plays. Astrologically 1588-9 was the time of Francis Bacon's 'Saturn return', an auspicious time for a new beginning.

1570, the date that Maier gives for the founding of the Fraternity of the Golden Rose-Cross, is the very year in which the chivalric cult of St George, King Arthur and the Virgin Queen was begun in earnest in England, immediately after the excommunication of Queen Elizabeth I by the Pope; and for this the Queen's Accession Day Tournaments were the prime focus. The principal

Building Paradise

person to design, inaugurate and then lead the Accession Day Tournaments for many years was Sir Henry Lee, the Queen's champion, who returned from France in 1570. These lavish annual tournaments, which continued on to the end of Elizabeth's reign, involved not only the Queen's courtiers but also all the most gifted poets, writers, artists, craftsmen and actors of the realm. The tournaments were not only great entertainments for the court and public but vehicles of culture and education, funded by aristocrats, wealthy courtiers and officials who gained social prestige and political influence thereby—although some of them were clearly aware of the higher cultural aims that they were in effect sponsoring. The story behind the tournaments had, from the start, an Arcadian theme, and it is Arcadia that was said to be the land of the Rosicrucians.

The heroes of Arcadia, heroes ofArcadia were poet-knights, sometimes called shepherd-knights. Of these, the poet and courtier Sir Philip Sydney (1554-86) was an outstanding example, who headed the English Areopagus of poets. In Spenser's *Faerie Queene* the author, who was a member of the Areopagus, epitomises the ideal poet-knight as the Red Cross Knight, a type of St. George who has to accompany the lady Una (the One Truth) to her land, to free it from the oppression of a frightful dragon.

In 1576 Francis Bacon was sent abroad to the French Court for three years. On Sir Nicholas' death in 1579 Francis returned home, aged eighteen, and it is possible that it was then that he became the President of the Society, inheriting what Sir Nicholas had begun and being given the moral support and encouragement of both the Queen and Burghley, although not the financial help for which he hoped and asked. Two other key dates were 1588/9, mentioned above, and 1593, Francis' thirty-third year and the year of publication of *Venus and Adonis,* when he first publicly used his Apollonian pseudonym, William Shakespeare. At the end of the following year, during the Gray's Inn Christmas/New Year Revels, his fraternity, or rather the ideal of it as a State institution, was announced to the lawyers of Gray's Inn and the Inner Temple, and the ministers and courtiers of the Queen, with the performance of *The Honourable Order of the Knights of the Helmet.* Quite rightly this highly praised entertainment has been called the germ of the House of Solomon or College of the Six Days' Work as

Solomon's House

described thirty-three years later in Bacon's *New Atlantis*.³ It is unlikely that the thirty-three year periods are by chance. (See Appendix C: 'Ciphers of Francis Bacon.)

It was Bacon's group that was truly the 'invisible' Rosicrucian College of the Six Days' Work, for they were dedicated to carrying out his scheme. In King James I's time, when Bacon took on the lease of Canonbury in 1616, the 'Invisible College' seems to have taken root there, howbeit for only a short period. Significantly, the Canonbury mansion was built in 1509-13 by William Bolton, a member of Gray's Inn and the prior of St. Bartholomew's Priory.

Bacon's mother lodge of Rosicrucians then spawned many children. For instance, in 1693 certain members of the principal Rosicrucian lodge in England, the Philadelphia Lodge in London, together with members from the Grand Lodge of the Rosicrucians in Heidelberg, set sail for North America in order to establish there not only a Rosicrucian colony but also the Rosicrucian sciences, arts and trades. Led by Grand Master Kelpius they were intent on carrying out a plan conceived by Lord Bacon. In due time, from this branch of the Rosicrucians arose the prominent Rosicrucian organisation known today as the Ancient and Mystical Order Rosae Crucis (AMORC).⁴

FREEMASONRY

Modern Freemasonry was established at the time of the Invisible College, born out of earlier Elizabethan origins and with Francis Bacon alluded to cryptically as the founder and first Grand Master.

Modern speculative Freemasonry can trace its beginnings in England to the latter part of the 16th century, with its fuller development taking place during the 17th century. When the Grand Lodge of English Freemasonry was formed in 1716 (the centenary of William Shakespeare's death) it was not the first Grand Lodge but a revival or rebirth of an earlier one—even though modern Freemasons generally understand the 1716 Grand Lodge to be the first Grand Lodge of their speculative system of initiation. According to the Freemasonic allegory concerning its origins, the original Grand Lodge of English Freemasonry was founded by St.

Building Paradise

Alban, which was Bacon's name as a viscount. Moreover, modern Freemasonry is described as a system of morality based on allegory and illustrated by symbol, and is specifically dedicated to charity. It works with what might be called certain proven axioms concerning the laws of love as well as with speculations. It employs an initiative method of teaching (Bacon's method), based on the example of the ancient Mystery schools but updated, and it uses all three types of poesie (*i.e.* narrative, dramatic and allusive) that Bacon identified and recommended for the upliftment of the mind and discovery of truth.

St. Alban, besides being reputed by the Church as the first Christian martyr in Britain, is claimed by Freemasonry in their legend of the Craft as the founder of Freemasonry in England. He was reputedly born in the 3rd century AD, near Verulamium (now St. Albans in Hertfordshire),[5] went to Rome as a young man where he served as a soldier under the Emperor Diocletian, and then returned to Verulamium in the company of Amphibalus, a Christian, by whom he was taught. When the persecution of Christians commenced, Amphibalus was sought after but was helped to escape by Albanus, who donned his preceptor's cloak and gave himself up to the soldiers instead. After being imprisoned and tortured, Albanus' real identity was discovered. Amphibalus was also found and both men suffered martyrdom for being Christians. The Abbey church of St. Albans was later erected over the site where St. Alban's body had been interred.

Freemasonry adds to this story. Its legend concerning St. Alban was first mentioned in the Cooke manuscript (*c.*1490) and repeated, with modifications and additions, in the Dowland manuscript (*c.*1500), the form and details of which were preserved in all the subsequent manuscript Charges of the 16th and 17th centuries.[6] When Dr. Anderson published the Legend of the Craft in his *Constitutions of the Free-masons* in 1723 and 1738,[7] certain significant details were added to or altered.

The legend declares that Masonry flourished in Britain since before the time of the Druids, and that during the Roman rule lodges and conventions were regularly held. However, continual wars reduced Masonry to a low ebb. It was then that Masonry was reintroduced into England by St. Amphibal, a Christian monk, who first communicated it to St. Alban, who was a knight.

Solomon's House

The story goes that when Carausius revolted from the Roman Emperor Maximilian and set himself up as the Emperor of Britain, he employed St. Alban to environ the city of Verulam with a wall and to build for him a splendid palace. To reward his diligence in executing these works, the Emperor Carausius appointed St. Alban as Steward of his household and chief ruler, after himself, of the realm. He also made St. Alban the paymaster and Governor of the King's (Emperor's) works. Then, in order to make himself and his government acceptable to the people of Britain, Carausius assumed the character of a Mason and raised the Masons to the first rank as his favourites, appointing St. Alban as the Principal Superintendent of their assemblies. St. Alban gave the fraternity the Charges and Manners as St. Amphibal had taught him (*i.e.* framed for them a constitution), assisted them in making Masons, treated them with great kindness and increased their pay. Later on, in the year AD 287, Carausius granted the Masons a charter and commanded Albanus to preside over them as Grand Master.

According to the Masonic record, which until recently has been largely accepted as historically accurate, St. Alban was martyred in the year AD 303. Modern scholarship, however, has convincingly shown that the historical St. Alban was martyred on 22nd June 209 by Geta, eldest son of the Emperor Severus, when they visited Britain in AD 208-9. It is also clear that St. Alban was certainly never a knight (knighthood was a chivalric honour invented much later in history), nor the steward of an emperor's household and chief ruler (after the emperor) of the realm. Moreover, it would seem that Amphibalus is a personification of the ecclesiastical cloak or vestment, *amphibalum,* which St. Alban donned (just as St. Veronica is a personification of Christ's true image imprinted on the handkerchief which covered his face).

However, the strange elements of the story, when applied allegorically to the later St. Alban—Viscount St. Alban—fit like a glove. Sir Francis Bacon was a knight and he was also St. Alban—Viscount St. Alban. This was a unique title and an honour deliberately bestowed on him by King James on the occasion of Bacon's sixtieth birthday (21st January 1621), with a special ceremony of investiture performed on 27th January 1621.[8] Moreover, in his speech to the King during the ceremony, recorded as a letter to his

Building Paradise

Majesty, Bacon made special mention of the vestment of St. Alban as being something of major significance to him:-

> So this is the eighth rise or reach, a diapason in music, even a good number and accord for a close. And so I may without superstition be buried in St. Alban's habit or vestment.[9]

Bacon served a king, James Stewart (James VI of Scotland and I of England), who was considered by many Englishmen to be a usurper of the throne of England[10] and who was the first to bear the title of Emperor of Great Britain. Lord St. Alban was his faithful 'steward' and proxy chief ruler of the realm. The 'continual wars' that reduced Masonry to a low ebb were the many centuries of foreign wars, the civil wars (romantically named the Wars of the Roses) and religious persecution. Moreover, King James did support the Masons in the manner described, and it was in his reign that Freemasonry became established (or revived) in England. The 'palace' that St. Alban (Bacon) built for the king was a house of learning, a temple of light, constructed by Bacon's fraternity in learning and illumination.

Bacon's temple is a temple of the Holy Spirit—the 'house *Sanctus Spiritus*'; his method is the 'perfect Method of all Arts'; his *Natural History* is the *Librum Naturae* or Book of Nature; and his fraternity in learning and illumination is the 'Fraternity of the Rosie Cross', all as mentioned in the famous Rosicrucian manifesto, the *Fama Fraternitatis Rosae Crucis, or Discovery of the Brotherhood of the most laudable Order of the Rosie Cross*. In his *New Atlantis* Bacon, the Second Solomon, calls his temple the House of Solomon or College of the Six Days' Work, founded by himself in the guise of Solamona (*i.e.* Solomon II) and comprised of a society of philosopher-priests whose badge is a red cross and who maintain a secrecy or invisibility from the world at large. Robert Boyle, writing in 1646-7, referred to the College as the 'Invisible College' or 'Philosophical College'.

According to the *Freemason's Guide and Compendium*, the modern history of English Freemasonry starts with the record of Elias Ashmole's admittance into Freemasonry in 1646, although it is recognised that speculative as well as operative Freemasonry existed in England long before this. Moreover, artefacts exist sug-

Solomon's House

gesting that the Royal Arch degree as well as the basic Craft degrees of initiation existed in the time of Queen Elizabeth I; but whether all these formed part of speculative Freemasonry as it emerged in the following century is not certain. They may at that early date be purely Rosicrucian.

The legendary dates of St. Alban, given so precisely as if factual, are part of the allegory. In the Kaye (*i.e.* Key) cipher used by Bacon, 287 = FRA ROSI CROSSE. The mythical year of 303 is likewise a cipher, which reduces to 33 since 0 is traditionally counted as a null. In the Baconian and Cabalistic Simple cipher, 33 = BACON. The number 33 is also the count of the word 'FREE', as in Freemason, which signifies love (*free* is derived from Sanskrit *pri* meaning 'love' or 'loving kindness'). Since a mason is a craftsman and builder in stone, and a stone is an ancient alchemical symbol of the heart,[11] a Freemason is a loving builder of love, whose temple is Solomon's temple, the heart temple of light and peace (the name *Solomon* is associated with the name of the sun, *Sol*, and with the Hebrew word *shalom* meaning 'peace'). In the Masonic Capital Letter cipher the initial or capital letters of the number Thirty-Three signify the 33rd degree of initiation, the highest degree of Freemasonry and the number signifying in Cabala the complete knowledge of the Tree of Life. This cipher 'T.T.' is to be found as a signature carved on the Shakespeare Memorial that was erected in Westminster Abbey in 1741,[12] as also on the title-

'TT' DETAIL: SHAKESPEARE MEMORIAL, WESTMINSTER ABBEY

TO.THE.ONLIE.BEGETTER.OF.
THESE.INSVING.SONNETS.
Mr. W. H. ALL.HAPPINESSE.
AND.THAT.ETERNITIE.
PROMISED.

BY.

OVR.EVER-LIVING.POET.

WISHETH.

THE.WELL-WISHING.
ADVENTVRER.IN.
SETTING.
FORTH.

T. T.

DEDICATION PAGE ('TT'): 1609 SHAKESPEARE'S SONNETS

page and dedication to the first edition of *Shake-speares Sonnets* published in 1609.

'Free' is the meaning of the name 'Francis'. 'FRANCIS' counts to 67 in the Simple cipher, so that the full signature of 'FRANCIS BACON' is 100 (*i.e.* 67 + 33), the traditional cipher of a Great Master—a highly illuminated soul who has completed thrice thirty-three degrees plus the crowning, all-embracing One. (See Appendix C: 'The Ciphers of Francis Bacon'.)

The Shakespeare plays, besides being authored by Francis Bacon and signed many times on significant pages with the above cipher signatures, are full of Masonic symbolism, meanings and

Solomon's House

words. In addition the number 100 is used in other ways to link Freemasonry with Shakespeare and thus with Francis Bacon. For instance, the founding (or refounding) of the English Grand Lodge of Freemasons took place in 1716, the centenary of the actor William Shakspere's death. But it was also in 1616 that the 'Invisible College' was said to have been founded by Bacon (*i.e.* his College of the Six Days' Work),[13] marked by his taking on a forty-year lease of Canonbury House, with its unique tower building complete with winding staircase and symbolic Freemasonic-Rosicrucian carvings.[14]

THE THREE PRINCIPALS AND SYMBOLS OF FREEMASONRY
Headpiece: The Benson Medley Edition of *Shakespeare's Sonnets* (1723).

In 1723, the centenary of the publication of the Shakespeare Folio of plays, modern Freemasonry emerged into the open with the publication of Anderson's *The Constitutions of the Free-masons*, in which the legend of the founding of Freemasonry by St. Alban is given. Anderson tells the reader that the book contains much that is cryptic. Also in the same year was published the Benson Medley edition of *Shakespeare's Sonnets*, the title-page headpiece of which depicts the symbols of the higher degrees of Freemasonry. The three principals of the higher degrees are shown in the centre as naked children observing the sun through telescopes, thereby representing three 'Cupids', the three Rosicrucian principals of the revived ancient society of magi or wise men. Alexander Pope, together with Dr. Sewell, was responsible for publishing this edition of Shakespeare's sonnets. Pope, a leading authority on both Bacon and Shakespeare as well as a poet, was involved as a key person in the design and erection of the Shakespeare Memorial in Westminster Abbey, which portrays Shakespeare standing, leaning on a Janus altar (*i.e.* the high altar of the Mysteries), with his legs crossed in the fashion of a knight.

Building Paradise

SHAKESPEARE, THE ROSICRUCIAN MASTER
The Shakespeare Memorial, Westminster Abbey.

Solomon's House

THE ROSICRUCIAN FATHER

The same Freemasonic symbols and artistic style employed in the headpiece of the Benson Medley edition of *Shakespeare's Sonnets* were used ten years later in the tailpiece of Dr. Peter Shaw's Collected Edition of Francis Bacon's Prose Works (1733), the first set of Bacon's works to be published after the emergence of the Freemasons in 1723. The Rosicrucian eagle of St. John spreads its wings over this engraving, casting its shadow and protecting all that lies beneath its wings. The famous Rosicrucian motto, *'Sub umbra alarum tuarum, Jehovah'* ('Beneath the shadow of thy wings, O Lord'), is associated with this emblem of an eagle with outstretched wings.

The motto and eagle can be found depicted together in Emblem 6 of the emblem book, *The Mirror of Modestie*, published

SYMBOLS OF FREEMASONRY
Tailpiece: Dr. Peter Shaw's Collected Edition of
Francis Bacon's Prose Works (1733).

EMBLEME 6.

NEuer should any thinke himselfe so sure
Of friends assistance, that he dares procure
New enemies: for vnprouok'd they will
Spring out of forg'd, or causelesse malice still.
Else, why should this poore creature be pursu'd,
Too simple to offend, a beast so rude.
Therefore prouide (for malice danger brings)
House-roome to find vnder an *Eagles* wings.
You are this *Eagle*, whcih ore-shades the *sheepe*
Pursu'de by *humane wolues*, and safe doth keepe
The poore mans honest, though might-wronged cause,
From being crushed by oppressions pawes.
Faire Port you are, where euery *Goodnesse* findes
Safe shelter from swolne *Greatnesse*, stubborne winds
Eager to drench it: but that feareless rest
Dwels in your harbour, to all good distrest.
I bid not you prouide, you are compleate,
The good for to protect, or bad defeate.

C 2

BENEATH THE SHADOW OF THY WINGS, O LORD
Emblem 6: *The Mirror of Modestie* (1618).

Solomon's House

in 1618. The emblem is assigned to Sir Francis Bacon and equates him with the eagle who o'ershades the sheep pursued by human wolves, keeps safe the honest man's cause from being crushed by oppression's paws, defeats the bad and protects the good.

The Rosicrucian motto is derived from Psalm 91:-

> He that dwelleth in the secret place of the Most High [*Elyon*]
> Shall abide under the shadow of the Almighty [*Shaddai*].
> I will say of the Lord [*Jehovah*], 'He is my refuge and my fortress:
> My God [*Elohim*]; in Him will I trust.'
> Surely He shall deliver thee from the snare of the fowler,
> And from the noisome pestilence.
> He shall cover thee with his feathers,
> And under His wings shalt thou trust:
> His truth shall be thy shield and thy buckler...[15]

The four distinct divine names form a Cabalistic sequence related in ascending order to the higher principles (*Sephiroth*) of the Tree of Life:-

Elyon ('the Most High') refers to Christ as the Son of 'the Highest', the possessor of heaven and earth, and dispenser of God's blessings in the world (*Sephira* 5).

Shaddai ('Almighty') refers to the All-bountiful—the grace, mercy or compassion that is the blessing of God (*Sephira* 4).

Jehovah ['Lord'] is the 'Name' or form of God and means 'the Everlasting', the One who was, who is and who is to come—the Renewer, Redeemer, Saviour and Shepherd—the Divine Intelligence (*Sephira* 3).

Elohim ['God'] refers to the 'Word' or Son of God as Creator (or Maker)—the Divine Wisdom (*Sephira* 2).

Bacon's private prayer that he made for his Great Instauration, which was eventually published in 1679 by Bacon's 'successor', Archbishop Tennison, incorporates the meaning of these divine principles and the Rosicrucian motto:-

Building Paradise

Crown
Power/Will

Life

Elohim
Wisdom
Word

Zodiac

Stars

Jehovah
Intelligence
Name

Knowledge

Right-hand

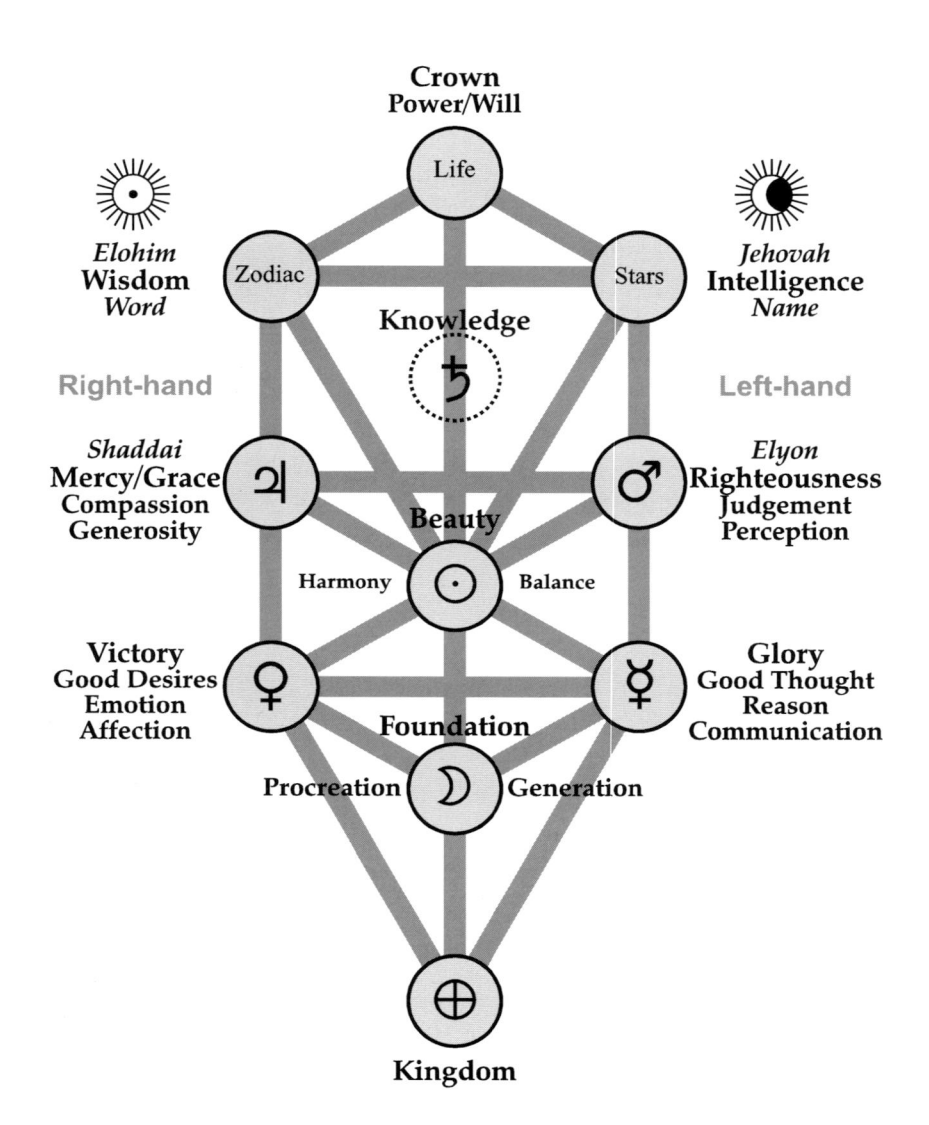

Left-hand

Shaddai
Mercy/Grace
Compassion
Generosity

Beauty

Elyon
Righteousness
Judgement
Perception

Harmony

Balance

Victory
Good Desires
Emotion
Affection

Foundation

Glory
Good Thought
Reason
Communication

Procreation

Generation

Kingdom

THE CABALISTIC TREE OF LIFE

Solomon's House

May God the Maker, the Preserver, the Renewer of the Universe, of His love and compassion to man protect and guide this work, both in its ascent to His glory and in its descent to the good of man, through His only Son, God with us.[16]

The eagle is especially the emblem of *Shaddai*, the Almighty, the grace of God that protects and preserves us, with the help of *Elyon*. The grace of God is symbolised by Jupiter, 'Father of Light', and Jupiter's emblem is the eagle. The idea that the grace of God throws a shadow is derived from the Orphic and Ancient Egyptian concept that God is truth and light is His shadow. Whereas the Greeks and Romans used the symbolism of the eagle, the Egyptians used the falcon, depicting the god of light, Ra (or Horus), as a solar disk with outstretched falcon wings. Ra, the spiritual Sun, equates with *Shaddai*, whilst Horus, the falcon god who dispenses the light of Ra on earth, equates with *Elyon*.

Grace or Mercy (*i.e. Shaddai*) is referred to in Cabala as the right-hand of God and is depicted on the right-hand side of the Tree of Life, standing immediately beneath Wisdom, the Word of God (*i.e. Elohim*), which heads the right-hand 'pillar' of creative force. Its counterbalance is made by Righteousness or Holiness (*i.e. Elyon*), which includes true perception and judgement and which is called the left-hand of God. This is shown on the left-hand side of the Tree of Life, placed immediately beneath Intelligence, the Name of God (*i.e. Jehovah*), which heads the left-hand 'pillar' of form. Whereas Jupiter signifies the grace or mercy of God, Mars is used to represent the divine righteousness or holiness. For this reason the Rosicrucian initiate is symbolised as a knight who wears the breastplate of righteousness and the helmet of illumination, and who has emblazoned on his chest the emblem of a rose blooming from the centre of a red (or golden) cross. The cross signifies the light of truth: the rose signifies the knight. Such a knight both distributes and protects goodness and truth. The equivalent symbol of the holy, illumined person is that of the astronomer/astrologer-magus who accurately and clearly sees the light of truth, such as depicted in the headpiece of the 1723 edition of *Shakespeare's Sonnets* (see above).

Significantly, Bacon refers to Jupiter as being the planet of civil society and action.[17] Equally significantly, Bacon equates

Building Paradise

THE CONSTITUTIONS OF THE FREE-MASONS.

CONTAINING THE

History, Charges, Regulations, &c. of that moſt Ancient and Right Worſhipful *FRATERNITY.*

For the Uſe of the LODGES.

L O N D O N:

Printed by WILLIAM HUNTER, for JOHN SENEX at the *Globe,* and JOHN HOOKE at the *Flower-de-luce* over-againſt *St. Dunſtan's Church,* in *Fleet-ſtreet.*

In the Year of Maſonry ——— 5723
Anno Domini ——— ——— 1723

THE JOHANNINE EAGLE
Title-page: Anderson's *The Book of Constitutions of the Free-masons* (1723).

Solomon's House

grace or mercy with charity—that is to say, with love in action. In other words, Bacon's idea of a true civil society is charity, in which everyone is merciful or compassionate, and illumined as a result.

Besides being the symbol of Jupiter and *Shaddai*, the Almighty, the eagle is also the emblem of St. John the Divine, the apostle of love and the 'beloved' of Christ. In the Christian trinity of the chief apostles, St. Peter represents faith, St. James stands for hope, and St. John personifies charity. St. John is also associated with the biblical Apocalypse or Book of Revelation and known as the great seer (*i.e.* magus). Not for nothing, therefore, is St. John the Divine the patron saint of Rosicrucianism and the higher degrees of Freemasonry. Notably Francis Bacon, the 'eagle', is associated with this attribution.

The Johannine, Rosicrucian eagle can be seen adorning the title-page of the 1723 *Constitutions of the Free-masons*, spreading its wings over the lion and unicorn of England and Scotland, exoterically understood, and of heart and mind, wisdom and intelligence (strength), esoterically understood.[18]

INITIATION AND THE PILLARS

Bacon's method is initiative. The initiative method employs an ages-old method of initiation, marked by degrees of attainment (or initiation) in which the secrets of the higher degrees are veiled from the lower ones, the whole making an unfolding system of teaching in the nature of a treasure hunt or game of hide and seek. In Freemasonry this takes form as a training in morality or human ethics, using allegory, symbolism and ritual drama. For instance, from a foundation of love and friendship (the 1st degree), the Freemason is exhorted to advance his learning by means of studying the seven liberal arts and sciences (the 2nd degree), culminating with charity or a life lived self-sacrificially in loving, wise service (the 3rd degree). The 4th or Arch degree lifts all this to an even higher level of consciousness and operation, which might well be called the gateway to the Rosicrucian level.

The first three degrees of initiation are known as the Craft degrees, whilst the 4th degree is called the Royal Arch of Solomon. The 1st degree is called 'Entering' and the initiate of this degree is styled an entered apprentice. The 2nd degree is called 'Passing' and the initiate is referred to as a fellow craftsman. The 3rd degree is the master mason's degree and is called 'Raising'. To become a Royal Arch mason, the master mason is 'exalted' and the initiation ceremony is called 'Exalting'.

The Craft sequence forms a complete set in itself and is referred to as moving from darkness to light, from a state of ignorance to a state of knowledge and illumination, by degrees. The three Craft degrees are related to the Christian sequence of faith, hope and charity. Faith enables the Freemason to ascend the first step of the ladder of initiation, hope enables the second, whilst charity, the third and last, 'comprehends the whole'.

Each Craft degree is associated with a pillar, whose symbolic name is used as the password of that degree. The pillars are named after those of Solomon's Temple, and represent those same pillars philosophically. Two of them are known as the Great Pillars, which were freestanding and stood each side of the entrance to the porch of Solomon's Temple. (The Great Pillars are also known as the Pillars of Hercules, Hermes or Enoch.) The third pillar is associated with the altar of incense that stood in the centre of the temple, on which was made the symbolic offering or sacrifice of the soul to God (*i.e.* as represented by the burning of incense on the altar).[19]

Since Solomon's Temple is an architectural expression of Cabala, and in particular of the Cabalistic Tree of Life, the pillars are also symbolic representations of the three 'pillars' of the Tree of Life. Freemasonry, therefore, also uses the Cabalistic names for these pillars—*viz.* Wisdom, Strength and Beauty. Wisdom is the right-hand pillar of the Tree of Life and of Solomon's Temple, Strength is the left-hand pillar and Beauty is the central or middle pillar.[20] Wisdom is the light of love, also known as the Word, which designs, creates and illuminates the universe. Strength is the Holy Intelligence or Understanding that provides the space and material that enables the Wisdom to take form, thereby supporting the universe and allowing illumination to take place. Beauty is the perfect harmony and balance of the other two. In one sense Beauty is the result of Wisdom and Intelligence (Strength), the poles of the universe, uniting and combining with each other in love, and for that reason Wisdom and Intelligence

Solomon's House

are known Cabalistically as the Father and Mother, with Beauty as the Son. Sometimes the middle pillar is referred to as Benignity, signifying moral beauty, which helps explain its meaning better. It is the ideal character of the master mason.

The Freemasonic names of the side pillars or Great Pillars are derived from the biblical Hebrew names as given in I Kings xii, 21, and II Chronicles iii, 17. The right-hand pillar is called *Jachin* and the left-hand pillar is called *Boaz*. *Maha-On* ('the Great One') or *Mahabone* is the name of the middle pillar. *Boaz* means 'In it is Strength'.[21] *Jachin* means 'I (*Jah*) establish'.[22] In combination they mean 'In strength I shall establish this mine house to stand firm forever'—a biblical statement derived from I Kings ix, 5. These 'secret' names are used as passwords of the Craft degrees.

The Cabala teaches that in order to advance in the study of the written and oral laws, and to attain to knowledge of God, man must unite the Blessed Name and Mystery of *Jachin* and *Boaz*. There are many references to this mystery in the Bible, each of which helps to explain it further. For instance, the prophet Samuel writes, 'I will establish the throne of his kingdom for ever' (II Samuel vii, 8-17), where 'his' refers to Solomon, a prototype of the Messiah. Jesus put it another way when he said, 'Upon this rock I will build my church' (Matthew xvi, 18).

> And if thou wilt walk before me, as David thy father walked, in integrity of heart, and in uprightness, to do according to all I have commanded thee, and wilt keep my statutes and judgements, then I will establish the throne of thy kingdom upon Israel for ever.
>
> I Kings ix, 4-5.

The throne or house or church of Christ, the Messiah, is Beauty. Integrity of heart is associated with wisdom, and uprightness with intelligence. Likewise the divine statutes or laws are associated with Wisdom, and the divine judgements with Intelligence.

It is Wisdom which, as the Creator, establishes or builds the universe. It is Strength that is the rock upon which, or in which, the universe is built. That which is built is Beauty, represented by Solomon's Temple, built of philosophical stone. Wisdom is creative love, which is associated with compassion and affection. It is also the divine will or desire. Strength or Intelligence is the pure mind that receives that light of love, intuits it, perceives it, reflects it, and comes to understand and know it. This Intelligence is also referred to as Understanding or Reason.

> Two mights are in a man's soul, given of the Father, from whom all good cometh. The one is in Reason, the other is Affection whom through Reason we know, and through Affection we feel and love. Man's soul though light of knowing in the Reason, and sweetness of love in the Affection, is espoused unto God.
>
> Richard St. Victor, *The Cell of Self-Knowledge*.

> The understanding of man and his will are twins by birth as it were; for the purity of illumination and the liberty of will began together.
>
> Francis Bacon, *Advancement of Learning*, Bk V (1640).

Wisdom is referred to as the pure being of God, whilst Intelligence is associated with the knowledge of that being. Traditionally these are given the symbols of sun and moon, referred to in Freemasonry, Cabala and the Bible as the Great Lights; hence Francis Bacon writes:-

> The truth of being and the truth of knowing are one, differing no more than the direct beam and the beam reflected.
>
> Francis Bacon, *Advancement of Learning*.

> But we are not dedicating or building any Capitol or Pyramid to human Pride, but found a holy temple in the human Intellect, on the model of the Universe… For whatever is worthy of Existence is worthy of Knowledge, which is the Image (or Echo) of Existence.
>
> Francis Bacon, *Novum Organum*, Bk I, Aph.120.

Wisdom is known as the light which illuminates the work of the Freemason, Strength as the light which sustains the work, and Beauty as the light which makes the work manifest. Wisdom plans the work, strength (intelligence) is needed to execute the work, and beauty is that which adorns the work. This is the Trinity that lies in all things and which, according to the First Tracing Board lecture of Freemasonry, 'guides us in all our undertakings, supports us under all our difficulties, and adorns the inward man'.

Whereas the sign of Wisdom and the right-hand pillar is the sun, and the sign of Intelligence (Strength) and the left-hand pillar is the moon, the sign of Beauty and the middle pillar is the blazing six-pointed star (or a constellation of seven stars). The six-pointed star, known as the Blazing Star or Christ Star or Star of David, is derived geometrically from the fusion of two triangles, the upward pointing one representing 'fire' and the right-hand pillar, and the downward pointing one signifying 'water' and the left-hand pillar. Their fusion creates, first, Solomon's Seal and then the Blazing Star.

Freemasonry associates the three pillars and what they signify with the classical orders of Greek architecture—*viz.* Doric, Ionic and Corinthian. (The Roman Composite Order is used for the 4th degree of the Royal Arch.) The most usual Freemasonic allocation of this architectural symbolism is that the Ionic represents Wisdom (*Jachin*), the Doric signifies Strength (*Boaz*) and the Corinthian refers to Beauty (*Mahabone*).

Even though the 1st degree comes under the light of Wisdom (*i.e.* creative love or friendship), and the 2nd degree comes under the light of Strength (*i.e.* understanding), yet Freemasonry 'builds' these pillars in sequence in the same manner that they were built classically—*i.e.* the ground storey of Doric first, the middle storey of Ionic second, and the top storey of Corinthian third. This means that *Boaz* is the password of the 1st degree, *Jachin* the password of the 2nd degree, and *Mahabone* the password of the 3rd degree. From this architectural symbolism, Understanding supports Wisdom, which is in the centre or heart of the edifice, which itself is crowned by Beauty. But degree-wise we have to have wisdom (*i.e.* faith), which is a kind heart full of love, before we can develop understanding of that wisdom (*i.e.* hope). Then we crown it with beauty of character, which comes by means of charity. To use an Eastern expression, there is a kind of *yin-yang* in this, so that balance is maintained in all things.

Building Paradise

THE PILLARS OF INITIATION
Frontispiece: Anderson's *The Book of Constitutions of the Free-masons* (1723).

Entry to the temple is via the archway in the background. Each subsequent pair of columns shows, via their classical order, the progressive degrees of initiation: (1) Doric, (2) Ionic, (3) Corinthian; culminating with the Composite order of the Royal Arch in the foreground. Apollo is in his sun-chariot overhead.

Solomon's House

THE CABALISTIC TITLE-PAGES OF BACON'S WORKS

Most of the early editions of Bacon's works were printed with beautifully illustrated title-pages, each of them designed Cabalistically and revealing a great wisdom and knowledge, including a cryptic portrayal of the Freemasonic degrees of initiation.

Ideally the illustrations need to be read as well as the text, or else the text cannot be fully understood. The illustrations also give us far more, in many ways, than the text does, although both are needed. As pictures they are associated with the eye and therefore with the imagination which is the eye of the mind. Bacon tells us that he equates imagination with Janus, the revealer and door-keeper of heaven, who interprets the wisdom to the mind so that it can be understood. In other words, Janus (the imagination) is the agent by means of which the twin Great Pillars of the human being (*i.e.* Wisdom and Understanding) can communicate with each other.[23] Furthermore, according to Bacon, imagination is also associated with the poetic faculty, which has the ability to raise our minds to levels beyond the ordinary mortal understanding so as to grasp great truths.[24]

It is the first three books of Bacon's Great Instauration, representing Parts 1-3 of the Instauration, that portray the first three degrees of Freemasonry in their title-pages. Significantly, the Great Pillars are a major feature of each of these title-page illustrations. The three books are: Part 1 – *De Dignitate et Augmentis Scientiarum* (*i.e.* 'Of the Advancement and Proficience of Learning'), Part 2 – *Novum Organum* (*i.e.* 'New Method'), and Part 3 – *Sylva Sylvarum or a Natural History.*

Yet, despite the fact that the *Advancement of Learning* is the first part of the Great Instauration, and that Bacon had already written and published the first version of the book in 1605, the first editions of these three books were published in the same sequence as the passwords in the Craft degrees of initiation—*i.e.* Part 2, *Novum*

ENTERING THE TEMPLE
Title-page: Francis Bacon's *Novum Organum*
(1620).

PASSING BEYOND THE PILLARS
Title-page: Francis Bacon's *Of the Advancement and Proficience of Learning* (1640).

RAISED INTO LIGHT
Title-page: Francis Bacon's *Sylva Sylvarum or A Natural History* (1626).

Solomon's House

Organum (1620), Part 1, *De Augmentis Scientiarum* (1623) and Part 3, *Sylva Sylvarum* (1626). It is also worth noting that the three books were published in three-year time intervals.

The picture is not, however, totally straightforward, as Bacon was always concerned about not giving too much away too soon. The 1620 *Novum Organum* and 1626 *Sylva Sylvarum* were printed with the Cabalistic Great Pillars title-pages. However, the 1623 *De Dignitate et Augmentis Scientiarum* had a fairly simple title-page, illustrated only with a woodcut of a flaming heart set within a wreath of bays. It was not until seventeen years later (fourteen years after Bacon's death) that the missing Great Pillars illustration appeared. This was printed as the title-page of the 1640 *Advancement and Proficience of Learning*. As this was the first English translation of Bacon's Latin version, its Cabalistic title-page engraving can be properly understood to substitute for, or explain in better detail, the earlier 1623 *De Augmentis* illustration, completing the Freemasonic Great Pillars sequence.

First of all, the sequence of title-page illustrations depicts the three Craft degrees in terms of their Freemasonic titles: that is to say, Entering (1st degree), Passing (2nd degree) and Raising (3rd degree). The 1620 *Novum Organum* portrays the ship of the soul entering between the Great Pillars; the 1640 *Advancement of Learning* depicts the ship passing behind the Great Pillars; and the 1626 *Sylva Sylvarum* has a globe, signifying the mind or soul, being raised up above the sea and illuminated with the supernal light from on high.

Secondly, the lighting effects in the pictures likewise indicate the same sequence of initiation, progressing from the semi-dark gloom of early dawn in the *Novum Organum* title-page, to partial light provided by the sun, moon and stars in the *Advancement of Learning* title-page, to the fullness of illumination in the *Sylva Sylvarum* title-page.

Thirdly, the Great Pillars indicate the sequence of Craft degrees, and, moreover, in a subtle way that makes us take note of the 2nd degree illustration (*i.e.* the *Advancement of Learning* title-page) and work to understand it—which is the meaning of the 2nd degree.

The 1623 *Novum Organum* and 1626 *Sylva Sylvarum* display two of the three classical orders of architecture in the design of

Building Paradise

their pillars. The *Novum Organum* has the Doric order—the *Boaz* of the 1st degree. The *Sylva Sylvarum* has the Corinthian order—the *Mahabone* of the 3rd degree. One is left to infer, therefore, that the 1623 *De Augmentis Scientiarum* should have had the Ionic order associated with it—the *Jachin* of the 2nd degree—so as to produce the Freemasonic sequence of symbolism. In fact the reserved illustration for this book, printed as the title-page to the 1640 *Advancement of Learning*, has some extraordinary Great Pillars that are specifically Baconian and immensely revealing in what they teach. They hold real wisdom, which is what *Jachin* signifies, and teach about the Great Instauration. They also emphasise the fact that in the 2nd degree the fellow craftsman is informed that the pillars are the archives of Masonry and should be studied. Near the top of the picture, representing the joining together of the two Great Pillars, as mentioned in the 2nd degree explanation of the passwords, are two hands clasped in a Masonic handshake.

To summarise, Part 1 of the Great Instauration, *The Advancement and Proficience of Learning*, which represents the Baconian Wisdom, is marked by the Ionic order, itself both masked and confirmed by the Baconian order. Part 2, *The New Method*, representing the Baconian Intelligence, is marked by the Doric order. Part 3, *A Natural History*, representing the Beauty of Nature, is marked by the Corinthian order. In publishing the first editions of these books as examples of the first three parts of the Great Instauration, they were presented in the sequence of Freemasonic passwords, with each picture depicting the appropriate degree. Thus the *New Method* was published first (in Latin), its Doric order representing *Boaz*, the password of the 1st degree, and its picture portraying the early dawn gloom and 'entering' of the 1st degree. The *Advancement of Learning* was published second (in Latin), but with its appropriate title-page appearing in 1640, its special Baconian order standing in for *Jachin*, the password of the 2nd degree, and its picture portraying the celestial lights and 'passing' of the 2nd degree. The *Natural History* was published third, its Corinthian order representing *Mahabone*, the password of the 3rd degree, and its picture portraying the illumination and 'raising' of the 3rd degree.

In this way the three Baconian title-pages uniquely illustrate the three Craft degrees of modern Freemasonry.

Solomon's House

Appropriately, the motto on the second, inner title-page of the 1640 *Advancement of Learning* declares: 'God has disposed all things in proportion, number and order'. It would seem that the author of the work has done his best to imitate his Creator, in order to fulfil the divine decree that makes man the image of God.

APPENDIX A
TITLES AND OFFICES

Honorary Titles
Sir Francis Bacon, Baron Verulam, Viscount St. Alban

Knighted (23 July 1603)
Created Baron Verulam (12 July 1618)
Created Viscount St. Alban (3rd February 1621)

Member of Parliament
Parliament of 1581	MP for Bassiney, Cornwall
Parliament of 1584	MP for Melcome Regis, Dorset
Parliament of 1586	MP for Taunton
Parliament of 1589	MP for Liverpool
Parliament of 1593	MP for Middlesex
Parliament of 1597	MP for Southampton & Ipswich
Parliament of 1604	MP for St Albans & Ipswich
Parliament of 1614	MP for St Albans, Ipswich & Cambridge University

Member of Gray's Inn
27 July 1576	Admitted *de societate magistrorum*
27 June 1582	Utter Barrister
10 Feb.1586	Bencher
23 Nov.1587	Reader
1589	Dean of the Chapel
1594	Deputy Treasurer
14 Nov.1599	Double Reader
17 Oct.1608–26 Oct.1617	Treasurer

Official Positions under Queen Elizabeth I
*c.*1591–24 March 1603	Queen's Counsel Extraordinary
1594–24 March 1603	Member of the Queen's Counsel Learned in the Law

Appendix A

Official Positions under King James I

July 1603–25 Aug.1604	King's Counsel Extraordinary
25 Aug. 1604–25 June 1607	King's Counsel Learned
25 June 1607–26 Oct.1613	Solicitor-General
1608	Clerk to the Star Chamber
1611	Judge of the Marshal's Court
1611	President of the Court of the Verge
1613	Chief Advisor to the Crown
26 Oct.1613–3 Mar.1617	Attorney General
9 June 1616–3 May 1621	Privy Councillor
3 March 1617–3 May 1621	Lord Keeper of the Great Seal
4 Jan.1618–3 May 1621	Lord High Chancellor

Building Paradise

APPENDIX B

DATES OF FRANCIS BACON'S WORKS

The following chart gives the dates of composition and publication of Francis Bacon's works—philosophical, poetic, legal and literary. The dates are given as accurately as possible, although some of these (such as for the writing of the Shakespeare plays) can only be approximate. The dates of certain key events in Bacon's life are included so as to provide an overview of his life and work, and of the influences of the one on the other.

Properly speaking, the Shakespeare works of poesie (drama and poetry) are part of Bacon's philosophical work, with the Folio of Shakespeare plays forming a record of his example of Part 4 of the Great Instauration. The fact that all the plays were written and performed before Bacon wrote his final, definitive philosophical treatises on the Great Instauration is because he derived and tested out the rules of his philosophy by means of the plays themselves. The year in which the Shakespeare plays began to be written and performed was the same year in which Bacon began work on his New Method.

It is interesting to note that: (a) the Shakespeare plays were begun after Francis Bacon had finished his legal studies and become firmly established as a barrister, Bencher and Reader of Grays Inn, with his own chambers and assistants; (b) the Shakespeare name and mask was first used publicly shortly after Anthony Bacon had returned to England and joined his brother; (c) the light-hearted comedies were written during the time that Anthony Bacon was with Francis; (d) the so-called 'dark' tragedies were written in the years immediately following Essex's insurrection and execution and Anthony Bacon's subsequent tragic death, and continued until Francis' marriage to Alice Barnham; (e) the great plays—the so-called 'romances'—began to be written soon after Francis married; and (f) no more Shakespeare plays were written once Francis had been appointed to the demanding office of Attorney General.

It is also clear to see that Bacon had very little time to write when he held high office, but that as soon as he was relieved of his duties as Lord Chancellor he set to with fervour to complete as

Appendix B

much of his philosophical work as possible, knowing that time left to him was short.

Key to the Chart:

Ph	=	Philosophical & Literary
P#	=	Great Instauration, (# referring to which Part of the G. I. the writings belong)
L	=	Legal
O	=	Other
*	=	Works of Poesie:-

Shakespeare: *P = Poetry, *H = History, *C = Comedy, *T = Tragedy
Bacon: *O

† = publications during Bacon's lifetime

Building Paradise

FRANCIS BACON'S LIFE AND WORKS - 1561-1626		
22 Jan. 1561		Birth
April 1573-1575		Student at Trinity College, Cambridge
June 1576		Admitted *de societate magistrorum* of Grays Inn
Sept. 1576-1579		Resident in France, with the French Court
March 1579		Entered Grays Inn to study law
1581		MP for Bassiney, Cornwall
1581-2		Travels in France, Italy, Spain
1582	O	*Notes on the State of Christendom*
June 1582		Utter Barrister of Grays Inn
March 1584		Visit to Scotland
1584		MP for Melcome Regis, Dorset
1585-6	L	*Letter of Advice to the Queen* (issued in Burghley's name)
Feb. 1586		Bencher of Grays Inn
1586		MP for Taunton
1586-9	L	*An Advertisement Touching the Controversies of the Church of England*
Nov. 1587		Reader of Grays Inn
1587/8	*O	Dumb show in the Gray's Inn Christmas Revels
1589		Dean of the Chapel of Grays Inn
1589		MP for Liverpool
1589-90	Ph	New Method begun.
1589-90	*T	*Titus Andronicus*
1589-90	*C	*The Taming of the Shrew*

Appendix B

1590	*H	King John
1590	*H	1 Henry VI (Henry VI Part 1)
1590	*H	2 Henry VI (The First Part of the Contention)
1590-1	*H	3 Henry VI (Richard Duke of York)
1591	*H	Richard III
c.1591-2		FB commanded by Queen to act as advisor to Essex
Feb. 1592		Anthony Bacon returns to England - joins FB
1592	*O	A Conference of Pleasure (Speeches composed for the Earl of Essex for the Queen's Accession Day Tilt, 17 Nov.): In Praise of Knowledge, In Praise of Fortitude, In Praise of Love, In Praise of Truth.
1592	L	Certain Observations made upon a Libel
1592-3	*C	The Two Gentlemen of Verona
1593		Theatres closed because of the plague
1593	*P	†Venus and Adonis
1593	Ph	Temporis Partus Maximus ('The Greatest Birth of Time')
1593		MP for Middlesex - FB fights for Parliament's rights
1593-4		FB in disgrace re. his stand as MP against the Queen
Jan. 1594		FB pleads his first case in the King's Bench
1594-1603		Queen's Counsel Extraordinary
1594		Deputy Treasurer of Grays Inn
July 1584		Visit to Scotland
1594	L	A True Report of the Detestable Treason intended by Dr Roderigo Lopez
1594	*P	†The Rape of Lucrece
1594	*O	The Device of the Indian Prince (Speeches composed for the Earl of Essex for the Queen's Accession Day Tilt, 17 Nov.): Squire, Hermit, Soldier, Statesman.

Building Paradise

1594	*C	*The Comedy of Errors* (written for the Grays Inn Revels)
1594	*C	*Love's Labour's Lost* (prob. written for Gray's Inn or the Court)
1594	*C	*Love's Labour's Won* (a lost play)
1594-5	*C	*A Midsummer Night's Dream* (prob. composed for the marriage of Elizabeth Vere and William, Earl of Derby on 26 Jan. 1595 at Greenwich)
1594/5	*O	*The Prince of Purpoole and the Honourable Order of the Knights of the Helmet* + *Comedy of Errors* (Gray's Inn Christmas/New Year Revels)
1595	*T	*Romeo and Juliet*
Aug. 1595		Anthony Bacon's services 'knit' to Essex (at Essex House)
1595	*H	*Richard II*
1595	*O	*The Sussex Speech* (composed for the Earl of Sussex, probably for the Queen's Accession Day Tilt, 17 Nov.)
1595	*O	*The Philautia Device* (Speeches composed for the Earl of Essex, probably for the Queen's Accession Day Tilt, 17 Nov.)
1596	L	*Maxims of the Law*
1596	*H	*1 Henry IV*
1596	*H	*2 Henry IV*
1597	*C	*The Merry Wives of Windsor* (composed for the election of Lord Hunsdon, the new Lord Chamberlain, as Garter Knight on 23 April)
1597	Ph	†*Essays* (1st ed.) + †*The Colours of Good and Evil* + †*Meditationes Sacrae*
1597		MP for Southampton & Ipswich
1597-8		Courtship with Elizabeth Hatton
1597-8	*C	*The Merchant of Venice*
Sept. 1598		Arrested for debt
1598	*C	*Much Ado About Nothing*

172

Appendix B

1598	*C	*As You Like It* (poss. written for the marriage of the Earl of Southampton to Elizabeth Vernon in 1598)
1599	*H	*Henry V* (deliberately likens Essex to Henry V)
Mar. 1599		Essex leads military expedition to Ireland
1599		Interview with the Queen re Hayward's book & *Richard II*
1599	*T	*Julius Caesar* (prob. written for the opening of the Globe Theatre at midsummer)
1599	*P	†*Shake-speare's Sonnets*
Nov. 1599		Double Reader of Grays Inn
June 1600		Essex arraigned before the Council
1600-1	*C	*Twelfth Night, or What You Will* (prob. written for the Grays Inn Christmas/New Year revels 1600/1, after which it was performed in the Middle Temple at the beginning of Feb. 1601.)
Feb. 1601		Essex's Insurrection, Trial and Execution
1601	L	†*Declaration of the Practices and Treasons attempted and Committed by the late Earl of Essex*
May 1601		Death of Anthony Bacon
1601	*T	*Hamlet*
1601	*P	†*The Phoenix and Turtle* (publ. in *Love's Martyr*)
1602-3	*T	*Troilus and Cressida* (prob. written for the Grays Inn Christmas/New Year revels 1602/3)
1593/1600	*H	*Sir Thomas More*
Mar. 1603		Queen Elizabeth I dies: King James I succeeds.
July 1603		Knight
1603	Ph	*Valerius Terminus of the Interpretation of Nature*
1603	L	*A Brief Discourse touching the Happy Union of the Kingdoms of England and Scotland*
July 1603-1604		King's Counsel Extraordinary

Building Paradise

1603-4	*C	*All's Well That Ends Well*
1604	*C	*Measure for Measure*
1604	*T	*Othello*
1604	*T	*Timon of Athens*
1604	Ph	*Cogitations de Natura Rerum* ('Thoughts on the Nature of Things')
1604	O	†*Apologie concerning the late Earl of Essex*
1604	L	*Certain Considerations touching the better pacification and Edification of the Church of England*
Aug. 1604-1607		King's Counsel Learned
1604		MP for St Albans & Ipswich
1604-5	*T	*King Lear*
1605	Ph	†*The Advancement and Proficience of Learning* (2 Books)
1605	Ph	*Temporis Masculus Partus* ('The Masculine Birth of Time')
1605-6	*T	*Macbeth* (prob. composed for James I and King Christian of Denmark: perf. at Hampton Court, 7 Aug. 1606)
1606	Ph	*Filium Labyrinthi sive Formula Inquisitionis* (written in English)
1606	O	*In Felicem Memoriam Elizabethae* ('In Happy Memory of Queen Elizabeth')
May 1606		Marriage to Alice Barnham
1606-7	*T	*Anthony and Cleopatra*
early 1607		Visit to Scotland
1607	*C	*Pericles*
1607	Ph	*Cogitata et Visa de Interpetatione Naturae* ('Thoughts and Conclusions on the Interpretation of Nature')
June 1607-1613		Solicitor-General

Appendix B

1608	*T	*Coriolanus*
1608	Ph	*Redargutio Philosophiarum* ('The Refutation of Philosophies')
Oct. 1608-1617		Treasurer of Grays Inn
1608		Clerk to the Star Chamber
1608-9	L	*The Plantation of Ireland*
1609	P5	†*De Sapientia Veterum* ('Wisdom of the Ancients')
May 1609		First Charter of Government for the Virginia Colony
1609-10	*T	*Cymbeline*
July 1610		Report to the Virginia Company Council of the shipwreck
1610	*C	*The Tempest*
1611	*C	*The Winter's Tale*
1611		Judge of the Marshal's Court
1611		President of the Court of the Verge
1611	Ph	*Phaenomina universi* ('Phenomena of the universe')
1611	Ph	*De Fluxu et Refluxu Maris* ('Of the Ebb and Flow of the Sea')
1612	Ph	*De viis mortis* ('Of life and death')
1612	Ph	*Descriptio Globi Intellectualis* ('A Description of the Intellectual Globe')
1612	Ph	*Thema Coeli* ('Theory of the Heavens')
1612	Ph	†*Essays* (2nd edition -38 essays)
1612-13	*H	*Henry VIII (All Is True)* (last complete Shakespeare play: poss. written for the marriage of Princess Elizabeth to Prince Frederick, Elector Palatine, on 14 Feb. 1613)
1612-13	*H	*The History of Cardenio* (a lost play) (co-authored by Fletcher)

Building Paradise

1613	*C	*The Two Noble Kinsmen* (co-authored by and title-paged to Fletcher)
Oct. 1613-1617		Attorney General
1614	L	†*Charge...touching Duels*
1614		MP for St Albans, Ipswich & Cambridge
Jun. 1616-1621		Privy Councillor
Mar. 1617-1621		Lord Keeper of the Great Seal
Jan. 1618-1621		Lord High Chancellor
July 1618		Baron Verulam of Verulam
1620	P3	*Parasceve ad Historiam et Naturalem* ('Preparative towards a Natural and Experimental History'
1620	P2	†*NOVUM ORGANUM* ('New Method') - Books 1 & 2
Jan. 1621		Viscount St. Albans
March 1621		Impeachment (+ Banishment from London, June 1621 - March 1622)
1621	*O	*The Fable of the New Atlantis*
1622		†*HISTORIA NATURALIS* ('Natural History')
	P3	†*Introduction to six Natural Histories*
	P3	†*Historia Ventorum* ('History of Winds')
1622	P3	†*HISTORY OF THE REIGN OF KING HENRY VII*
1622	Ph	*Abcedarium Naturae or a Metaphysical Piece*
1623	L	*A Discourse of a War with Spain*
1623	L	*A Dialogue touching an Holy War*
1623	L	*A Digest of the Laws of England*
1623	P3	†*Historia Vitae et Mortis* ('History of Life and Death')

Appendix B

1623	P3	*Historia Densi et Rari* ('History of Density and Rarity')
1623	P3	*Historia Gravis et Levis* ('History of Gravity and Levity')
1623	P3	*History of the Sympathy and Antipathy of Things*
1623	P3	*History of Sulphur, Salt and Mercury*
1623	P3	*History of the Reign of King Henry VIII* (unfinished)
1623	P4	†*SHAKESPEARE'S COMEDIES, HISTORIES & TRAGEDIES* (First Folio)
1623	P1	†*DE DIGNITATE ET AUGMENTIS SCIENTIARUM* ('Of the Advancement and Proficience of Learning') - 9 Books
1624	P5	*Cogitationes de Natura Rerum* ('Thoughts on the Nature of Things')
1625	P5	†*ESSAYS, OR COUNSELS CIVIL AND MORAL* (3rd/final edition - 58 essays)
1625	P3	†*Apothegms New and Old*
1625	*O	†*Translation of Certain Psalms into English Verse*
1625	P3	Translation into Latin of *History of the Reign of King Henry VII*
1625	P3	Translation into Latin of *Counsels Civil and Moral, or Essays*
1625	L	Translation into Latin of *Dialogue touching an Holy War*
1625	*O	Translation into Latin of *The Fable of the New Atlantis*
1625	P5	Revision of *De Sapientia Veterum* ('Wisdom of the Ancients')
1625	P3	*Inquisitio de Magnete* ('Enquiries into Magnetism')
1625	P3	*Topica Inquisitionis de Luce et Lumine* ('Topical Inquisitions into Light and Luminosity')
1626	P3	†*SYLVA SYLVARUM, OR NATURAL HISTORY* (publ. after FB's death)
9 April 1626		Death (Easter Day)

Building Paradise

FRANCIS BACON'S WORKS PUBLISHED AFTER HIS DEATH		
1626/7	P3/O	*SYLVA SYLVARUM* and *NEW ATLANTIS* published together by Rawley
1629		**CERTAIN MISCELLANY WORKS** (publ. by Rawley):-
	L	*Considerations touching War with Spain*
	L	*An Advertisement touching an Holy War*
	L	*An Offer to our Late Sovereign King James of a Digest to be made of the Laws of England*
	P3	*The History of the Reign of King Henry VIII*
1629	L	*Use of the Law*
1629	L	*Elements of the Common Laws*
1638		**OPERUM MORALIUM ET CIVILIUM** (publ. by Rawley):-
	P3	*Historiam Regni Henrici Septimi, Regis Angliae*
	P5	*Sermones Fideles, sive Interiora Rerum*
	P5	*De Sapientia Veterum*
	O	*Dialogum de Bello Sacro*
	*O	*Novam Atlantidem*
	P1	*De Augmentis Scientiarum*
	P3	*Historia Ventorum*
	P3	*Historia Vitae et Mortis*
1641	L	*Cases of Treason*
1641	O	*Confession of Faith*
1641	L	*Speech concerning Naturalisation*
1641	L	*Office of Constables*
1641	L	*Three Speeches: 1) Post-Nati; 2) Naturalisation; 3) Union of England & Scotland*

Appendix B

1641	L	*Discourse concerning Church Affairs*
1642	L	*An Essay of a King*
1642	L	*The Learned Reading of Sir Francis Bacon (to Gray's Inn)*
1642	L	*Ordinances*
1648		**THE REMAINS OF THE RIGHT HONORABLE FRANCIS LORD VERULAM**:-
	O	*Letters*
	O	*Confession of Faith*
1651	L	*Relation of the Poisoning of Overbury.*
1653		**SCRIPTA IN NATURALI ET UNIVERSALI PHILOSOPHIA** (publ. by Isaac Gruter):-
		An important collection of Bacon's minor writings including:-
	P4	*Scala Intellectus sive Filum Labyrinthi* (Intro. to Part 4)
	P5	*Prodromi sive Anticipationes Philosophiae Secundae* (Intro. to Part 5)
1653	Ph	*Cogitationes de Natura Rerum*
1653	Ph	*De Fluxu et Refluxu Maris*
1656		**THE MIRROR OF STATE AND ELOQUENCE (= REMAINS)**
1657		**RESCUSCITATIO** Part 1 (publ. by Rawley):-
		The Life of the Honourable Author
	O	*Speeches in Parliament*
	O	*Certain Treatises written or referring to Queen Elizabeth's times*
	O	*Certain Letters*
	P3	*Fragment of an Essay Of Fame*
	O	*Confession of Faith*

1658		**OPUSCULA VARIA POSTHUMA, PHILOSOPHICA, CIVILIA ET THEOLOGIA** (publ. by Rawley):-
	P3	Historia Densi et Rari ('History of Density and Rarity'
	O	In Felicem Memoriam Elizabethae
	O	Imago Civilis Iulii Caesaris
	O	Imago Civilis Augusti Caesaris
	O	Confessio Fidei
1661	O	Letter of Advice to the Duke of Buckingham
1662	L	Charge given for the Verge
1663		**OPUSCULA VARIA POSTHUMA, PHILOSOPHICA, CIVILIA ET THEOLOGIA** (publ. by Rawley):-
	O	In Felicem Memoriam Elizabethae
	O	Imago Civilis Iulii Caesaris
	O	Imago Civilis Augusti Caesaris
	O	Confessio Fidei
	L	Dialogus de Bello Sacro
1665		**OPERA OMNIA:-**
	P1	De Dignitate et Augmentis Scientiarum
	P2	Novum Organum Scientiarum, cum Parasceve ad Historiam Naturalem & Experimentalem
	P3	Historia Ventorum
	P3	Historia Vitae et Mortis
	P5	Scripta de Naturali & Universali Philosophia
	P3	Sylva Sylvarum, sive Historia Naturalis
	*O	Nova Atlantis
	P3	Historiam Regni Henrici VII, Regis Angliae

Appendix B

	P5	*Sermones Fideles, sive Interiora Rerum*
	P5	*De Sapientia Veterum*
	O	*Dialogus de Bello Sacro*
	O	*Opus Illustre in felicem memoriam Elisabethae Reginae*
	O	*Imago Civilis Iulij Caesaris*
	O	*Imago Civilis Augusti Caesaris*
1670		**RESCUSCITATIO** Part 2 (publ. by Rawley):-
		The Life of the Honourable Author
	O	*Speeches in Parliament*
	O	*Certain Treatises written or referring to Queen Elizabeth's times*
	O	*Certain Letters*
	P5	*Fragment of an Essay Of Fame*
	O	*Confession of Faith*
1679		**BACONIANA** (publ. by Archbishop Tennison):-
	Ph	incl. *Abcedarium Naturae, or a Metaphysical piece*
1734		**LETTERS AND REMAINS**:-
	Ph	incl. *Valerius Terminus or the Interpretation of Nature.*
1861	Ph	*Promus*

Building Paradise

APPENDIX C
CIPHERS OF FRANCIS BACON

Francis Bacon and his Rosicrucian fraternity made use of several different kinds and types of cipher, some of them to sign various published works issued outwardly under different names or pseudonyms, and some of them to give messages or teachings.

Francis himself was a secretive person, both by choice and by necessity. He learnt the use of ciphers early in his youth when he was employed by Lord Burghley and Sir Francis Walsingham, on behalf of the Queen, on intelligence matters both at home and abroad. Francis' brother Anthony likewise was employed on intelligence matters and was sent as an intelligencer to France and elsewhere for over twelve years. When Anthony finally returned to England in 1592 Francis 'knit' his services to Essex, by request of the Queen. Anthony thereafter acted as a virtual 'Secretary of State' to the Earl, running his own network of spies and, with the help of Francis, feeding both the Earl and the Queen with intelligence.

Francis Bacon not only used cipher but also invented several ciphers of his own, one of which he describes in Book VI of the 1623 Latin edition of his *Advancement of Learning* (the *De Augmentis Scientiarum*, first published in English translation in 1640). This particular cipher he calls the Biliteral Cipher, which he says he invented in his youth whilst in Paris (1576-9). From the principles of this cipher Morse code was later developed and ultimately the binary system that computers use nowadays.

The simplest of the ciphers used by Francis Bacon and his Rosicrucian fraternity were numerical ones, wherein each letter of the alphabet has an equivalent numerical value. This is an ancient Cabalistic cipher method, used in both the Hebraic Old Testament and the Greek New Testament for instance, but which has many possible variations. One which is recorded in Bacon's time is the Latin Cabala, adopted in Italy in 1621 by a circle of literary ecclesiastics, who established it on the occasion of the left arm of the blessed Conrad—a famous hermit—being brought with ceremony from Netina to Piacenza. (The record of this is in a rare pamphlet entitled *Anathemata B. Conrado,* issued in Placentia in 1621.)

Appendix C

There are two versions of this Latin Cabala described, one 'Simple' and the other 'Ordinary', the 'Simple' having twenty-two letters for its alphabet and the 'Ordinary' having twenty-three (the letter 'K' being added).

Bacon's Cabalistic ciphers are very similar to the Latin Cabala, but based on the twenty-four letters of the Elizabethan alphabet rather than the twenty-two or twenty-three of the Latin Cabala. Three main variations are used—the Simple Cipher, the Reverse Cipher and the Kay (*i.e.* the 'K' or Key) Cipher. There are two variations of the Kay Cipher and it is the second one that is the most important and used, for instance, in the Shakespeare Folio of plays.

The basic Simple Cipher (*i.e.* A = 1, B = 2, ...Z = 24) is illustrated on page 141 in Gustavus Selenus' great cipher book, *Cryptomenitices et Cryptogaphiae*, published in Germany in 1624. This Simple Cipher was developed by Francis Bacon into what he called a four-fold structure, in which the twenty-four letter alphabet is repeated four times so that the corresponding numbers continue to 96 (*i.e.* 4 x 24) and each of the numbers/letters in the four sets relates both to a Greek letter and word, and also to an element or celestial body. Francis left a record of this cipher for posterity, to be published eventually by 'T.T.' (who is usually assumed to be Archbishop Thomas Tenison) in his *Baconiana* of 1679 under the title of *Abecedarium Naturae* ('The Alphabet of Nature').

Kay Ciphers are first mentioned by Francis Bacon in his 1605 version of the *Advancement of Learning*, but not described. In his 1623 Latin edition (the *De Augmentis Scientiarum*) he refers to them as the 'Ciphrae Clavis' (Key Ciphers). The Baconian, Mr. W. E. Clifton, discovered the working of this cipher with the help of two particular volumes from his collection of 17th century books—Thomas Powell's *The Repertorie of Records* (1631) and a special edition of Rawley's *Resuscitatio* (1671) of Bacon's works—which alerted him to the fact that the cipher uses the twenty-six characters of the old alphabet primers, in which the Ampersand ('&') followed by 'et' was added to the twenty-four letter alphabet, and that K (which starts the counting) equals 10. Since the numbers 25 and 26 (which correspond to the '&' and 'et') are treated as nulls, then A equals 27, B equals 28, etc..

The Reverse Cipher is simply the Simple Cipher in reverse (*i.e.* A = 24, B = 23, ...Z = 1), and its use seems to be as an occa-

Building Paradise

sional double-check to the veracity of cipher signatures in the other two main Cabalistic ciphers.

SIMPLE CIPHER											
A	B	C	D	E	F	G	H	I	K	L	M
1	2	3	4	5	6	7	8	9	10	11	12
N	O	P	Q	R	S	T	V	W	X	Y	Z
13	14	15	16	17	18	19	20	21	22	23	24

REVERSE CIPHER											
A	B	C	D	E	F	G	H	I	K	L	M
24	23	22	21	20	19	18	17	16	15	14	13
N	O	P	Q	R	S	T	V	W	X	Y	Z
12	11	10	9	8	7	6	5	4	3	2	1

KAY CIPHER (2)											
A	B	C	D	E	F	G	H	I	K	L	M
27	28	29	30	31	32	33	34	35	10	11	12
N	O	P	Q	R	S	T	V	W	X	Y	Z
13	14	15	16	17	18	19	20	21	22	23	24

The principal Cabalistic signatures used on monuments and in the various published works of Francis Bacon or 'Shakespeare', or the Rosicrucian fraternity in relationship to Bacon-Shakespeare, are as follows:-

Appendix C

BACONIAN CIPHER SIGNATURES			
Signature	Simple	Kay	Reverse
FRANCIS	67	171	108
BACON	33	111	92
FRANCIS BACON	100	282	200
FRA. ROSI. CROSSE	157	287	168

FRA. ROSI. CROSSE stands for 'Fratres Rosi Crosse' (Brothers of the Rosy Cross) or 'Frater Rosi Cross' (Brother of the Rosy Cross). Other Cabalistic signatures based on Francis Bacon's titles are also used.[1]

The cipher signature method is unusual in that it often uses a count of letters per word per column (or page), or else of the number of words per column (or page), or both, to give the cipher signature. As Bacon stated in his *Advancement of Learning* (1605), 'For Cyphars; they are commonly in Letters or Alphabets, but may be in Wordes'.

For instance, in Francis Bacon's *Advancement of Learning* (1640) there are 287 letters on the Frontispiece page, 287 letters on the Dedication page, and 287 letters on page 215, which is falsely numbered and should in reality be page 287, just to make sure we get the message. Each of these key pages is therefore signed FRA. ROSI. CROSSE in Kay Cipher.

Ben Jonson's Portrait Poem on the first page of the 1623 Shakespeare Folio has 287 letters, the count of FRA. ROSI. CROSSE in Kay Cipher. The title page of the Folio, containing Shakespeare's portrait, has 157 letters in its words, the count of FRA. ROSI. CROSSE in Simple Cipher. The first page of the Dedication in the Shakespeare Folio has 157 words in italic font, the count of FRA. ROSI. CROSSE in Simple Cipher. The Catalogue of plays has exactly 100 Roman letters on the full page, and 100 complete italic words in its second column, the count of FRANCIS BACON in Simple Cipher. The page also has 111 capitals in italic font, the count of FRANCIS BACON in Kay Cipher. The first page of the Comedies, (*i.e.* the first page of *The Tempest*) in the Shakespeare Folio has 287 words in regular font in its second column, whilst its first column has 100 italic font letters (actors' character names discounted) and 257 words in regular font. 100 = FRANCIS BACON (Simple Cipher), whilst 257 − 100 = 157 = FRA. ROSI. CROSSE (Simple Cipher). That is to say, 257 = 100 + 157 = FRANCIS BACON, FRA. ROSI. CROSSE.

The eight main lines of text on the inscription of the Shakespeare Monument at Stratford-upon-Avon have 287 letters (*i.e.* FRA. ROSI. CROSSE in Kay Cipher) in their 50 complete words. 50 has a highly significant meaning in the Cabalistic cipher system (see below), and at the same time is the number of the Argonauts, the symbolism of which Bacon uses to describe his seekers after truth—the Rosicrucian fraternity. (*N.B.* The ship Argo is prominently shown on several title pages of his works.) Complementing this, the garbled quotation on the scroll of the Shakespeare Memorial in Westminster Abbey is made up of 33 complete words (*i.e.* BACON in Simple Cipher) containing 157 letters (*i.e.* FRA. ROSI. CROSSE in Simple Cipher), whereas the original six lines from *The Tempest* (Act 4, scene 1) in the Shakespeare Folio from which the Memorial quotation is derived are composed of 40 words containing 167 letters. The Westminster Abbey memorial was erected in 1741, but the project was launched in 1726, the centenary of Bacon's death.

Francis Bacon's first name, Francis, means 'Free'. He used this both as a teaching and as a cipher signature, for FREE = 33 = BACON (Simple), or FREE = 67 = FRANCIS (Reverse), or FREE = 111 = BACON (Kay). 'Free' also has the connotation of Master and was used in the Orphic Mysteries to hail the resurrected initiate as 'Liber Bacchus!' ('Bacchus the Free!'), and in the Vedic teachings as the title of the Master (*i.e. Jivanmukta*, 'the Free'). The English word 'free' is from the Sanskrit root *pri*, meaning 'to love', and so fundamentally FREE = LOVE. (*e.g.* Freemason means 'Builder of Love' or 'Loving Builder'). In both Simple and Reverse Cipher, LOVE = 50, the number of the Argonauts. In the 1623 Shakespeare Folio Francis Bacon signs the very first play of the Folio, *The Tempest*, with this signature, for the text begins with '*Master*' and ends with '*Free*'. It is especially meaningful, as the play is all about attaining true mastery as a master of love, a master of compassion, with the help of Ariel, the spirit of love, which Prospero has set free.

The full signature, FRANCIS BACON, counts to 100, divided neatly into thirds by FRANCIS (33) and BACON (67), providing a fun-

Appendix C

damental (1:1), an octave (1:2) and a fifth (2:3) in music. 100 is the Cabalistic number of universality, used for instance as the overall measure of the Globe Theatre, which is 100 feet in diameter. 33 is the number of the personal master (*e.g.* Jesus was said to be 33 years old at his crucifixion and resurrection)—the first stage of universal mastership. 100 is the number of the universal master, the fully ascended soul of love, enthroned in heaven.

33 is also represented by the initials 'T.T.' (*i.e.* Thirty-Three). As such it is used to represent the Thirty-Third Degree of Initiation, and thus is used as a sign or signature of the master. Like the initials 'B.I.' (which sign the Shakespeare Folio's Portrait poem and represent the names of Solomon's Pillars, Boaz and Jachin, as well as being the initials of Ben Jonson), 'T.T.' also signifies the Twin Pillars that stand before the porch of Solomon's Temple, the Temple of Light. 'T.T.' forms the capital letters of *The Tempest*, the introductory play of the Shakespeare Folio. The Dedication in *Shake-speare's Sonnets* (1609) is signed 'T.T.' (which, like 'B.I' in the Folio, is also associated with an appropriate person—in this case, Thomas Thorpe). The signature of 'T.T.' is carved into the base of the Shakespeare Memorial in Westminster Abbey, at Shakespeare's feet. The collection of Bacon's previously unpublished manuscripts, published in 1679 under the title of *Baconiana*, in which the keys to Bacon's Cabalistic cipher are given, is signed 'T.T.', which initials are generally assumed to be those of Archbishop Thomas Tenison, the 'appropriate person' as editor or front man for those responsible for preserving and publishing Bacon's manuscripts.

'AA' is likewise an important signature of the Rosicrucian fraternity, used since the time of the Ancient Egyptians. It represents the polarity of all life—the Creator and Created, as well as the Alpha and Omega. Moreover, Apollo and Athena, the two Spear-Shakers, also stand for this Double A sign, or the Double A sign stands for them. The Double A was used as a headpiece in several books of the Rosicrucian fraternity, mostly during Bacon's time. It is used, for instance, to head certain pages in the Shakespeare Folio, as also in Bacon's philosophical works.

The 'AA' headpiece used in the Shakespeare Folio has within it two conies (rabbits) squatting back to back, giving the rebus signature of back-cony. 'Bacon' is one of the ways in which Bacon's name was used in Latin editions of his acknowledged works: for instance, the very first work of his published in Latin, *De Sapientia Veterum* (1609), has 'Francisci Baconi' on its title-page (meaning 'of' or 'by Francis Bacon'), as also his *Latin Opera* (1638) and *Opuscula Varia Posthuma* (1658). Its Cabalistic cipher is used frequently, FRA BACONI counting to 66 in Simple Cipher and 222 in Kay Cipher, which numbers are exactly double the values of BACON in Simple and Kay ciphers respectively.

The boar, a symbol of Apollo, the divine swineherd, is said to imprint the ground with the sign of 'AA'. The boar is Bacon's heraldic animal, referred to cryptically in Mistress Quickly's line in *The Merry Wives of Windsor* (IV, i.): 'Hang-hog is latten for Bacon, I warrant you'. This 'parable' is from a story told about Sir Nicholas Bacon, Francis Bacon's father, which Francis records in his *Apophthegm 10*, published in *Resuscitatio* (1671): '...Hog is not Bacon until it be well hanged.'

This is a sample of straightforward Baconian ciphers, Cabalistic and symbolic, which provide the signatures of Francis Bacon and the Rosicrucian fraternity, of which he was the President. Some other Baconian ciphers have also been discovered and are in the process of being researched, such as those that are based on the Cardano Grille, a cipher method invented by Geronimo Cardano (1501-1576) and adapted by Francis Bacon, plus Caesar ciphers, a logarithmic cipher, and others.

---

[1] See *Francis Bacon's Cipher Signatures* by Frank Woodward (1923) for a detailed study.

POETRY

Extract from Francis Bacon's *Advancement of Learning* (1640), Bk. II, ch xiii.

> As for Narrative Poesie, or if you please Heroical (so you understand it of the matter, not of the verse) it seems to be raised altogether from a noble foundation; which makes much for the dignity of man's nature. For seeing this sensible world is in dignity inferior to the soul of man, Poesie seems to endow human nature with that which History denies; and to give satisfaction to the mind, with, at least, the shadow of things, where the substance cannot be had. For if the matter be thoroughly considered, a strong argument may be drawn from Poesie, that a more stately greatness of things, a more perfect order, and a more beautiful variety delights the soul of man, than any way can be found in Nature since the Fall. Wherefore seeing the acts and events, which are the subject of true History, are not of that amplitude as to content the mind of man, Poesie is ready at hand to feign acts more heroical. Because true History reports the successes of business, not proportionable to the merit of virtues and vices; Poesie corrects it, and presents events and fortunes according to desert, and according to the law of Providence: because true History, through the frequent satiety and similitude of things, works a distaste and misprision in the mind of man; Poesie cheereth and refreshes the soul, chanting things rare, and various, and full of vicissitudes. So as Poesie serveth and conferreth to delectation, magnanimity, and morality; and therefore it may seem deservedly to have some participation of divineness; because it doth raise the mind, and exalt the spirit with high raptures, by proportioning the shews of things to the desires of the mind; and not submitting the mind to things, as Reason and History do. And by these allurements, and congruities, whereby it cherisheth the soul of man, joined also with consort of music, whereby it may more sweetly insinuate itself, it hath won such access that it hath been in estimation even in rude times, and barbarous nations, when other learning stood excluded.

Building Paradise

Dramatical, or Representative Poetry, which brings the world upon the stage, is of excellent use, if it were not abused. For the instructions and corruptions of the stage may be great, but the corruptions in this kind abound; the discipline is altogether neglected in our times. For although in modern commonwealths, stage-plays be but estimed a sport or pastime, unless it draw from the satyr and be mordant; yet the care of the Ancients was that it should instruct the minds of men unto virtue. Nay, wise men and great philosophers have accounted it as the archet or musical bow of the mind. And certainly it is most true, and as it were a secret of nature, that the minds of men are more patent to affections and impressions, congregate, than solitary.

But Poesie Allusive, or Parabolical, exceeds all the rest, and seemeth to be a sacred and venerable thing, especially seeing Religion itself hath allowed it a work of that nature, and by it traffics divine commodities with men. But even this also hath been contaminate by the levity and indulgence of men's wits about allegories. And it is of ambiguous use, and applied to contrary ends. For it serves for obscuration, and it serveth also for illustration: in this it seems there was sought a way how to teach; in that an art how to conceal. And this way of teaching which conduceth to illustration was much in use in the Ancient times: for when the inventions and conclusions of human reason (which are now common and vulgar) were in those ages strange and unusual, the understandings of men were not so capable of that subtilty, unless such discourses, by resemblances and examples, were brought down to sense. Wherefore in those first ages all were full of fables, and of parables, and of enigmas, and of similitudes of all sorts... So even at this day, and ever, there is, and hath been much life and vigour in parables; because arguments cannot be so sensible, nor examples so fit. *There is another use of Parabolical Poesie, opposite to the former, which tendeth to the folding up of those things; the dignity whereof deserves to be retired and distinguished, as with a drawn curtain: that is when the secrets and mysteries of religion, policy and philosophy are veiled, and invested with fables and parables...*

NOTES ON THE TEXT

CHAPTER 1

[1] Paracelsus was the byname of Philippus Aureolus Theophrastus Bombastus von Hohenheim (1493-1541 or 1544), a famous German-Swiss physician and alchemist who established the role of chemistry in medicine.

[2] Paracelsus, *Buch von den Mineralien*, (Book of Minerals), ch 8. See also *De Minerabilis, Opera Omnia,* Geneva, Vol. II, 1656, quoted in Arthur Edward Waite's *Real History of the Rosicrucians*, 1887, p 34:-

> 'God will permit a discovery of the highest importance to be made; it must be hidden till the advent of Elias the Artist…'

> '…there is nothing concealed which shall not be revealed, for which cause a marvellous being shall come after me, who as yet lives not, and who shall reveal many things.'

[3] Tycho Brahe (1546-1601) was not the first to notice the star but he was the first to observe it scientifically as an astronomer (on 11 November 1572) and to declare that it was a genuine new star lying beyond the moon in the realm of the fixed stars—an idea which was disquieting to the intellectual community of his day who believed in the Aristotelian harmony of the world ruled by a perfect and unchanging celestial realm. Tycho published his observations in *De nova stella* (1573). His more esoteric comments were written down in a small tract on 'the new and much admired star' that was eventually published in 1602, dedicated to Rudolf II, the Holy Roman Emperor and occultist.

[4] Genesis i, 14-19.

[5] The *Fama Fraternitatis* and *Confessio Fraternitatis*. The earliest known printed editions of the *Fama* and *Confessio* appeared in 1614 and 1615 respectively; but the manifestos had been in circulation some years prior to this, at least as early as 1610, if not earlier. Taken together, the manifestos supply the information that father C.R.C. was born in 1378 and had lived 106 years (and therefore died and was buried in 1484), and that his tomb was rediscovered and opened 120 years later (*i.e.* 1604).

[6] 33 is the Simple (Cabalistic) cipher for BACON. It is also the number of the degrees in a complete process of illumination, related to the Cabalistic Tree of Life, and of the bones in the spine of a human being up which the dragon energy or *kundalini* flows in order to produce illumination. Jesus Christ, for instance, was said to be aged thirty-three when he was crucified and rose again from the dead, reborn in glory.

[7] From *The Works of Francis Bacon* (London: 1860), edited by James Spedding, translation by Robert Ellis.

[8] In rabbinical tradition John the Baptist is equated with the great prophet Elijah and also with Enoch, the Idris of Sufi tradition. He is referred to as the Great Teacher, who, as Enoch, was the first human being to complete all the initiations and ascend bodily into the highest heaven, where he is said to have become the great archangel

Building Paradise

Metatron, chief of all the Archangels, the Great Angel of the Presence and Guardian of the seven-pillared Temple of Wisdom. There, out of love for humanity, he chose to remain with and teach those below rather than rise and reunite totally with *En Sof*, the Godhead. His role is to announce and prepare people for the coming of the Messiah, whilst not being the Messiah himself. He prepares souls for their resurrection—for the dawning of the great Light. For this purpose he incarnates from time to time, as well as guiding from 'above'.

John the Baptist, together with his counterpart, John the Beloved, is the patron saint of Freemasonry and Rosicrucianism.

CHAPTER 2

[1] The 'new star' was a supernova in the constellation of Cassiopeia, 'the Virgin Queen'. The star blazed in the sky from August 1572 until March 1574, appearing brighter than Venus. The general public across Europe believed it meant that the end of the world had come and the Second Coming of Christ would occur, whilst the sages recognised it as the sign of the birth or appearance of a great light in the world. Paracelsus had forecast it a century earlier, speaking of the star as 'the sign and harbinger of the approaching revolution: there is nothing concealed which shall not be revealed, for which cause a marvellous being shall come after me, who as yet lives not, and who shall reveal many things'. He named this marvellous being as Elias the Artist, who would renovate all the sciences and teach the transmutation of all the metals. Tycho Brahe wrote that the star marked the entrance of the world into the seventh revolution that would inaugurate the golden age, adding that 'Some great light is now at hand which shall enlighten and by degrees expel the former darkness'. He linked this with his forecast of a major conjunction of planets that would occur in 1602-4, when the actual prophecies of the star would be released. Robert Fludd, writing later about the planetary conjunctions, said that the supernova marked the beginning of the Rosicrucian work that continued in secrecy until the planetary conjunctions, the latter being a sign to the Brotherhood to emerge into the open, expand their membership and begin the restoration of the world.

See Peter Dawkins, *The Great Vision* (Francis Bacon Research Trust, 1985).

[2] Edward Tirrell, one of Sir Nicholas Bacon's wards, also went with them, plus a servant.

[3] Sir Amyas Paulet succeeded Dr Dale as ambassador in France in February 1577.

[4] Francis Bacon, *Sylva Sylvarum*, Century X, No 986.

[5] Sir Nicholas Bacon died on 20 February 1579.

[6] Sir Nicholas Bacon's funeral took place on 9 March 1579.

[7] Dr William Rawley, *The Life of the Right Honourable Francis Bacon*. (First published 1657 as an introduction to *Resuscitatio*.)

[8] Sir Nicholas Bacon had put aside a large sum of money before his death, meaning to buy an estate with which to endow his son Francis. However, he died before this

Notes on the Text

was done, with the result that Francis only received one fifth of the legacy intended by his father.

9 The poems of 'Immerito' were attributed to Edmund Spenser when they were published, but there are strong indications that Edmund Spenser was used as a mask for Bacon's poems, just as Will Shakspere was a mask for Bacon's plays. To begin with, however, the pseudonym of 'Immerito' was used.

10 Bodley (the founder of the Bodleian Library at Oxford), himself travelled a great deal. In 1583 he became 'Gentleman-Usher' to the Queen, and in 1588 was appointed by the Queen as Resident Minister at the Hague.

11 A letter exists from Sir Thomas Bodley to Francis Bacon from which it appears that Francis travelled through Italy, Spain, Germany and Denmark, and that his expenses were met by Bodley and his 'friends', who desired him to keep a record of all he observed and learnt, and to report from time to time. (See W T Smedley, *Mystery of Francis Bacon*, p.85.)

12 Nicholas Faunt had likewise spent 1581 in France, Germany, Switzerland and the north of Italy gathering political intelligence. Back at the English court in 1582, Faunt collected and arranged the observations he had made abroad. From 1582 onwards Anthony kept in close contact with Faunt, who had become a secretary of Sir Francis Walsingham, the Queen's Secretary of State and head of the intelligence service.

13 Now in the Harleian Collection in the British Museum: Harl. MSS. 7021. 1.

14 The *Notes on the Present State of Christendom* were transcribed (from a collection of Bacon's MSS in the care of the Earl of Oxford) and printed by Robert Stephens in the supplement to his second collection of Bacon's papers, published in 1734 and reprinted by Mallet in 1760.

15 Francis Bacon was elected as an MP in successive Parliaments until his appointment as Lord Keeper in 1617.

16 Mentioned by Bacon in the French edition/translation of *Sylva Sylvarum*, 1631.

17 As a Bencher, Francis Bacon was allowed a place with the Readers at their table.

18 Francis Bacon, letter to Lord Burghley (c.1591): printed in Rawley's *Resuscitatio*, Supplement, p 95.

19 Letter from Essex to the Queen (1594). *Henry IV*, Parts I and II, are estimated to have been written in 1596.

20 Sir Philip Sydney, *Astrophel and Stella*.

21 Bruno was a spy as well as a hermeticist and cabalist.

22 Michel de Montaigne, *Essayes on Morall, Politike, and Militarie Discourses* (1603), translated from French by John Florio.

23 Francis Bacon, *Promus of Formularies and Elegancies*, fol. 103 (written c.1594).

24 Francis Bacon, *Apology concerning the Earl of Essex* (1604).

Building Paradise

[25] The *Promus* consists of a collection of manuscripts, or folios, written in Bacon's own hand, which are now kept at the British Museum (Harleian Collection, No. 7017). These folios, numbered from 83 to 132, appear to have been written in the years 1594-6 and form part of what must have been a much larger collection. Folio 85 is dated 5th December 1594, and folio 114 is dated 27th January 1595.

[26] *Titus Andronicus* and the three parts of *Henry VI* were owned first by Lord Strange's Men and then in 1592 by Lord Pembroke's Men, before being passed on to the Lord Chamberlain's Men in 1594. *The Taming of the Shrew* is also identified as having been with Pembroke's Men. In addition, the other Shakespeare plays identified as having been written by 1592—*King John, Richard III* and *The Two Gentlemen of Verona*—were in all probability owned by these companies.

[27] Robert Greene, *Greene's Groatsworth of Wit* (1592), written in the last months of his life and published posthumously:-

> There is an upstart crow beautified with our feathers that, with his 'tiger's heart wrapped in a player's hide', supposes that he is as well able to bombast out a blank verse as the best of you: and, being an absolute *Johannes Factotum*, is in his own conceit the only Shake-scene in the country.

The quotation Greene uses is a parody of a line from Shakespeare's *Henry VI*, Part 3.

[28] Henry Wriothesley, the third Earl of Southampton (1573-1624), was a ward of Lord Burghley, Bacon's uncle and the Queen's Lord Treasurer. From 1585 to 1589 Southampton studied at St John's College, Cambridge, before becoming a member of Gray's Inn. In 1594 he came of age and inherited a fortune, enabling him to become a generous patron of poetry and drama, which he loved. He became a special friend of Robert Devereux, the Earl of Essex, and of the two Bacon brothers, his 'cousins' Anthony and Francis, and become a member of the Essex-Pembroke group who patronised the group of writers involved in Bacon's literary-dramatic project.

[29] Venus and Adonis are cabalistic symbols of the Grand Pillars that stand at the gateway of the Temple of Light.

[30] The land was sold for £1800.

[31] 60 acres in the forest of Zelwood, Somerset, at a nominal rent of £7.10s.0d. per annum.

[32] The reversion of the lease of the lands in Twickenham Park was due to fall in Michaelmas 1624, and Francis Bacon's lease from that date was to be for twenty-one years, at the same terms (*i.e.* 12 guineas a year) as the lease formerly held by Edward Bacon and then (in 1595) held by Milo Dodding. The grant of the reversion of the lease is dated 17 November 1595. The fact that Milo Dodding held the lease after Edward Bacon did not interfere with Francis Bacon's occupation of Twickenham Lodge, which continued as before.

[33] Francis Bacon, *Apology concerning the Earl of Essex:-*

> From the time I had any rime or reason…I loved my country more than was answerable to my fortune and I held at that time my Lord to be the fittest instrument to do good to the State and therefore I applied myself to

Notes on the Text

him in a manner which I think rarely amongst men… And when not long after I entered into this course, my brother Master Anthony Bacon came from beyond the seas…I did likewise knit his Service to be at my Lord's disposing…

[34] *The First Part of the Life and Raigne of King Henrie IIII*, by John Hayward (publ. Feb 1599).

[35] Francis Bacon, *Apologie in certaine imputations concerning the late Earle of Essex* (1604).

[36] Francis Bacon's advice had been to pour money and education into Ireland, and help of all kinds, to raise the Irish people from their situation of dire poverty to one of prosperity. This advice was not carried out. Instead the Catholic Irish were systematically subjugated and terrorised by the Protestant Scots and English rulers, rather than being befriended and respected.

[37] Hepworth Dixon, *Story of Lord Bacon's Life*, p 218. Daphne Du Maurier, in her book *The Winding Stair* (p 31) gives the amount as £300.

[38] Francis Bacon, *Letter to Lord Salisbury* (March 1606) (Spedding Vol 3, ch 8).

[39] Bacon was assisted by Sir Henry Hobart and Sir Edwin Sandys, who helped draft the document.

[40] *The True Repertory of the Wracke and Redemption of Sir Thomas Gates*, dated 15 July 1610, written as a private letter by William Strachey. This confidential report was not published until 1625, when it was included in *Purchas His Pilgrimes*,[41] but it is quite clear that the author of the Shakespeare play, *The Tempest*, was privy to it, for he used details from the report in his play.

[42] The play's first recorded performance took place before the King at Whitehall on the night of Hallowmas, 1611. It was acted again before the court during the winter of 1612-13 by the King's Men, as part of the grand and prolonged entertainments provided for the visit of Frederick, the Elector Palatine, on his betrothal and subsequent marriage to King James' daughter, the Princess Elizabeth, on St Valentine's Day 1613.

[43] *The Two Noble Kinsmen*, to which Bacon contributed, was mainly Fletcher's play and title-paged to Fletcher when published.

[44] Francis Bacon, *Advancement of Learning* (1623), 'Plan of the Work' (Part IV):-

> And now that we have surrounded the intellect with faithful helps and guards, and got together with most careful selection a regular army of divine works, it may seem that we have no more to do but to proceed to philosophy itself. And yet in a matter so difficult and doubtful there are still some things which it seems necessary to premise, partly for convenience of explanation, partly for present use.
> Of these the first is to set forth examples of inquiry and invention according to my method, exhibited by anticipation in some particular subjects; choosing such subjects as are at once the most noble in themselves among those under enquiry, and most different one from another; that there may be an example in every kind. I do not speak of those examples which are joined to the several precepts and rules by way of illustration (for of these

Building Paradise

I have given plenty in the second part of the work); but I mean actual types and models, by which the entire process of the mind and the whole fabric and order of invention from the beginning to the end, in certain subjects, and those various and remarkable, should be set as it were before the eyes. For I remember that in the mathematics it is easy to follow the demonstration when you have a machine beside you; whereas without that help all appears involved and more subtle than it really is. To examples of this kind—being in fact nothing more than an application of the second part in detail and at large,—the fourth part of the work is devoted.

[45] The report, entitled *The True Reportory of the wracke and Redemption of Sir Thomas Gates*, dated 15 July 1610, was not published until 1625 when it was included in *Purchas His Pilgrimes* (Pt 2, Bk x). Strachey also wrote the report, *The History of Travaile in Virginia Britannia*, which he dedicated to Sir Francis Bacon as the 'encourager, pattern and perfection of all virtuous endeavours'.

Chapter 3

[1] Translation from the Latin.

[2] Joseph Hall, *Satires Virgidemiarum* (1597).

[3] Ben Jonson, Tributary Poem, Shakespeare Folio (1623):-

> ...Or when thy socks were on,
> Leave thee alone, for the comparison
> Of all, that insolent *Greece* or haughty *Rome*
> sent forth, or since did from their ashes come.

[4] *Memoriæ Honoratissimi Domini Francisci, Baronis de Verulamio, Vice-Comitis Sancti Albani Sacrum. Londini In Officina Johannis Haviland, 1626*. Copies in the British Museum, Trinity College Library, Cambridge, and the Libraries of Jesus College and All Soul's, Oxford. Limited facsimile edition published privately in 1950, edited by W.G.C.Gundry of the Middle Temple, Barrister-at-Law.

[5] Francis Bacon, *Advancement of Learning* (1605), Bk I.

[6] Ben Jonson, *Ode for Lord Bacon's Birthday* (1621), publ. in *Underwood*, No.51.

Chapter 4

[1] William Rawley, 'The Life of the Honourable Author', prefixed to *Resuscitatio, Or, Bringing into Publick Light severall Pieces of the Works...of the Right Honourable Francis Bacon* (1657).

[2] The Hebraic Scriptures—the written Wisdom or Word of God—are known as the written *Torah*, 'the Law'. The wisdom itself is not exclusively Hebraic, but it was first written down in Hebrew for the tribes of Israel by Moses, who also taught the oral

Notes on the Text

counterpart to Joshua. Joshua then transmitted it to the elders of Israel. Originally this Written Torah consisted of the Pentateuch (the five books of Moses), but was later expanded to include the Prophets (*Nebiim*) and the Writings (*Ketubim*). Hand in hand with the Written Torah is the *Mishna* which, with the *Talmud* ('Commentary on the Scriptures') and *Gemarah* ('Commentary on the Mishna'), comprises the Oral Torah or Doctrine, transmitted by word of mouth from generation to generation. In a broader sense it also includes the *Haggadah* (historical and symbolic 'Narration') and *Midrashim* (rabbinical 'Explanations').

The Written Torah is the 'law', studied by all children of Israel. The Mishna is known as the soul of the law, studied by rabbins and teachers. The Cabala (*Kabbala*– 'Received Wisdom') is an even deeper esoteric level of knowledge, known as the soul of the soul of the law, which is studied and practised by the highest initiates. The Cabala is, in effect, the fourth and final level of interpretation of the Scriptures by the Oral Doctrine—the level known as *Sod* ('Mystery'), which concerns the spiritual interpretation and application of the *Maaseh Bereshith* ('the Work of the Beginning').

The Cabala is said to have first been taught by God to a school of angels before the fall of man. After the fall, the archangel Ratziel taught it to Adam and Eve, so that mankind might find redemption. The knowledge was handed down, with further revelations by successive archangels, to the great Initiates of mankind: for instance, the archangel Tophiel to Shem, the archangel Raphael to Isaac, the archangel Metatron to Moses and the archangel Michael to David. The earliest form of it as a book, written in hieroglyphics, is attributed by the Hebrews to Enoch, the seventh master of the world after Adam, by the Egyptians to Thoth (or Hermes), and by the Greeks to Cadmus.

In the time of the Hebrew prophets, the first chapter of Ezekiel's prophecies, containing the vision of the divine throne as a celestial chariot (*Maaseh Merkabah*, 'the Work of the Chariot'), was made part of the Cabala. With the additional revelation brought by Jesus, the mystery teachings of the Messiah were incorporated into what later became known as the Christian Cabala.

3 Birch MSS, 4263, f.110, copy in contemporary hand, published in James Spedding's *The Letters and the Life of Francis Bacon,* Vol. VII, p 229. This prayer was found among Bacon's papers. According to Spedding, this prayer was composed 'certainly before the 18th April [1621], and most probably at this very time'. This time was during the period when Bacon's impeachment was being proposed and discussed in the House of Lords, and he had just written his will, dated 10th April 1621. On the 18th April Bacon had an interview with the King concerning the charge about to be brought against him.

4 Proverbs xxv, 2.

5 In the Freemasonic Royal Arch Degree, the 'Second Solomon' is referred to as Zerubbabel, its allegory being based on the story in the Bible of the physical rebuilding of Solomon's Temple under the leadership of Zerubbabel.

6 Spedding, *Lord Bacon's Works,* III, p 248.

7 Spedding, *Lord Bacon's Works,* IV, p 53.

8 Spedding, *Lord Bacon's Works*, IV, pp 449-450. The final sentence can more properly read: 'or have wits of such sharpness and discernment that they can of themselves pierce the veil'.

9 Francis Bacon, 'Of Truth', *Essays* (1625).

10 Spedding, *Lord Bacon's Works*, IV, p 106-7.

11 Spedding, *Lord Bacon's Works*, IV, p 119.

12 Eccles. 3:11 — '(No man can find out) the work that God maketh from the beginning to the end.'

13 Spedding, *Lord Bacon's Works*, IV, p 119.

14 Quoted from *The Way of Hermes*, translated by Clement Salaman, Dorine van Oyen and William D. Wharton (London: Duckworth, 1999).

15 Ecclesiastes iii, 11.

16 Francis Bacon, *Advancement of Learning* (1605), Bk II.

17 Romans xii, i.

18 See Peter Dawkins, *The Master*, Pt 2, 'AI and the Boar' (FBRT 1993) and *Arcadia*, Ch 8, 'The AA Signature of Light' (FBRT 1988).

19 Matthew xxii, 29.

20 *Psalm* 123: 2

CHAPTER 6

1 Ecclesiastes iii, 11.

2 For a good discussion of this see Julian Martin, *Francis Bacon, The State and the Reform of Natural Philosophy* (Cambridge University Press, 1992).

3 Spedding, *Lord Bacon's Works*, IV, p 112.

4 Spedding, *Lord Bacon's Works*, V, p 22.

5 *e.g* the Rosicrucians and Freemasons.

6 *Ecclesiastes* iii, 11.

7 Genesis i, 2.

8 Hebraic tradition teaches that the Mother aspect of Divinity is signified by spiritual Water ('the waters') and the Father aspect by spiritual Fire. The former is represented by the letter *Mem* ('M') the latter by the letter *Shin* ('Sh'). Their union forms spiritual Air, the name for which is *Shamaim*, a word compounded of *Shin* and *Mem*. It is represented by the Hebrew letter *Aleph* ('A'), the sign of the Creator. *Shamaim* ('Fire-Water') is the spiritual Æther, which is Light.

Notes on the Text

In Alchemy this *Shamaim* or Æther is known as the Quintessence, the Universal Agent and Powder of Projection. It is represented by Mercury, whose creative 'father' aspect is the Logos (*i.e.* invisible Fire or Light) and whose receptive 'mother' aspect is uncreated substance (*i.e.* invisible Water or Darkness).

In the act of creation, the Logos aspect of Mercury becomes active as the Holy Spirit whilst the substantial aspect of Mercury responds by becoming, or making, primal matter that can give form to the otherwise formless light as the universe or 'Nature'.

Bacon refers to this inherent duality, which is yet a Oneness, in his essay on Pan in *The Wisdom of the Ancients*:-

> Pan (as his name imports) represents and lays open the All of things or Nature. Concerning his original there are two only opinions that go for current; for either he came of Mercury, that is, the Word of God, which the Holy Scriptures without all controversy affirm, and such of the philosophers that have any smack of Divinity assented unto; or else from the confused seeds of things. For they that would have one simple Beginning, refer it unto God; or if a materiate Beginning, they would have it various in power. So that we may end the controversy with this distribution, that the world took Beginning either from Mercury or from the seeds of all things.

> Virgil Eclogue 6
>
> > *Namque canebat uti magnum per inane coacta.*
> > *Semina terrarumque, animaeque, marisque suissent,*
> > *Et liquidi simul ignis: et his exoerdia primis*
> > *Omnia, et ipse tener mundi concreverit Orbis.*
>
> > For rich-vein'd Orpheus sweetly did rehearse
> > How that the seeds of Fire, Air, Water, Earth,
> > Were all pack'd in the vast void Universe:
> > And how from these as firstlings, all had birth,
> > And how the body of this Orbick frame,
> > From tender infancy so big became.

> But, as touching the third conceit of Pan's original, it seems that the Grecians (either by intercourse with the Egyptians, or one way or other) had heard something of the Hebrew Mysteries; for it points to the state of the World, not considered in immediate Creation, but after the Fall of Adam, exposed and made subject to death and corruption: for in that state it was (and remains to this day) the offspring of God and sin. And therefore all these three narrations concerning the manner of Pan's birth may seem to be true, if it be rightly distinguished between things and times. For this Pan or Nature (which we suspect, contemplate, and reverence more than is fit) took beginning from the Word of God by means of confused matter, and the entrance of prevarication and corruption.

(Francis Bacon, 'Pan, or Nature', *Wisdom of the Ancients* – 1619 English translation by Sir Arthur Gorges of the original Latin edition published in 1609.)

[9] Ecclesiastes iii, 11.

Building Paradise

CHAPTER 7

1. As such these seekers after truth have been known as the 'Sons of Truth', 'Sons of the Doctrine' or 'Sons of Wisdom'—a formula which occurs in the *Sefer Ha-Zohar* ('Book of Splendour'), the prime Cabalistic treatise on the Pentateuch or written *Torah* (the first five books of Moses).

2. England is the dowry of the Virgin Mary, according to Roman Catholic tradition.

3. See Francis Bacon, *The Advancement of Learning and New Atlantis*, edited by Arthur Johnston (Oxford University Press, 1974), Introduction, p x.

4. See H. Spencer Lewis, *Rosicrucian Questions and Answers*, (AMORC, 1929, 1977), Ch VII.

5. N.B. Gorhambury, Bacon's estate, is 'near' Verulamium.

6. Halliwell MS (supposed 1390). Cooke MS (supposed 1490). Dowland MS (supposed 1500). Lansdowne MS (supposed 1560). York MS No. 1 (supposed 1600). Harleian MS No. 2054 (supposed 1625). Grand Lodge MS (supposed 1632). Sloane MS No. 3848 (1646). Sloane MS No. 1942 (1659). Harleian MS No. 1942 (supposed 1660). Aitcheson-Haven MS (1666). Edinburgh-Kilwinning MS (supposed 1670). York MS No. 5 (supposed 1670). York MS No. 6 (supposed 1680). Lodge of Antiquity MS (1686). York MS No. 2 (1693). Alnwick MS (1701). York MS No. 4 (1704). Papworth MS (supposed 1714).

7. The first edition of Anderson's *Constitutions of the Free-masons* was published in 1723, the second edition in 1738.

8. Chamberlain, writing on the 3rd February 1621, records that 'On Saturday the Lord Chancellor was created Viscount St. Alban's, with all the ceremonies of robes and coronet, whereas the rest were only done by patent'. See Spedding, *Letters and Life of Francis Bacon*, Vol. XIV, pp 167-8.

9. Spedding, *Letters and Life of Francis Bacon*, Vol. XIV, p 168.

10. If Francis Bacon were truly the eldest and only living son of Queen Elizabeth, as the evidence seems to indicate, then Francis would have been the legal heir to the throne of England, not James Stewart. James, therefore, could rightly be considered a usurper. See Peter Dawkins, *Dedication to the Light* (FBRT, 1984) for more information on this.

11. *e.g.* such as in the symbolism of the Philosopher's Stone.

12. The Westminster Abbey Shakespeare Memorial was erected in 1741 under the auspices of Richard Boyle, the 3rd Earl of Burlington, Alexander Pope, Dr. Richard Mead and Dr. Martin. Dr. Martin was the founder of the Society of Antiquaries. Dr. Mead was a well-known patron of literature and a former Vice-President of the Royal Society. He was considered to be one of the greatest authorities on Bacon at that time, to whom several recent editions of Bacon's works (including the 1740 Mallet edition) had been dedicated. Alexander Pope, the English poet and satirist who had recently edited and published a new volume of Shakespeare's works, was a leading authority on both Bacon and Shakespeare. Richard Boyle, the 3rd Earl of Burlington, was a patron of literature and leader of the Palladian group who included the above.

Notes on the Text

[13] According to Rix and Rutter's *History of the Royal Society*.

[14] Canonbury House is located in Islington, London, on the summit of Islington's hill. In Bacon's time it was in the country. Canonbury Tower is now the home of the Canonbury Masonic Research Centre.

[15] Psalm 91, 1-4.

[16] Francis Bacon, prayer printed at end of *Abecedarium Naturae, or a Metaphysical Piece*, first published by Archbishop Tennison in *Baconiana* (1679).

[17] Francis Bacon, *The Advancement and Proficience of Learning* (1605):-

> But this is that which will indeed dignify and exalt knowledge: if contemplation and action may be more nearly and straitly conjoined and united together than they have been; a conjunction like unto that of the two highest planets, Saturn, the planet of rest and contemplation, and Jupiter, the planet of civil society and action.

[18] The lion is a symbol of the heart and emotion, whilst the unicorn is a symbol of the mind and thought. The former signifies the right-hand pillar and the latter the left-hand pillar of the Tree of Life. In this particular emblem on the title-page of the *Constitutions of the Free-masons* the Jewish presentation is adopted whereby the pillars are seen as from inside the temple looking out, or as from the stage by an actor looking at the audience.

[19] Since the third pillar of beauty is associated with Hiram Abif, the symbol of the 'broken column' is also used to refer to this central pillar. Various editions of Bacon's books were adorned with pictures of the broken column in conjunction with swans, the emblem of Apollo, Orpheus and Shakespeare.

[20] Solomon's Temple was orientated east-west, with the entrance porch in the east and the holy of holies in the west. The symbolism of a temple is such that it represents the divine mother lying down on the ground on her back, with her head represented by the holy of holies (equivalent to the chancel in a church). So in Solomon's Temple the right-hand side was to the south and the left-hand side was to the north. This meant that the right-hand great pillar of Wisdom was in the south-east and the left-hand great pillar of Strength was in the north-east. In Christian churches, which are orientated in the opposite direction (*i.e.* with the chancel to the east), the right-hand side is to the north and the left-hand side to the south. Freemasonic lodges tend to follow the Christian pattern.

[21] The Hebrew word *Boaz* is kin to the Greek word *Boue* meaning primeval chaos—the dark womb of time.

[22] The Hebrew word *Jachin* is kin to the Greek word *Iacchus* (*i.e.* Bacchus), the god of wisdom or light and all creative and procreative powers.

[23] Francis Bacon, *Advancement of Learning* (1605), Bk.II:-

> The knowledge which respecteth the faculties of the mind of man is of two kinds; the one respecting his Understanding and Reason, and the other his Will, Appetite, and Affection; whereof the former produceth Position or Decree, the latter Action or Execution. It is true that the

Building Paradise

> Imagination is an agent or nuncius in both provinces, both the judicial and the ministerial. For Sense sendeth over to Imagination before Reason hath judged: and Reason sendeth over to Imagination before the decree can be acted: for Imagination preceedeth Voluntary Motion. Saving that this Janus of Imagination hath differing faces: for the face towards Reason hath the print of Truth, but the face towards Action hath the print of Good; which nevertheless are faces...

In the above quotation it is useful to understand that Bacon equates action as well as will, appetite, affection and sense with the right-hand pillar, whilst position or decree is equated with understanding and reason and the left-hand pillar.

[24] Francis Bacon, *Advancement of Learning* (1605), Bk.II:-

> Neither is the Imagination simply and only a messenger; but it is invested with, or at least wise usurpeth no small authority in itself, besides the duty of the message. For it was well said by Aristotle, 'That the mind hath over the body that commandment which the lord hath over a bondman; but that reason hath over the imagination that commandment which a magistrate hath over a free citizen', who may come also to rule in his turn. For we see that, in matters of Faith and Religion, we raise our Imagination above our Reason; which is the cause why Religion sought ever access to the mind by similitude, types, parables, visions, dreams. And again, in all persuasions that are wrought by eloquence, and other impressions of like nature, which do paint and disguise the true appearance of things, the chief recommendation unto Reason is from the Imagination.

> ...so as it appeareth that poesy serveth and conferreth to magnanimity, morality, and to delectation. And therefore it was ever thought to have some participation of divineness, because it doth raise and erect the mind, by submitting the shows of things to the desires of the mind; whereas reason doth buckle and bow the mind into the nature of things.

SELECT BIBLIOGRAPHY

Francis Bacon's Life
Baker, H. Kendra, *The Persecution of Francis Bacon* (Francis Bacon Society, 1978).
Barber, Richard (ed.), *John Aubrey's Brief Lives* (London: Folio Society, 1975).
Bevan, Bryan, *The Real Francis Bacon* (London: Centaur Press, 1960).
Cockburn, N. B., *The Bacon Shakespeare Question* (Surrey: Cockburn, 1998).
Dawkins, Peter, *The Pattern of Initiation* (FBRT, 1981).
Dawkins, Peter, *The Virgin Ideal* (FBRT, 1980).
Dawkins, Peter, *Dedication to the Light* (FBRT, 1984).
Dawkins, Peter, *The Great Vision* (FBRT, 1985).
Dawkins, Peter, *Arcadia* (FBRT, 1988).
Dawkins, Peter, *The Master*, Pt 2, 'AI and the Boar' (FBRT, 1993).
Dixon, William Hepworth, *Personal History of Lord Bacon* (London: John Murray, 1861).
Dodd, Alfred, *Francis Bacon's Personal Life-Story* (London: Rider, 1949, 1986).
Fuller, Jean Overton, *Sir Francis Bacon: A Biography* (London: East-West Publications, 1981).
Gundry, W. G. C. (ed.), *Manes Verulamiani* (London: 1950).
King, Norah, *The Grimstons of Gorhambury* (Chichester: Camelot Press, 1983).
Mathews, Nieves, *Francis Bacon: The History of a Character Assassination* (London: Yale University Press, 1996).
Maurier, Daphne du, *Golden Lads* (London: Victor Gollancz, 1975).
Maurier, Daphne du, *The Winding Stair* (London: Victor Gollancz, 1975).
Pott, Mrs. Henry, *Francis Bacon and his Secret Society* (London: Robert Banks & Son, 1911).
Rawley, Dr. William, 'The Life of the Honourable Author', prefixed to *Resuscitatio, Or, Bringing into Publick Light severall Pieces of the Works...of the Right Honourable Francis Bacon* (1657).
Spedding, James (ed.), *The Letters and the Life of Francis Bacon* (London: Longman, Green, Longman & Roberts, 1861-74).
Steeves, G. Walter, *Francis Bacon: A Sketch of his Life, Works and Literary Friends, chiefly from a bibliographical point of view* (London: Methuen, 1910).

Francis Bacon's Philosophy
Bowen, Catherine Drinker, *Francis Bacon: The Temper of the Man* (London: Hamish Hamilton, 1963).
Hall, Manly P. (ed.), *New Atlantis, Begun by the Lord Verulam and Continued by R. H. Esquire* (Los Angeles, CA: The Philosophical Research Society, 1985).
Farrington, Benjamin, *Francis Bacon: Philosopher of Industrial Science* (London: Lawrence & Wishart, 1951).
Gundry, W. G. C. (ed.), *Manes Verulamiani* (London: Chiswisk Press, 1950).
Martin, Julian, *Francis Bacon: The State, and The Reform of Natural Philosophy* (Cambridge: Cambridge University Press, 1992).
Johnston, Arthur (ed.), *Francis Bacon: The Advancement of Learning and New Atlantis* (Oxford University Press, 1974).
McCutcheon, Elizabeth, *Sir Nicholas Bacon's Great House Sententiae* (Claremont, CA: English Literary Supplements, No. 3, 1977).
Peltonen, Markku (ed.), *The Cambridge Companion to Bacon* (Cambridge:

Cambridge University Press, 1996).
Pérez-Ramos, Antonio, *Francis Bacon's Idea of Science and the Maker's Knowledge Tradition* (Oxford: Clarendon Press, 1988).
Spedding, J., Ellis R.L., and Heath (eds.), *The Works of Francis Bacon* (London: Longman, 1857-8).
Urbach, Peter, *Francis Bacon's Philosophy of Science* (Illinois: Open Court, 1987).
Wigston, W. F. C., *The Columbus of Literature, or Bacon's New World of Sciences* (Chicago: F. J. Schulte, 1892).
Wormald, B. H. G., *Francis Bacon: History, Politics & Science, 1561-1626* (Cambridge: Cambridge University Press, 1993).

Ciphers

Dawkins, Peter, *Arcadia* (FBRT, 1988).
Dawkins, Peter, *The Master,* Pt 2: 'AI and the Boar' (FBRT, 1993).
Leary, Penn, *The.Cryptographic.Shakespeare.* (Omaha, USA: Westchester House, 1987).
MacDuff, Ewen, *The Sixty-Seventh Inquisition* (Shoreham, England: Eric-Faulkner-Little, 1973).
MacDuff, Ewen, *The Dancing Horse Will Tell You* (Shoreham, England: Eric-Faulkner-Little, 1974).
Woodward, Frank, *Francis Bacon's Cipher Signatures* (London: Grafton, 1923).

Cabalistic, Freemasonic, Rosicrucian

Best, Shabaz Britten (ed.), *Genesis Revised* (Farnham: Sufi Publishing Co., 1970).
Case, Paul Foster, *The True and Invisible Rosicrucian Order* (Maine: Samuel Weiser, 1981).
Castells, F. de, *The Genuine Secrets in Freemasonry* (Letchworth: A LEWIS, 1978).
Castells, F. de, *Historical Analysis of the Holy Royal Arch Ritual* (Letchworth: A LEWIS, 1929).
Cox, Rev. John Edmund (ed.), *The Constitutions of the Freemasons* (Bro. Richard Spencer, 1871).
Curl, James Stevens, *The Art and Architecture of Freemasonry* (London: B. T. Batsford, 1991).
Dawkins, Peter, *Francis Bacon – Herald of the New Age* (FBRT, 1997).
Dyer, Colin, *Symbolism in Craft Freemasonry* (Shepperton: A LEWIS, 1976).
Eisler, Robert, *Orpheus—The Fisher* (London: Watkins, 1921).
Fellowship of the School of Economic Science (ed.), *The Letters of Marsilio Ficino* (London: Shepheard-Walwyn, 1975).
Filby, F. A., *Creation Revealed* (Glasgow: Pickering & Inglis, 1963).
Frere, A. S. (ed.), *Grand Lodge* (London: United Grand Lodge of England, 1967).
Godwin, Joscelyn, *Robert Fludd, Hermetic Philosopher and Surveyor of Two Worlds* (London: Thames & Hudson, 1979).
Halevi, Z'Ev ben Shimon, *Tree of Life* (London: Rider, 1972).
Halevi, Z'Ev ben Shimon, *A Kabbalistic Universe* (London: Rider, 1977).
Hall, Manly P., *Masonic Orders of Fraternity* (Los Angeles: The Philosophic Research Society, 1950).
Hall, Manly P., *Orders of the Great Work – Alchemy* (Los Angeles: The Philosophic Research Society, 1949).

Bibliography

Hall, Manly P., *Orders of Universal Reformation* (Los Angeles: The Philosophic Research Society, 1949).
Hall, Manly P., *New Atlantis: Begun by the Lord Verulam and continued by R. H. Esquire* (Los Angeles: The Philosophic Research Society, 1985).
Hall, Manly P., *An Interpretation of the Myth of Dionysus,* printed with *The Dionysian Artificers* by Hippolyta Joseph da Costa (Los Angeles: The Philosophic Research Society, 1975).
Hamill, John, *The Craft: A History of English Freemasonry* (Wellingborough: Crucible, 1986).
Hancox, Joy, *The Byrom Collection* (London: Jonathan Cape, 1992, 1997).
Harvey, William, *The Complete Manual of Freemasonry* (Dundee: Sparks & Son, 1973).
Horne, Alex, *King Solomon's Temple in the Masonic Tradition* (Wellingborough: Aquarian Press, 1972).
Jones, Bernard E., *Freemason's Book of the Royal Arch* (London: Harrap, 1957).
Jones, Bernard E., *Freemason's Guide and Compendium* (London: Harrap, 1956).
Kalish, Rev. Dr. Isidor (ed.), *Sepher Yezirah* (New York: L. H. Frank, 1877; reprinted AMORC, 1970).
Leadbeater, C. W., *The Hidden Life in Freemasonry* (Adyar, Madras: Theosophical Publishing House, 1975).
Levi, Eliphas, *The Book of Splendours* (Wellingborough: Aquarian Press, 1981).
Lewis, H. Spencer, *Rosicrucian Questions and Answers* (AMORC, 1929, 1977).
Mackey, A. G., *The History of Freemasonry* (New York: Gramercy Books, 1996).
MacNulty, W. Kirk, *Freemasonry: A Journey through Ritual and Symbol* (London: Thames & Hudson, 1991).
Macoy, Robert, *A Dictionary of Freemasonry* (New York: Bell Publishing Co., 1989).
Maier, Michael, *Laws of the Fraternity of the Rosie Crosse* (Themis Aurea), facsimile reprint of original English edition of 1656 (Los Angeles: Philosophical Research Society, 1976).
Mead, G. R. S., *Thrice-Greatest Hermes* (Detroit: Hermes Press, 1978).
McIntosh, Christopher, *The Rosicrucians* (Wellingborough: Crucible, 1987).
Ponce, Charles, *Kabbalah* (London: Garnstone Press, 1974).
Pott, Mrs Henry, *Francis Bacon and his Secret Society* (London: Robert Banks & Son, 1911).
Rola, Stanislas Klossowski de, *The Golden Game: Alchemical Engravings of the Seventeenth Century* (London: Thames & Hudson, 1988).
Roob, Alexander, *Alchemy and Mysticism* (London: Taschen, 1997).
Schaya, Leo, *The Universal Meaning of the Kabbalah* (London: George Allen & Unwin, 1971).
Scott, Walter (ed.), *Hermetica: The Writings attributed to Hermes Trismegistus* (Bath: Solos Press, 1993).
Spratt, T, *The History of the Royal Society of London for the improving of natural knowledge* (London, 1667).
Taylor, Thomas (transl.), *The Cratylus, Phaedo, Parminides, Timaeus and Critias of Plato* (Minneapolis: Secret Doctrine Reference Series, Wizards Bookshelf, 1976).
Taylor, Thomas (transl.), *The Hymns of Orpheus* (Los Angeles: The Philosophic Research Society, 1981).
D. van Oyen, William D. Wharton, *The Definitions of Hermes Trismegistus to Asclepius*, transl. Jean-Pierre Mahé (London: Duckworth, 1999).
Philalethes, Eugenius, *The Fame and Confession of R.C.* (W.J. Parret, 1923).

Building Paradise

Waite, Arthur Edward, *A New Enclyclopaedia of Freemasonry* (Secausus, New Jersey: University Books, 1973).
Waite, Arthur Edward, *Emblematic Freemasonry* (William Ryder & Son, 1925).
Waite, Arthur Edward, *The Secret Tradition in Freemasonry* (Rebman, 1911).
Waite, Arthur Edward, *The Brotherhood of the Rosy Cross* (New York: Weathervanes Books, 1970).
Wigston, W. F. C., *Bacon, Shakespeare and the Rosicrucians* (London: Geaorde Redway, 1888).
Wilmshurst, W. L., *The Meaning of Masonry* (New York: Bell Publishing Co., 1980, facsimile of 1927 edition).
Yates, Frances A., *The Rosicrucian Enlightenment* (London: Routledge & Kegan Paul, 1972).
Yates, Frances A., *Astraea: The Imperial Theme in the Sixteenth Century* (London: Routledge & Kegan Paul, 1975).
Yates, Frances A., *The Occult Philosophy in the Elizabethan Age* (London: Routledge & Kegan Paul, 1979).
Yates, Frances A., *Giordano Bruno and the Hermetic Tradition* (London: Routledge & Kegan Paul, 1964).
Mystical Theology and the Celestial Hierarchies (The Shrine of Wisdom, 1965).
The Divine Pymander of Hermes Trismegistus (The Shrine of Wisdom, 1978).
The Way of Hermes: The Corpus Hermeticum, transl. Clement Salaman, Dorine van Oyen and William D. Wharton (London: Duckworth, 1999).

INDEX

Æneid 55
Æther 199
A Midsummer Night's Dream 10
Aaron 85
Académie des Sciences 133
Accession Day celebration 24
Accession Day tournaments 10
Active Philosophy 120
Active Science 75, 120, 123
Advancement of Learning 2, 35-36, 63, 69, 85, 103, 113, 120, 123, 126-127, 159, 163, 164, 195
All is True 38
All's Well That Ends Well 20
AMORC 139
Amphibalus 140-141
Anathemata B. Conrado 182
Anaxagoras 17
Ancient and Mystical Order Rosae Crucis 139
Ancient Wisdom 4
Anderson, Dr. 140
Aphorisms of the Interpretation of Nature or the Reign of Man 106
Aphorisms on the Interpretation of Nature and the Realm of Man 106
Apollo 48-49, 83, 127, 130, 187-188
Apology concerning the Earl of Essex 194
Apophthegm 10 188
Aquarian Age xiii
Arcadia, heroes of 138
Arcadian Woodstock Tournament 9
Arcadia 20, 138
Archangel Metatron 191, 197
Archangel Michael 136, 197
Archangel Raphael 197
Archangel Ratziel 197
Archangel Tophiel 197
Archbishop of Canterbury 10
Archbishop of York 43
Archbishop Tennison 56, 149, 183, 187
Areopagus of English lawyer-poets 11
Argonauts 54
Ariel 186

Aristotelian system of thought 10
Art of Discovery 3, 56, 63, 66, xiv
Art of Interpretation 104
Art of Science 5
Art of Transmission 66
Ascending and Descending Ladder of Axioms 105, 113
Asham, Roger 134
Ashley, Robert 47
Ashmole, Elias 142
Athena 49, 83, 130, 187
Athens 130
Atlantis 104, 131
Authorised Version 85
Auxiliares 133
Axiomata 68, 107-108
Bacchant 128
Bacchus 127-128, 186
Bacco 128
Bacon, Anthony 10-11, 14, 21, 24, 28
Bacon, Edward 16
Bacon, Lady Anne 12, 16
Bacon, Lady Ann 9
Bacon, Sir Nicholas 9, 12, 134-135, 137
Baconiana 187
Bacon's method 5
Bacon's science, based on love 3
Bacon's science 5
Barnham, Alice 29
Bassanio 24
Benignity 155
Bensalem 62, 132
Beza, Theodore 1
Bible 85
Binary system 182
Blazing Star 157
Blois 11
Boaz 155, 187, 201
Bodley, Sir Thomas 15, 193
Boener, Peter 36
Bolton, Edmund 33, 133
Bolton, William 139
Book M 107
Book of God's Word 83
Book of God's Works 83

Book of Nature 107
Book of Revelation 153
Book of the World 107
Borgia 64
Boswell, Sir William 39, 47
Boyle, Robert 142
Brahe, Tycho 1, 191-192
Brotherhood of Light 134
Bruno, Giordano 20
Burghley, Lord 9, 12-15, 17, 21, 25
Burghley, Robert 25
Cabala, Hebrew 117
Cabala, Moses' secret 132
Cabala 59-60, 118, 132-133, 151, 154-156, 182, 197
Cabalistic philosophy 113
        teaching 77
        worlds 76
Campion, Thomas 41
Canonbury Manor 33
Cardano Grille 188
Cassiopeia, supernova in 22
Cassiopeia 1, 192
Cecil Robert 23
Cecil, Anne 20
Cecil, Elizabeth 10, 26
Cecil, Robert 17
Cecil, Sir William 9, 11, 135
Celtic-Druidic tradition 136
Charity 120
Chenonceaux, 11
Christian trinity 153
Church teachings 117
Cicero 46
Cipher, bilateral 15, 182
Cipher, cabalistic 2, 182
    Kay 183
    reverse 183
    simple 143, 183, 191
Ciphrae Clavis 183
Clerke, William 10
Coke, Sir Edward 23, 26
College of the Six Days' Work 33, 62, 120, 131, 138, 142
Collins, Samuel 47
Comedy 128
Commedia dell'arte 12
Commentaries 133
Confessio Fraternitatis 191
Conrad 182
Constable, Sir John 39

Constitution of the United States of America 30, 38
Constitutions of the Free-masons 140, 153
Conubio jungam stabili 123
Cooke manuscript 140
Cooke, Sir Anthony 134
Corinthian order 164
Cornelius Agrippa von Nettesheim 135
Court of Love 12
Critias 136
Cross of Light 136
Cross of Truth 136
Cryptography 15
Cryptomenytices et Cryptographiae 135, 183
Cupid   116-118
        and Coelum 116
        and the Atom 116
Cygnus 2
Cymbeline 29
Daniel, Samuel 19-20
Dark Lady of the Shakespeare *Sonnets* 22
Davies, John 42
Daystar 49
De Armado, Don Adriana 21
De Augmentis Scientiarum 37, 63, 80, 120, 123, 127, 135
De Dignitate et Augmentis Scientiarum 36, 103, 126, 163
De Montaigne, Michel 20
De nova stella 191
De Vere, Edward, Earl of Oxford 11
Dee, Dr. John 14, 137
Delphic Oracle 54
Depository of the Mysteries of the Son 133
Devereux, Robert, Earl of Essex 17-18
Diana 130
Dionysian masquerades 128
Dodding, Milo 194
Doric order 164
Dowland manuscript 140
Drant, Thomas 14
Dudley, Earl Robert 10
Dudley, Robert, Earl of Leicester 19, 137
Dyer, Edward 14
E.F. 48

Index

Eastern wisdom teachings 117
Edward VI 134
Elias the Artist 192
Elias 4
Elijah 191, xiii
Ellesmere, Lord 31
Elyon 151
Emperor Augustus 43
Emperor Carausius 141
Emperor Diocletian 140
Emperor Maximilian 141
Emperor of Great Britain 142
Emperor Severus 141
English Areopagus 10, 14, 19, 137-138
English Church 137
English Grand Lodge of Freemasons 145
English language 3
Enoch 191, 197
Erasmus 135
Eros 117
Essays and Wisdom of Ancients 119
Essays, Bacon's 26
Essentials 133
Essex House 17, 137
Essex, Earl of 23, 26-27, 137
Essex, Lady Frances 19
Eupheus, the Anatomy of Wit 20
Euripides 54
Ezekiel 60, 197
Faerie Queene 138
Fama Fraternitas 68
Fama Fraternitatis 106, 114, 142, 191
Father C.R.C. 136
Faunt, Nicholas 15, 193
Ferne, Henry 47
Ficino, Marcilio 136
Final causes 76
First Vintage 112
Fletcher, John 31
Florio, John 19-20
Fludd, Robert 2, 192
Fontainebleau 11
Formal causes 76
Forms 105
Fourth Day of Creation 2
Fraternity of the Golden Rose-Cross 137
Fraternity of the Rosy Cross 131, 142, 136
Freemasonic degrees of initiation 159

Freemason's Guide and Compendium 142
Freemasonry, English 2
Freemasonry, Grand Lodge of English 139
Freemasonry 60, 118, 121, 139, 142, 156, xiii
French Academies 13
Fulwood House 12
Fulwood, Mr 12
Gates, Sir Thomas 30
Genesis 60
Georgics 55
Geta 141
Globe Theatre 38, 187
Golden Rose-Croix, brothers of 134
Good pens 88
Gorhambury 16, 34
Gospel of Bartholomew 132
Grand Company of Ancients 11
Gray's Inn Christmas Revels 25
Gray's Inn 11-12, 15-16, 137
Great Instauration 33, 66, 85, 88, 103-104, 115, 118-119, 121, 123, 126-127, 130-131, 159, 164
Great Pillars 154, 159, 163-164
Greene, Robert 14, 19
Greene's Groatsworth of Wit 194
Hall, Joseph 42
Hamlet 11, 20, 27
Harvey, Gabriel 10, 14
Hatton, Lady 25
Hatton, Sir William 26
Haviland, John 47
Hayward, John 27
Henri IV of France 21
Henry IV 18
Henry VIII 31
Henry VI 9, 194
Herbert, George 36, 38, 47
Herbert, Henry, Earl of Pembroke 19
Herbert, William 11
Hermes Trismegistus 56, 125
Hermetic wisdom 5
Heydon, John 131
Hippocrene 49
Hiram Abif 201
Historia Densi et Rari 110
Historia Gravis et Levis 110
Historia Naturalis 110
Historia Ventorum 36, 110

Building Paradise

Historia Vitae et Mortis 110
Historiam Regni Henrici VII, Regis Angliae 111
History of Density and Rarity 110
History of Gravity and Levity 110
History of Life and Death 110
History of Sulphur, Salt and Mercury 110
History of the Reign of King Henry VIII 111
History of the Reign of King Henry VII 110
History of the Sympathy and Antipathy of Things 110
Hobbes, Thomas 36
Hokhmah 60
Holland, Philemon 10
Holofernes 20
Holy Innocents' Day 25
Homer 54
Horace 46
Horus 151
Hotspur 18
House of Solomon 138, 142
House of the Holy Spirit 120
Idris 191
Iliad 55
Immerito (Edward Spenser) 14
Imperator of Sodalitium 135
Incomparable Paire 29
Inner Temple 137
Inns of Court, 137
Intelligence networks 14, 182
Invisible Brethren 133
Invisible College 133, 139, 142, 145
Ionic order 164
Isaac 197
Jachin 155, 187, 201
Jacob's Ladder 132, 184
Jamestown 30
Janus 159
Jehovah 151
Jesus Christ 63-64, 77, 136, 191
John the Baptist 4, 191-192
Jonson, Ben 19, 36, 41, 45-46, 56, xiii
Joshua 197
Jupiter 2, 121, 151
Kelpius, Grand-master 139
Kenilworth Entertainment 9
King Arthur 136-137
King James I 28, 34, 85, 133, xiii

King James VI of Scotland 28
King James' Academy or College of Honour 33
King James' Authorised Version of the Holy Bible 85
King James 60
King John 194
King Lear 20, 27
Knights of the Helmet, Honourable Order of 25, 138
Knights Templar 136
Kundalini 191
Labeo, Antistius 43
Laboratory of the theatre 119
Ladder of the intellect 71, 73, 112
Lady Fortune 22
Laelius 42
Latin Opera 188
Lee, Sir Henry 9, 138
Leicester House 17, 137
Leicester, Earl of 14, 17
Leicester's Men 22
Librum Mundi 107
Librum Naturae 68, 107, 142
Lodge, Thomas 14, 19
Logos 117-118
London Virginia Company 30
Lord Keeper of the Great Seal of England 9
Lord Pembroke's Men 19, 22, 194
Lord Strange's Men 22, 194
Love's Labour's Lost 12, 20-21
Lucrece 11
Lyly, John 10, 14, 19-20
Macbeth 27
Magi 136
Maha-On 155
Mahabone 155
Maier, Michael 134
Manes Verulamiani 47, 53, 55, 114
Marlowe, Christopher 14, 19
Maro 54-55
Mars 2, 130, 151
Masonic symbolism 144
Master of Trinity 10
Masters of Wisdom xiii
Matthew, Sir Tobie 33, 43-44
Meautys, Sir Thomas 36, 39
Mecænas 55
Medici, Catherine de 12
Mercury 118

Index

Messiah 121
Method of Discourse 66
Method of the Mind in the Comprehension of Things Exemplified 112
Milton 46
Minerva 48
Mistress Quickly 188
Montgomery, William, Earl of 29
More, Sir Thomas 134-135
Morse code 15, 182
Moses 59, 64, 85, 136, 197
Mount Helicon 49
Mountjoy, Lord 19
Mr. William Shakespeares Comedies, Histories, & Tragedies 118
Muses 49, 52
Mysteries of the Torah 59
Nashe, Thomas 14, 19
Natural History 66, 131, 142, 164
Navarre, Henri of 21
Navarre, Marguerite de 12
Nérac 12
Nestor, 54-56
New Age, Bacon as herald of 4
New Atlanteans 132
New Atlantis 33, 62, 104, 113, 121, 123, 131-133, 136, 139, 142
New Method 31, 88, 104, 112, 127, 137
New or Second Philosophy 120
Notes on the Present State of Christendom 15
Novum Organum 31, 37, 63, 106, 113, 159, 163
Odyssey 55
Olympus 53
Opuscula Varia Posthuma 188
Order of the Rosy Cross 137
Organum, Aristotle's 104
Orpheus 4, 136
Orphic Mysteries 55, 186
Orphic Mystery schools 128
Othello 27
Ovid 46
Oxford, Earl of 19
Oxford's Boys 20
Oxford's Men 20
Pallas Athena 25, 48
Pan 199
Paracelsus 136, 191-192
Parasceve ad Historiam et Naturalem 110
Paris 11
Paulet, Sir Amyas 11
Peele, George 14, 19
Pegasean arts 49
Pembroke, Philip, Earl of 29
Pentateuch 197
Perez, Antonio 21
Pericles 29
Philadelphia Lodge 139
Philosophia Moralis 114
Philosophical College 142
Philosophies—divine, human and natural 79
Phoebus 49
Phoenix 6
Pillars of Hercules 154
Platonic Academy of Marsilio Ficino 136
Platonic Academy 134
Platonic solids 78
Plato 136
Poesie 73, 140, 189-90
Poitiers 11
Polonius 11
Pope, Alexander 46, 145
Powell, Thomas 56
Practical Science 120
Preparative towards a Natural and Experimental History 110
Prerogative Instances 113
Promus of Formularies and Elegancies 21, 193
Prospero 78, 186
Protheus 68, 107
Purchas His Pilgrimes 196
Pylus 54
Pyramid of Divinity 85
Pyramid of Philosophy 73, 75, 81, 85, 104, 108, 115
Pythagoras 6, 136
Queen Anne of Denmark, 29
Queen Elizabeth I 9, 14, 18, 22-23, 26, 28, 136, 137, xiii
Queen's Accession Day Tournaments 137
Quirinal Hill, 49
Quirinus, spear of 49
Quirinus, temple of 49
R. H. Esquire 131
R.P. 48

Building Paradise

Ra 151
Randolf, Thomas 47-49
Rawley, Dr. William 12, 36, 39, 47, 110, 123, 131
Real History of the Rosicrucians 191
Red Cross Knight 138
Remaining Helps or Ministrations to the Intellect 106
Renaissance, English 3, 39
Renaissance, French 11
Resuscitatio 183, 188
Rich, Lord 19
Rich, Penelope 19
Richard III 17, 194
Richard II 26-27
Rogers, Daniel 14
Roman Composite Order 157
Romulus, 49
Rosicrucian
    College of the Six Days' Work 121, 123, 134
    Eagle of St. John 147
    'Invisible College' 33
    initiate 151
    manifesto 7, 68, 106, 110, 114, 120, 133, 136, 142
    motto 147, 149
    Order 137
Rosicrucians 2, 133, 136, 138
Rota Mundi 68, 107
Royal Academy 133
Royal Society 33, 133
Sagittarius 2
Sancti Spiritus 120
Satan 132
Saturn 2, 121
Scientia Activa 120
Scipio 42
Scourge of Folly 42
Sea Adventurer 38
Sea-Adventure 30
Second Philosophy 73
Secunda Philosophia 120
Seneca 55
Sephiroth 149
Serpentarius 2
Sewell, Dr. 145
Shaddai 151, 153
Shakespeare First Folio 11, 19
Shakespeare Folio 39, 46, 118, 123, 135, 168, 186
Shakespeare Memorial 143, 145, 187, 200
Shakespeare Monument 47, 53, 186
Shakespeare, pseudonym 4, 22, 42, 47, 138
Shakespeare, William 2, 16, 19, 26
Shakespeare's *Sonnets* 144-145, 147, 151, 187
Shamaim 199
Society of Magians 134
Society of Wise Men 135
Socrates 54-56
Sod 60
Solamona 132, 142
Solomon 9, 53, 59-60, 64, 143
    Ecclesiastes 79
    House 131-133
    Pillars 187
    157
    71, 73, 84, 154-155, 187, 197, 201
    Royal Arch of 153
    wisdom of 60
Southampton, Earl of 11, 19
Spanish Armada 17
Spear Shaker 48 (see also Athena)
Spenser, Edmund 10, 14, 19, 193
St Paul xiv
St. Alban 139-141, 143
St. Amphibal 140-141
St. Bartholomew's Priory 139
St. Bartholomew 132
St. George 136
St. James 153
St. John the Divine 153
St. Paul's School 135
St. Veronica 141
Stanley, William, 6th Earl of Derby 10
Star of David 157
Steganographia 135
Stella 19
Strachey, William 30, 38
Strange, Lord 11
Summary Law of Nature 76
Summary Philosophy 119
Supernova, prophetic 1
Supernova 10
Sussex's Men 22
Sydney, Mary, Countess of Pembroke 19

Index

Sydney, Sir Philip 10-11, 14, 19, 137-138
Sylva Sylvarum 110, 123, 131, 163
Table of Affirmations 112
Table of Degrees 108
Table of Deviation 108
Table of Essence and Presence 108
Table of Rejection or Exclusion 112
Tables of First Presentation 108, 112
Tables of Invention 105, 113
Tantric teachings 117
Templars' Outer Temple 137
Temple
    of light 120, 187
    of philosophy 120, 127, 130
    of Vesta 130
    of Wisdom 192
Terence 42
The Comedy of Errors 25
The Constitutions of the Free-masons 145
The Device of the Indian Prince 24
The History of the Reign of King Henry VII 36
The History of Travaile in Virginia Britannia 196
The Holy Guide 131
The Honourable Order of the Knights of the Helmet 138
The Intellectual Sphere rectified to the Globe 112
The Letters and the Life of Francis Bacon 197
The Life of King Henry the Eighth 38
The Merchant of Venice 24
The Merry Wives of Windsor 188
The Mirror of Modestie 147
The Rape of Lucrece 22
The Remaining Helps or Ministration to the Intellect 113
The Repertorie of Records 183
The Schoolmaster 134
The Taming of the Shrew 194
The Tempest 20, 29-31, 38, 78-79, 185-187
The True Reportory of the Wracke and Redemption of Sir Thomas Gates 195-196
The Two Gentlemen of Verona 194
The Two Noble Kinsmen 195
The Winter's Tale 29

Theophrastus von Hohenheim 136
Thirty-Third Degree of Initiation 187
Thoth 197
Thread of the Labyrinth 112
Three Heads 78
Timaeus 136
Titus Andronicus 22, 194
Tityrus 55
Torah 196
Tours 11
Tractatis Apoligetica 2
Transportata 133
Tree of Knowledge 132
Tree of Life 132, 151, 154, 191, 201
Trentham, Elizabeth 20
Trinity College 10
Trithemius, Abbot Johann 135-136
Trojan War 54
Turtledove 6
Tutelaires 133
Twickenham Lodge 16
Twin pillars 4, 6
Two Noble Brethren 19
Una (the One Truth) 138
University Wits 14, 19
Utopia 131, 136
Vaughan, Sir John 34
Venus and Adonis 10-11, 19, 22, 30, 43, 138
Venus 2, 10, 130
Vernon, Elizabeth 19
Verulamium 140
Virgil 46, 54-56
Virgin Mary 136
Virginia Colony 38
Virginia Company 29, 38
Walsingham, Sir Francis 11, 14, 19, 134
Western wisdom tradition 117
Wheel of the World (*Rota Mundi*) 108
White House 12
White Temple 12
Whitgift, John 10
William Shakespeare's Comedies, Histories and Tragedies 36
Williams, Bishop 34
Williams, John 47
Wither, George 19
Wolsey, Cardinal 38
Woodstock Tournament 10
World of Creation 77

Building Paradise

World of Emanation 77
World of Fact 77
World of Formation 77
Wriothesley, Henry 194
Yoga 6-7
Zerubbabel, 197
Zoroaster 136

BOOKS BY PETER DAWKINS

The Master Series
The Shakespeare Enigma
Building Paradise
Beyond the Veil
Life of the Master

The Wisdom of Shakespeare Series
The Wisdom of Shakespeare in 'As You Like It'
The Wisdom of Shakespeare in 'The Merchant of Venice'
The Wisdom of Shakespeare in 'Julius Caesar'
The Wisdom of Shakespeare in 'The Tempest'

FBRT Journal Series
The Pattern of Initiation
The Virgin Ideal
Dedication to the Light
The Great Vision
Arcadia

Other Books
Zoence, Science of Life
The Grail Kingdom of Europe
Sinai, Mountain of the Lord
Francis Bacon – Herald of the New Age
The Master